Friedrich von Hausen

UNC | COLLEGE OF ARTS AND SCIENCES
Germanic and Slavic Languages and Literatures

From 1949 to 2004, UNC Press and the UNC Department of Germanic & Slavic Languages and Literatures published the UNC Studies in the Germanic Languages and Literatures series. Monographs, anthologies, and critical editions in the series covered an array of topics including medieval and modern literature, theater, linguistics, philology, onomastics, and the history of ideas. Through the generous support of the National Endowment for the Humanities and the Andrew W. Mellon Foundation, books in the series have been reissued in new paperback and open access digital editions. For a complete list of books visit www.uncpress.org.

Friedrich von Hausen
Inquiries Into His Poetry

HUGO BEKKER

UNC Studies in the Germanic Languages and Literatures
Number 87

Copyright © 1977

This work is licensed under a Creative Commons CC BY-NC-ND license. To view a copy of the license, visit http://creativecommons.org/licenses.

Suggested citation: Bekker, Hugo. *Friedrich von Hausen: Inquiries Into His Poetry.* Chapel Hill: University of North Carolina Press, 1977. DOI: https://doi.org/10.5149/9781469657059_Bekker

Library of Congress Cataloging-in-Publication Data
Names: Bekker, Hugo.
Title: Friedrich von Hausen : inquiries into his poetry / by Hugo Bekker.
Other titles: University of North Carolina Studies in the Germanic Languages and Literatures ; no. 87.
Description: Chapel Hill : University of North Carolina Press, [1977] Series: University of North Carolina Studies in the Germanic Languages and Literatures. | Includes bibliographical references.
Identifiers: LCCN 76-16058 | ISBN 978-1-4696-5704-2 (pbk: alk. paper) | ISBN 978-1-4696-5705-9 (ebook)
Subjects: Friedrich von Hausen, 1150 (ca.)-1190 — Criticism and interpretation.
Classification: LCC PT1522 .F4B4 | DCC 831/ .2

FOR
STEPHANIE
AND
ANNE SARAH

CONTENTS

ACKNOWLEDGMENTS	x
ABBREVIATIONS	x
INTRODUCTION	1
I. ICH MUOZ VON SCHULDEN SIN UNFRO	4
II. MICH MÜET DEICH VON DER LIEBEN QUAM	17
III. AN DER GENADE AL MIN FRÖIDE STAT	27
IV. DIU SÜEZEN WORT HANT MIR GETAN	34
V. ICH SAGE IR NU VIL LANGE ZIT	40
VI. WAFENA, WIE HAT MICH MINNE GELAZEN	47
VII. SI WELNT DEM TODE ENTRUNNEN SIN	54
VIII. SI DARF MICH DES ZIHEN NIET	56
IX. MIN HERZE UND MIN LIP DIU WELLENT SCHEIDEN	65
X. MIN HERZE DEN GELOUBEN HAT	74
XI. IN MINEM TROUME ICH SACH	77
XII. DEICH VON DER GUOTEN SCHIET	82
XIII. MIR IST DAZ HERZE WUNT	88
XIV. ICH SIHE WOL DAZ GOT WUNDER KAN	95
XV. ICH LOBE GOT DER SINER GÜETE	100
XVI. SICH MÖHTE WISER MAN VERWÜETEN	107
XVII. ICH DENKE UNDER WILEN	116
CONCLUSION	123
NOTES	126
BIBLIOGRAPHY	149

ACKNOWLEDGMENTS

By kind permission of the editors, "Friedrich von Hausen: 'Lichte ein unwiser man verwuete,' " *Seminar*, 8 (1972), 147-59, and "Friedrich von Hausen: 'Ich muoz von schulden sin unfro,' " *Husbanding the Golden Grain: Studies in Honor of Henry W. Nordmeyer* (Ann Arbor, 1973), pp. 24-45, are incorporated into this volume as the first and sixteenth chapters respectively. These articles have been partly rewritten in order to bring their arguments into line with those of the other chapters.

A grant from the Graduate School and the College of Humanities of the Ohio State University made possible the publication of this volume.

ABBREVIATIONS

AfdA	Anzeiger für deutsches Altertum
Archiv	Archiv für das Studium der neueren Sprachen und Literaturen
Beiträge	Beiträge zur Geschichte der deutschen Sprache und Literatur
CL	Comparative Literature
DVjs	Deutsche Vierteljahrsschrift für Literaturwissenschaft und Geistesgeschichte
DU	Der Deutschunterricht
EG	Etudes germaniques
FuF	Forschungen und Fortschritte
GGA	Göttingische gelehrte Anzeigen
GLL	German Life and Letters
GRM	Germanisch-Romanische Monatsschrift
JEGP	The Journal of English and Germanic Philology
MLN	Modern Language Notes
MLR	The Modern Language Review
MP	Modern Philology
NM	Neuphilologische Mitteilungen
SG	Studium generale
WW	Wirkendes Wort
ZfdB	Zeitschrift für deutsche Bildung
ZfdPh	Zeitschrift für deutsche Philologie
ZfdA	Zeitschrift für deutsches Altertum
ZfDk	Zeitschrift für Deutschkunde

INTRODUCTION

The comments presented in the pages ahead are based on several considerations. First, it has been said that the scribe responsible for the C manuscript must have been somewhat of a poet in his own right.[1] This opinion is part of the argument that the C text is less reliable than B, since the C scribe dabbled with rhymes and rhythms and did not hesitate to rewrite whole lines in order to accommodate his own way of reading the text which had been transmitted to him. It could be argued, however, that the C scribe, precisely because he had a knack for poetry and presumably was highly intelligent, was keenly sensitive to some of the poetic devices characteristic of Hausen. On occasion he may have had a more acute understanding of these lyrics than his B counterpart, or more insight than the critics have accorded him. Hence it may be suggested that every so often the C text is perhaps more illuminating than the B text.[2] In such instances the text cited as a basis for discussion differs from that which has been given preference in the various editions of *Des Minnesangs Frühling* or elsewhere. As we shall see, this attempt at greater generosity with regard to the C text has an effect on the values of *hohe Minne* and other concepts with which Hausen's poetry has been long associated.

Second, a word should be said about the order in which the lyrics are discussed. Contrary to the rationale posited by critics such as Brinkmann,[3] we do not know whether the lyrics were meant to be read in a particular order so as to reveal a "plot" line indicating a development from one lyric to the next. By following an order which is roughly that of the manuscripts we seek to avoid any attempt to read Hausen's poems as a series.[4] Nothing prevents a "better" poem—however defined, whether by Brinkmann with his view of developmental features at stake, or by someone who applied a different criterion—from having been written at an early, inspired moment, or a less successful one at a later, lackluster hour. This is not to deny the possibility or even likelihood that at least some of these lyrics were composed in a specific order. For instance, it would be quite reasonable to argue that on the basis of the suggestions advanced in chapter IX, "Min herze und min lip diu wellent scheiden," should preferably be read after, rather than before, "Sich möhte wiser man verwüeten" (chapter XVI), though this would still not prevent the possibility that the former was composed before the latter. Similar reasoning could be applied to suggest that "this" poem may very well have been meant to come after "that" one. However, such reasoning cannot provide a valid criterion by which to arrange *all* the Hausen poems. As stated before, even *if* Hausen had intended that his lyrics be read in a specific sequence, this does not mean that he wrote them in that very same order. Besides, it is quite possible that some of the alleged components have been lost so that we can never be confident about the exact stages of the development he may have had in mind. All these considerations make it advisable to disregard, at least for the time being, any attempt at arranging the lyrics in a particular sequence.

The approach adopted here must therefore do without the insights that Brinkmann and others gain with the strict order in which they arrange the Hausen materials. Brinkmann, for instance, is able to use information obtained from one lyric to elucidate those that follow. The following discussions have no such benefits since it stands to reason that each lyric must be read without relying on "plot" data, gained elsewhere, about the situation developed in it. Such independence, in turn, has other consequences. For one thing, the desire to present a continuous argument during the discussion of a given poem may to a degree conflict with the equally valid desire to avoid repetition: in a realm of few thematic variations some poems are bound to yield suggestions that are similar to those advanced previously. For instance, during the discussion of many a lyric the question arises whether the lady around whom the speaker's thoughts revolve is aware of his ponderings, and the answer to this question may have a bearing on our way of understanding the entire poem. For another thing, unlike Baumgarten[5] or Müllenhoff[6] with their points of view, or Brinkmann with his, or Wechssler[7] with still another, we have no choice but to regard these lyrics as pure fiction. It is therefore impossible to learn from them a kind of biography of Hausen's love life. Indeed, we do not know whether he had or wanted one at all.[8] Since there are seventeen poems—MF 54,1 ("Wol ir, sist ein saelic wip") is considered spurious for reasons outlined elsewhere[9]—there are seventeen speakers and an almost equal number of ladies. "Poetic fiction" thus becomes a key term. Brinkmann and most critics with him, on the other hand, speak throughout of "the poet"; with this view, there is no need to distinguish between the poet as *Dichter* and the poet as *persona*. In the following readings, this distinction becomes an important and sometimes crucial one.

Further, it should be noted that it is not the purpose of these comments to provide counter-arguments to established criticism on Hausen's poetry. To be sure, attempts are made to gainsay those views that seem to be out of focus because of their bias; yet the following chapters do not seek to establish a totally new framework of poetic reference. Instead, they seek to point out *additional* levels of meaning, thus suggesting that Hausen was not a totally single-minded poet but was capable of providing variety. Indeed, ambiguity might thus become an important characteristic of his *oeuvre*.[10]

Then, too, the critics dealing with Hausen's poetry have again and again drawn attention to his penchant for working with antithetical statements. This view has long been a commonplace: "[Hausen] gefällt sich darin, Gegensätze aufzustellen, Möglichkeiten auszumalen, und durch unerwartete Wendungen zu überraschen."[11] It is but a short step to raise the question whether irony is at work in this poetry.[12] The quote from Scherer implies also that such irony would be the result of a considerable amount of self-awareness on the part of the poet; he would stand above his art. The discussions to follow will seek to delineate the implications of Hausen's antithetical procedure and the irony possibly flowing from it.

It must, of course, be left to the reader to judge whether a balanced view has been maintained or enhanced in these pages when they are read in conjunction with what other scholars have said about Hausen's poetry. And the reader ultimately will also be the judge on matters that lie either at the periphery or the very heart of a given discussion. Such matters deal with *hohe Minne*, Hausen's religious faith, his alleged attempts to harmonize *Frauendienst* and *Gottesdienst*, the concept of the poet as the bringer of *fröide*, the basic purpose behind the self-imposed task implied by this concept, and several other questions.

If one were to rely on the conviction that emendations have often been unwarranted, it would be logical to go back to the manuscripts and proceed from what they have transmitted. But there would be one or two drawbacks to such exclusive reliance on the manuscripts. It would compel us to discuss all the variants—thus adding considerably to the length of each discussion—even though they often do not affect the meaning of a given line. Hence many of the emendations that were brought about in the various editions of *Des Minnesangs Frühling* or elsewhere and have become part of the "established" readings are taken as acceptable in the context of the present work: our approach is deliberately narrow and refrains from seeking to deal with all the formal aspects that normally come the way of the reader of poetry. With this consideration it seems sensible to limit citations from the manuscripts to those instances in which they transmit lines differing in meaning from their counterparts in *Des Minnesangs Frühling* and warranting an argument in their favor.[13]

The aim of the following discussions, then, is to evaluate the texts for their contents. After all, "bei einer gedanklich so subtilen Kunst wie dem Minnesang wird bei aller textkritischen Arbeit doch letzten Endes immer das Bemühen um den Gedanken, das Logische und Rationale im Vordergrund des Interesses zu stehen haben."[14]

Needless to say, the discussions will not be equally fruitful. They are bound to be uneven, in length as well as persuasiveness. Part of this lack of homogeneity is no doubt due to the comparative lack of critical verve with which a given discussion is developed. Part of it may also be due to occasional and comparative lack of creative verve on the part of the poet. Besides, the approach used in these pages will yield more "value" with one lyric than with another. Their different lengths, too, contribute to unevenness.

To put all this differently: the following suggestions aim at being read in the spirit in which they are presented, that is to say, they are meant to cast *additional*, as opposed to (totally) *new*, light on Hausen's poetry. In this connection, the various discussions ought properly to be accompanied by strings of qualifiers connoting alternate possibilities: "but," "on the other hand," "in addition," "at the same time." Yet to enter every appropriate qualification in a book of this kind would bury the peruser under an avalanche of multiple readings. Hence the reader is asked to approach the various discussions with some sympathy regarding the stylistic problem I seek to avoid when, after the initial discussion of "Ich muoz von schulden sin unfro," I severely limit the use of such circumspect modifiers. In this first chapter they are thought advisable in order to establish clearly the kind of bifocal scrutiny brought to bear also on the successive evaluations. In the latter, the more or less traditional readings are largely represented by the secondary sources cited.

I. ICH MUOZ VON SCHULDEN SIN UNFRO

42, 1   I   1 Ich muoz von schulden sin unfro,¹   1 BC
               sit si jach do ich bi ir was,
               ich möhte heizen Eneas,
               und solte ab des wol sicher sin,
     5   5 si wurde niemer min Tido.
               wie sprach si so?
               aleine frömdet mich ir lip,
               si hat iedoch des herzen mich
               beroubet gar für elliu wip.

    10   II 10 Mit gedanke ich muoz die zit   2 BC
               vertriben als ich beste kan,
               und lernen des ich nie began,
               truren unde sorgen pflegen;
               des was vil ungewent min lip:
    15   15 durch elliu wip
               wande ich niemer sin bekomen
               in solhe kumberliche not
               als ich von einer han genomen.

         III   Min herze muoz ir kluse sin   3 BC
    20   20 al die wile ich habe den lip;
               so müezen iemer elliu wip
               vil ungedrungen drinne wesen,
               swie lihte si sich troeste min.
               nu werde schin
    25   25 ob rehtiu staete iht müge gefromen.
               der wil ich iemer gegen ir pflegen;
               diu ist mir von ir güete komen.

Aided by the measured rhythm, the first line strikes a tenuous balance:

> 1 Ich muoz von schulden sin unfro,

I have good cause not to be happy,²

The self-centeredness inherent in the immediate mention of the first personal pronoun³ is muted by the use of an innocuous adjective. A more forceful predicate would have given more force to the statement, would have elicited interest and aroused sympathy for the speaker's woe. As it is, he does not say that he is in despair, but merely that happiness is absent.⁴

This low-keyed opening allows us to focus attention on the remainder of the sentence with its reference to one of the famous pairs of lovers of Antiquity:

> 2 sit si jach do ich bi ir was,[5]
> ich möhte heizen Eneas,
> und solte ab des wol sicher sin,
> si wurde niemer min Tido.
>
> since she said when I was with her
> that, even if my name were Aeneas,
> I could be very certain
> she would never be my Dido.[6]

These lines, together with the following question:

> 6 wie sprach si so?
>
> why did she say that?

call for some scrutiny since their implications are multiple. To begin with, the sixth line constitutes an invitation to the audience to pay heed to and participate in what is perhaps best designated as a game. This game begs to be taken seriously; boisterousness is taboo, as are all allusions, snide or otherwise, that might rupture the frail framework of reference in which the game is to be played. The speaker pits himself against the audience. He will entertain his listeners with a display of verbal artistry; their task is to stay abreast of the manner in which he develops the motifs touched upon, and to observe whether he abides by the simple but basic rules. The cardinal rule is to remain polite in word and bearing. In this way, speaker and listeners entertain each other. They play a sophisticated game which requires intellectual exertion on each side.

Brinkmann makes perhaps a related point[7] when he finds that Hausen "mit gebildeten, wissenden Hörern rechnet, die seine Anspielung sofort verstehen."[8] It remains to be seen, however, whether this "sofort verstehen" demands the acquiescence in such views as Brinkmann propagates; he himself may have missed something, thus drastically altering the "message" of the lyric from what Hausen meant it to be. Since Brinkmann's is the lengthiest study, and purportedly profound,[9] there will be ample opportunity to cite some of his tenets.

The Aeneas-Dido reference immediately brings to mind the tragic end of an affair in which Dido was the victim. This lay-out of the "plot" material is necessary to present the problem to be resolved, and to provide the audience with the basic clue. The necessity of providing a plot on which to hinge matters accounts for the epic quality of the strophe; those that follow are reflective and hence more typical of Hausen's writings in general. The clue teases the anticipation of the listeners. How will this be developed without violation of the rules? The game is not unlike the solving of a riddle.

The question, "wie sprach si so?" is not only an invitation. It is effective on other levels as well—simultaneously. While calling upon the activity of the audience, it may be a bland inquiry, but it may also be spoken in dismay and amazement: Now, how could she ever say such a thing?[10] Why did she say what I just told you she said? Think about it! And the audience thinks and may find the answer obvious: the lady thought she would regret it if she ventured into the relationship which the speaker evidently urged upon her "do [er] bi ir was" (3)—there is room for doubt as to the exact nature of his intentions. It is also clear that the indirect and, at best, neutral manner in which the lady's words are conveyed licenses the audience, eager to enter into the spirit of the game, to wonder whether her fear was without basis or whether she knew for certain she had good reason to safeguard herself against Dido's fate.[11] Her statement tells the listeners also that, whatever her feelings toward the speaker, they are not necessarily of coldness and utter indifference, or even enmity; for all they know, her decision may be full of regret. This much, at any rate, is certain: whatever love prevails,[12] whether or not on his side alone, he was with her, and it is therefore not love from afar.[13]

There are many cases of a lady's dreading love in *Minnesang*. These lines, for example, are from Reinmar:

> 178, 29 Des er gert daz ist der tot
> und verderbet mangen lip;
> bleich und eteswenne rot
> also verwet ez diu wip.
> minnent heizent ez die man,
> und möhte baz unminne sin.
> we im ders alrest began!

This motif of fear resulting from an envisioned intimate bond between a woman and a man is hence not an isolated phenomenon in medieval literature. It is similar also to Kriemhild's reaction to her falcon dream in the *Nibelungenlied* when she vehemently denies that she will ever fall victim to love.[14]

It may thus be the lady's lack of confidence in the desirable outcome of love, her lack of trust in the speaker's *staete*,[15] that led her to allude to the Aeneas-Dido story rather than to that of any pair of famous lovers who remained mutually faithful. Obliquely but sententiously, doubt is raised in the minds of the listeners: will the lady turn out to be correct in her judgment?[16] We may also wish to infer that the possible amazement with which the speaker asks, "wie sprach si so?" is motivated by the necessity that he adopt a stance in public regarding the lady's doubt about his *staete*, and that his reaction in public is different from his private one. With this, the lyric acquires some of the aspects of a little psychological drama. The speaker's stance, too, is part of the plot design, and the audience must take it into account when making its assessment as to the truth of the story.

From the lady's point of view, then, it may be inevitable that she avoids the speaker:

> 7 aleine frömdet mich ir lip,

Schönbach suggests that "aleine" stands for "obgleich";[17] all the commentators have followed him in this:

> although she avoids me

However, it would seem perfectly legitimate to wonder whether "aleine" could be read as a qualifier to "ir lip": "only she avoids me" or "she alone avoids me." These readings suggest a period rather than a comma—as used in *Des Minnesangs Frühling*—after the seventh line. With the emphasis on "ir lip" thus resulting we must contend with the implication that other ladies do *not* avoid the speaker. This, in turn, raises the spectre that he is the ladies' man against whom Jungbluth polemicizes because the idea that the speaker is thus exposed to the temptation to engage in "extracurricular" sidetrips constitutes an uncourtly notion.[18] Jungbluth notwithstanding, we could suggest as alternate readings (with emphasis automatically falling on the possessive adjective) "only her person avoids me" or "her person alone avoids me." These renditions carry into the stream of associations a barely veiled allusion to the speaker's possible interest in celebrating love on the physical plane.[19]

Of course, the present line of reasoning takes the lady's lack of trust in the speaker's *staete* as fully justified; and it is also evident that it takes the strophe out of the realm of *hohe Minne* with which it has long been identified. The speaker, however, claims:

> 8 si hat iedoch des herzen mich
> beroubet gar für elliu wip.

All the commentators have given "für" the value of "before":

> she has nevertheless robbed me
> of my heart before all women.

If this is mandatory, it must be possible to make a little change and turn "before all women" into "before all other women," as Brinkman does: "Eine bleibt ihm fremd, sie hat aber dafür gesorgt, daß er allen andern fremd bleibt."[20] Braun seems to be of the same opinion: "Dennoch hat gerade die sich Versagende allein (für elliu wip) den Dichter des Herzens beraubt."[21] Sayce translates the phrase as "before all (other) women."[22] Schönbach, incidentally, wonders whether " 'elliu wip' einen Verstecknamen für die Frau enthält, wie sie bei den Provençalen beliebt waren."[23] With these readings, the closing lines of the strophe are in harmony with the rule that a courtly bearing toward the lady must be maintained despite her obviously aloof demeanor.

At first glance, the second strophe offers little new:

> 10 Mit gedanke ich muoz die zit[24]
> vertriben als ich beste kan,
> und lernen des ich nie began,
> truren unde sorgen pflegen;
> des was vil ungewent min lip:

> I must pass the time thinking
> as best I can,
> and learn what I never learned,
> grieving and worrying;
> I was totally unaccustomed to that:

These lines present the speaker in a reflective mood. This turning inward leads to a hazy form of communication; the passage is somewhat repetitive: the fourteenth line roughly restates what the twelfth has to say—"des ich nie began"—thus underscoring the novelty of the situation referred to. Schönbach finds that the fourteenth line is necessary because the twelfth is "zu wenig nachdrucksvoll."[25] This suggestion either constitutes an excuse for an inept line of poetry or it fails to do justice to the intention behind the repetitive ring, and it may therefore be more felicitous to think that repetition is deliberately applied to relay the speaker's pondering the new experience that has come his way.[26] On a totally different plane of evaluation, of course, repetition may also be interpreted as an indication that Hausen is not far removed from the earlier *Minnesang* poets.[27]

Thus "gedanke" (10) shows the pensiveness involved in the speaker's endeavor to relay his thoughts. It is therefore small wonder that no firm, reliable data are presented and that the listeners have cause to wonder what the actual connections are between the various statements. If, for instance, we translated "min lip" of the fourteenth line with "my person" or even "my body" rather than with a pronoun, we might have to understand from these lines that the speaker has had experiences with other women who never gave him cause to "truren unde sorgen pflegen"—the notion of the ladies' man again. In this way, the lady's possible mistrust in the speaker's *staete* would indeed be justified.

Brinkmann sees things differently; he says of "des ich nie began . . . des was vil ungewent min lip": "Das darf nicht mißverstanden werden. Es soll kein Zeugnis dafür sein, daß er zum ersten Male Umgang mit sorge hält. Es ist vielmehr Ausdruck einer seelischen Verwandlung."[28] From Brinkmann's point of view this is a logical insight since he sees the Hausen poems as interrelated so that each lyric is to an important degree determined by the information gathered from the preceding poems. He places "Ich muoz von schulden sin unfro" as the thirteenth in the Hausen corpus, entitles it "Eine vor allen," and gives "sorgen pflegen" (13) a kind of metaphysical twist to distinguish it from previous occasions on which a speaker in a Hausen lyric talks about his "sorgen." Incidentally, it is impossible for Brinkmann to see these lyrics as so many examples of "Spiel"; with his view regarding interrelations between the poems, he would have to think in terms of a long game performed on the installment plan—he does not.

Brinkmann's view does enable him to utilize fully what we may call the epic backdrop behind these poems. Whereas for him this backdrop equates with (historical) reality pertaining to the poet's personal life, to us these epic elements (largely presupposed in the poetic process) are constituted by the background data which the game with the audience presupposes; hence these make-believe elements function only as backdrop materials against which the poet spins out his make-believe realities.

This is what Becker has to say: "Im übrigen gewährte der Dienst bei der sorgsamen Behütung der Mädchen meist Trauer und Sehnsucht, wie Hausen, 42, 11 ff. zeigt."[29] In a day when virtually all critics have followed Neumann's article on *hohe Minne* and the philosophy accompanying it,[30] there is something poignant about Becker's argument that the lady of *Minnesang* should be thought of as unmarried. However sympathetic to Becker's view an occasional reader might be—he should be prepared to feel totally isolated—the Hausen reference hardly supports Becker's thesis. He might have served his own purpose better by pointing out that the lady of "Ich muoz von schulden sin unfro" evokes the notion that the "inner" probability of the situation developed suggests that she is "zu haben," that is, is free and unencumbered.

It is worthwhile to remember that the reflection in the second strophe is not reflection in isolation, but is proclaimed in public, and that there is little private about it. The audience, in fact, is forced to reflect also. At the same time it is of course still involved with the self-imposed task of playing the detective regarding the Aeneas-Dido reference and, if possible, of guessing ahead, or at least staying abreast of, the denouement of that riddle before the speaker solves it.

Reflecting together—"mit gedanke die zit vertriben"—is a learning process— "lernen" (12)—and leads to increased insight. And again, this process turns out to be a startlingly private affair: "truren unde sorgen pflegen" (13). The audience is provided another clue with which to unravel the Aeneas-Dido teaser, and the speaker has managed another dichotomy, not only because private dolor becomes public property, but also because entertainment and "truren unde sorgen pflegen" (before and with a public) have virtually become synonymous. Brinkmann makes a similar point; it deserves citing at some length because it acquaints us with an example of what the "tiefe Auslegung" recommended by him[31] amounts to:

Der Dichter ist nicht durch eine gemeinschaftliche Erfahrung gesichert, an die er sich nur anzuschließen braucht, sondern immer wieder auf sich selbst gestellt. *Die Haltung, zu der sich die Menschen der Gesellschaft vereinen sollen, bietet sich ihnen im Liede des Dichters dar,* das dadurch eine besondere Bedeutung für sie erhält. *Er stiftet das Gemeinsame, nämlich die Haltung, aus der gelebt werden soll, durch sein Beispiel.* Das macht ihn für die Gesellschaft unentbehrlich, so daß sie ohne ihn nicht bestehen kann. Wenn der Dichter einen Anschluß sucht, dann knüpft er nicht mehr an einen Erfahrungssatz, sondern an ein literarisches Beispiel an, an Tristan, Salomo und Eneas (Hausen, 32,1;[32] italics added).

Is Brinkmann saying that by virtue of his poetry Hausen is safeguarding his society against some existential plight? However that may be, the italicized items receive an ironic twist when confronted with the ultimate unraveling process of the lyric's "message" as delineated below.

The second part of the second strophe seems to provide at least a partial answer to the Aeneas-Dido problem. Not the speaker, but the lady inflicts pain:

> 15 durch elliu wip
> wande ich niemer sin bekomen
> in solhe kumberliche not
> als ich von einer han genomen.

> for the sake of all women
> I never expected to end
> in such distress
> as I have incurred from one.

The audience can relax and make up its tally as to how far ahead or behind it was in its endeavor to stay with the development of the theme. The only possible question remaining is how this ill-fated speaker will react to the treatment the lady has given him. And so, despite the lack of epic flow, the strophe is of consequence after all. Aside from conveying the public quality of "truren unde sorgen pflegen," it serves to develop further the antithesis between the lady ("einer" of the eighteenth line) and "elliu wip" of the fifteenth.

The third strophe is no longer part of the reflection proper. It is projected into the future and brings the resolve stemming from the learning process mentioned in the previous strophe. It brings also the final solution to the Aeneas-Dido riddle:

> 19 Min herze muoz ir kluse sin
> al die wile ich habe den lip;
> so müezen iemer elliu wip
> vil ungedrungen drinne wesen,

> My heart must be her shrine
> as long as I shall have life;
> thus all women must forever
> be in there totally uncrowded.

Regarding the shrine-reference Braun speaks of a "der geistlichen Sphäre entlehnten Bild."[33] Schönbach finds that it is not "ein 'verschluss' im Allgemeinen, wie die Wörterbücher sagen, sondern: cellula, in qua degit monachus inclusus. . . . also eine für alle Zeit (20) verschlossenes Örtchen, wo einer allein drinnen ist."[34] Sayce states: "There is the twofold idea that the lady is enclosed in his heart, and that she is enshrined there alone."[35] All other commentators have agreed with these views, though Mowatt's procedure suggests that he does not feel quite comfortable.[36] The difficulties begin with 21 f. Paul translates: "So lange ich lebe, soll kein Weib in meinem Herzen (von der Geliebten) gedrängt werden, keine sich um den Platz darin mit ihr streiten."[37] Schönbach states: "Nach 20 setze ich Strichpunkt; 21 f. übersetze ich: 'Dagegen sollen für alle Zeit alle Frauen ganz und gar nicht in Bezug darauf gedrängt werden, daß sie in mein Herz sollen.' "[38] This is not Schönbach's most elegant sentence; its wording may spring from his sensible determination to state matters circumspectly. Ehrismann reads thus: "Es müssen immer elliu wip (von mir) ungedrängt in meinem Herzen sein, ohne daß ich mich zu ihnen dränge, mich um ihre Gunst bemühe; d.h., sie sind mir gleichgültig."[39] Neunteufel says: "Das Bild [in 19] ist in den folgenden Versen in einer ironischen Entgegnung [der Dame], die der Dichter einflichtet, weiter fortgesetzt."[40] This is Vogt: "Keine von allen Frauen braucht sich jemals dadrinnen mit ihr zu drängen (soll sich je dort neben sie eindrän-

gen),"⁴¹ and this is Kraus' reaction to Vogt's view: " 'müezen' bedeutet nicht 'brauchen.' "⁴² Sayce feels uneasy: " 'Therefore all (other) women will never be jostled in it by me, however easily she can dispense with me.' These lines are not entirely satisfactory, but the sense seems to be: 'I will never trouble other women with my attentions, however little she cares for me.' "⁴³ Brinkmann does something drastic; he emends: "so müezen *niemer andriu* wip/ vil ungedrungen drinne wesen"⁴⁴ (italics added), thus harmonizing the line with the way he decides the lyric should be read. It is the integrity of the sensitive reader—of a specific kind—that leads Brinkmann to advocate this solution to what elsewhere has remained an act of acquiescence in a nettlesome little problem. It forces Brinkmann to disregard, however, that "elliu wip" serves as an important unifying element between the three strophes, and that it is the mainstay in the antithetical development between "all women" and the lady. The conclusion is clear: Brinkmann's solution is not a solution; we lose as much, if not more, with it as we gain and have reason to remain unsatisfied.

And then there is Mowatt, who sees things this way: "The impasse is resolved once the manuscripts are consulted.... The passage has suffered interpretative emendation, in the substitution of 'müezen' present for 'muossen' preterite.... Each stanza is built on an opposition between the present and the past situation of the speaker. In each case, 'elliu wip' is the mark of an earlier, more generalized type of service, and is contrasted with the present exclusive devotion."⁴⁵ This argument is lucid and clearly suggests that we serve ourselves (and Hausen of course) by returning to the manuscripts which agree on this point. Ingenious though it is, however, Mowatt's view does not solve the matter entirely. The translation he cites indicates that the distinction made, though correct, does not prevent the employment of a verb form that has nothing to do with the preterite: "Thus (or nevertheless) all women shall always be unjostled in my heart." Obviously, with this view "elliu wip" are not in the speaker's heart any longer. But the translation of "so" as "thus" or "nevertheless" does nothing to establish the contrast between past and present situations as mentioned by Mowatt. And to be sure, it is difficult to see what else could be done with "so" with the above view at stake; the little word stubbornly refuses to yield to another way of reading these lines. Then, too, "iemer" (21) would seem to refer to the future, as does "iemer" of 26 (see below). In addition to all this, Mowatt's elucidation contradicts the closing lines of the first strophe. In order to accommodate his evaluation, these would have to state that the lady robbed the speaker's heart *away from* all (other) women. The conclusion seems fair: Mowatt's endeavor to do justice to the manuscripts harbors a blemish, and the solution to the problem remains as elusive as ever.⁴⁶

Regarding the following lines:

> 23 swie lihte si sich troeste min.
> nu werde schin
> ob rehtiu staete iht müge gefromen.⁴⁷
>
> however easily she may console herself.
> let it now become apparent
> whether true steadfastness is of any avail.

Kraus takes 23 to be a continuation of 22, from which he separates it with a comma, and he emends the manuscripts' "getroeste" by substituting for it "troeste." The other critics have followed him in this. Lexer gives "troeste" the value of "zuversichtlich machen," "ermutigen." Schönbach, perhaps not too logically, renders "sich troeste min" as "console herself for the loss of me"—"die Frau meint, sie will sich gewiß trösten."[48] Mowatt reminds us that the manuscripts have "sich getroeste min"[49] which carries the value Schönbach imputes to "sich troeste min." Whatever the meaning ultimately to be derived from these lines, they are the end product of the way in which the speaker has regaled his audience by manipulating its thinking. While abiding by the rules of the game, he has brought about a complete reversal: the lady acts as Aeneas acted, he himself has followed Dido, except that there is not the profound despair to warrant Dido's solution to the problem. The verisimilitude of his refraining from this last step is motivated, in retrospect, by the fact that he is (merely) without happiness—"unfro" (1).

Because of the verb, "rcht[e] staete pflegen" (25 f.) may almost be equated with "truren unde sorgen pflegen" (13); trapped in his own language, the speaker becomes his own victim.[50] This relationship indicates that the learning process in which speaker and audience are involved, and by which they entertain each other, makes their game a decorous one. Wechssler makes a related point when he speaks of "Lieder der Trauer, gesungen zur Freude der Gesellschaft, zu deren Unterhaltung und Erheiterung."[51]

Whatever our success in reading "Ich muoz von schulden sin unfro," with the required amount of acquiescence and naiveté, but ever on the alert for implications and complications in this would-be real situation, the closing statement *must* clinch the matter:

> 26 der wil ich iemer gegen ir pflegen;
> diu ist mir von ir güete komen.
>
> I shall practice that toward her always;
> it has come to me because of her goodness.

To hear that the speaker's *staete* stems from the lady's "güete" *must* be a complete motivation; it cannot be a *deus ex machina*. To acquiesce and take it piously at face value, therefore, or simply refuse to pay attention to it would amount to doing the poet an injustice, for it would prevent us from appreciating fully this last gesture of courtly bearing toward the lady, would tempt us to evaluate it as a hollow gesture, or would compel the view that its use is not merely ironic, but blatantly sardonic. One thus could imagine the speaker as delivering his last line with tongue in cheek, and, with a degree of defiance toward his audience, daring it to call him a violator of the rules.

The understanding thus gained from this poem remains unsatisfactory, primarily in view of the way the critics have dealt with the litotes in the third strophe—"vil ungedrungen drinne wesen" (22)—and our own doubt that full justice has been done to the "güete" of the closing line; this doubt led to some ungainly thrashing about with subjunctives. The conclusion seems inevitable: something has gone wrong, and the only thing left to do is return to the instances in which "elliu wip" occurs. For this "elliu wip," I suggest, has caused the problem.[52]

In the first strophe we were told that "si hat iedoch des herzen mich/ beroubet gar für elliu wip." We had already some difficulty with the second part of this strophe and saw how, depending on our evaluation of "aleine" (7), it was possible to gain two different readings—with far-flung and in part mutually exclusive implications—since we, late ones, *may* have lost the clarity of view that Hausen could call his own.

Now, "für elliu wip" is no less ambiguous, though in a different way, since it is deliberate. Whereas the first reading conforms to that of previous commentators reading this phrase as "before all (other) women," the fact remains that "für" at times carries the meaning "for." And thus we detect that with this value in mind we can think of the lady as a representative of all women. Because of her, despite her enmity toward the speaker, he has become receptive to all women.[53] He is not only devoted to the lady, but has also become a devotee of (all) womankind (in general). To be sure, we realize immediately, once it is stated, that this motif is a commonplace in *Minnesang*.[54] However, the critics dealing with the litotes in the third strophe—see the citations above—have forgotten it, and their evaluations may hence not quite do justice to what Hausen may have had in mind. Indeed, we now are ready to appreciate more fully "das ganze sorgfältige Gewebe" of the first strophe about which Kraus has taught us.[55]

With this evaluation obtained from the first strophe, which now says two different things because its key phrase can be evaluated in two different ways, we have reason to turn once again to the third strophe, and find that a punctuation different from that applied in *Des Minnesangs Frühling* may be possible:

> 19 Min herze muoz ir kluse sin
> al die wile ich habe den lip.
> so muossen[56] iemer elliu wip
> vil ungedrungen drinne wesen.
> swie lihte si sich getroeste[56] min,
> nu werde schin
> ob rehtiu staete iht müge gefromen.

Now 21 f. are capable of yielding a totally different value which tells us that the opposite of our first reading is also possible: because of the lady's effect on the speaker, the capacity of his heart is such that it can harbor all her sisters. With this, the full meaning of "swie lihte si sich getroeste min" remains effective. The line may even say that the lady is capable of adopting Aeneas' role completely: just as Aeneas found solace away from Dido and eventually married Lavinia, so the lady is capable of finding solace elsewhere. In this manner, we have another antithesis emerging that is not clearly revealed with the Kraus punctuation: despite the lady's possible readiness to find solace elsewhere, the speaker declares his everlasting *staete* to her.

This time, of course, we cannot speak of a mutually exclusive contrast between the lady on the one hand and all other women on the other. Instead we see a simultaneous accommodation brought about. In the third strophe, this simultaneity is not only revealed in the personal references—"*ir* kluse" (italics added) and "elliu wip"—but is enhanced by the time elements employed: "al die wile ich habe den lip" is identical to "iemer" of 21. Precisely because "such and such" is the case with respect to the lady, it is the case also with respect to "elliu wip." This means that the litotes of 22 now has the opposite meaning from what it is given in the critics' elucidations as cited above. Logically, "so" (21) has the meaning of "hence," "therefore," "consequently" in our reading.

The speaker's closing statement that his intended "rehtiu staete" is the result of the lady's "güete" now shows this "güete" to consist in her being effective on the speaker in such a way as to compel him to open his heart to all women—a courtly compliment indeed.

Incidentally, on the present level of evaluation it would not alter things too much if we interpreted the speaker's "rehte staete" as a tribute in memory of the lady's beneficial effect on his heart: "rehtiu staete" *in memoriam*. With this, "muossen" (21) of the manuscripts should indeed be reintroduced, though for reasons other than those advanced by Mowatt (see above). In fact, his argument is thus turned upside down.

In this manner, in the third strophe, too, we have instances of ambiguity enabling us to read simultaneously various mutually exclusive and yet equally valid meanings from the key terms employed. It seems therefore safe to conclude that Hausen's procedure in this lyric is a variation of a theme touched upon by Andreas Capellanus; the latter puts this statement into the mouth of a man of the middle class: "One should not be a lover of several women at the same time, but for the sake of one should be a devoted servant to all."[57] It also follows from within the present way of reading the lyric that the lady is narrow-minded and egocentric, and has no appreciation for the speaker's impeccably lofty terms.

This poem, then, turns out to be an exercise in *double entendre*, and it becomes evident in retrospect that the very opening line may be ambiguous. If we translate it as "I have good reason not to be happy," it sets the tone of the lyric as evaluated in our first reading. But the line may also mean "I am not happy because of my own fault (because she had reason to say when I was with her....)."[58] The first meaning ties in with the speaker's claim that he is *staete* so that his lack of happiness is unfair and unwarranted. The second meaning stems from the possible inference that the lady thinks he is *unstaete* because he squanders his affections, whatever their exact nature, amongst the multitudes, and must bear the consequence of this lack of focus and concentration in love:[59] she therefore shuns him. In either reading tension vibrates between the lady's *güete* and the speaker's being "von schulden unfro."

The possible tenuousness of this particular detail of our argument may stem from the fact that the speaker stands between the lady and the audience. He thus has an advantage over her that prevents her statement from coming through as immediately and directly convincing as his own to an audience which wonders about the possible reasons behind anybody's statements. Whereas the speaker's own manner of delivery allows him to scrutinize his (carefully chosen) considerations from various sides, her words sound no less than blunt. It is even possible that they are cutting, particularly if it is fair to translate the third line as "*even if* my name were Aeneas," thus possibly insinuating the speaker's total lack of (physical?) qualifications. It is therefore all the more gallant that he provides a counterbalance to his advantage by using the subjunctive mood when leaving room for the lady's possible readiness to console herself "lihte" (elsewhere?), thus giving her a benefit of the doubt.

The evaluation here presented suggests that the title which Brinkmann gives to the lyric—"Eine vor allen"—tells only half the story since there turns out to be equally valid reason to cap it under the phrase "Eine für alle." Then, too, we have reason to draw attention to a dictum advanced by Lehfeld: "Vor allem zeichnet Hausen sich aus durch seine Gewandtheit, mit entgegengesetzten Gedanken *gleichsam zu spielen*" (italics added),[60] which turns out to be correct in a manner more radical than Lehfeld himself may have intended. For now we have on the one hand a lady envisioned as possibly consoling herself readily—"lihte"—elsewhere and hence as potentially *unstaete*, but who on the other hand is also the catalyst bringing about the speaker's receptivity to all women.

It is interesting to note how Kraus comes close to bringing an evaluation very similar to that suggested in these pages, but then turns into the opposite direction:

Eneas ist der 'minnesaelige Troian' (En. 10023), dem die Frauen ihre Liebe entgegentragen. Aber wenn der Dichter auch so verführerisch wäre wie er, so würde sie sich ihm doch nicht hingeben wie Dido. Darauf erwidert er: "wie kommt sie dazu, so etwas zu sagen?": es liegt ja gerade umgekehrt: sie ist es, die ihn "frömedet" (wie Eneas die Dido) und er ist es, dem sie alle Gedanken an andere Frauen beraubt hat (während Eneas die Dido verläßt). Deshalb beteuert er in der zweiten Strophe die Größe seines Kummers, den ihm alle anderen Frauen nie hätten bereiten können, und deshalb betont er . . . seine Unbekümmertheit um alle anderen Frauen, seine "rehte staete," die ihm nicht verlassen wird: "swie lihte si sich troeste min" (wie Eneas sich der Dido "getroestet" hat).[61]

With the twofold meaning argued in these pages, a quaint light falls on a sentiment like that pronounced by Korn. His view is representative of the views of many; it speaks of the poet's self-imposed task, "das ursprüngliche Individual-Erleben in ein hohes Minneverhältnis zu verwandeln, das heißt, zu überpersönlicher, ideeller Wesenhaftigkeit aufzuhöhen."[62] With the notion of the "performance" of a game, of course, Korn's view fails to do justice to the possibly important element of irony in Hausen's method, and therefore may not be an entirely reliable gauge by which to measure the full quality and "meaning" of this lyric.

However that may be, the lady's possible fear may have turned out to be justified: her suitor, contrary to her possible wishes and bearing out her fear, did not abide by her alone. Perhaps from her point of view,[63] his heart has not become a shrine for one, but an abode for many. The compliment coming in the wake of his claim in the closing line that she herself is the cause of this state of affairs leaves her less than appeased; presumably, whereas he speaks of "*rehte* staete"[64] (italics added), she finds his argument to be mere verbiage. Along a similar line of reasoning, however, the speaker is also correct. The lady, to his sorrow, does not accept him on the (flawlessly) courtly terms advanced by him, and from his point of view she is *unstaete* if she is to

15

console herself "lihte" regarding him. In this way, each can be envisioned as using the same terms to argue his or her own *staete* while (obliquely) accusing the other of the lack of it. This device highlights the art of Hausen's antithetical procedure, as well as the outcome of it in this poem.

So far, little issue has been taken with previous elucidations of "Ich muoz von schulden sin unfro." Some questions emerge, however. Some of these touch upon the concept of *Minnesang* as that body of poetry which celebrates *hohe Minne*. This baffling term has been encumbered with many connotations, and for the moment, at any rate, there is room for doubt regarding the acceptability of some of them. By way of example, the generally prevailing view that *staete* and endurance are part of *hohe Minne*, or even constitute *hohe Minne*, would not give license to tag this lyric with the *hohe Minne* label without bringing severely limiting reservations to bear on the term. Nowhere is it said, for instance, that the exercise of *staete* is an ideal to be attained. It is, instead, a state to be endured. Considering the irony encountered in the lyric's *double entendre*, even that statement is limited in value. He who endures this state would rather have his reward.[65]

Other questions deal with the fact that "Ich muoz von schulden sin unfro" is an exercise in deliberate ambiguity. Hence irony of a high and sophisticated caliber becomes a feature of immediate and compelling consequence with Hausen, though it remains to be seen whether perhaps it is germane to this one poem only. In this connection we cite Spanke: "Hausen bildet keinen Fremdkörper in der Geschichte der mittelhochdeutschen Lyrik; eher ist er als Pfadfinder zu bezeichnen. Das fremde Gut, das er aufnahm ... hat er zu *Kunstwerken* geformt, *die dem Gefühls- und Gedankenkreis des damaligen deutschen Rittertums entsprachen*"[66] (italics added). Insofar as this statement is also applicable to the content of the poem under discussion, the question arises what that "Gefühls- und Gedankenkreis" amounts to. And on the basis of the same axiom that form and content are one, Ehrismann[67] may be said to have investigated this matter. In view of the nature of our poem, however, his is not necessarily the most authoritative statement on the problem; it may need additional investigation. Curtius, for one, thought it good to question some of Ehrismann's basic findings.[68]

This study does not advocate that on the basis of a single lyric we should modify our more or less codified and established way of viewing Hausen's poetry in general. There is, after all, a vast difference between this lyric and, say, "Min herze und min lip diu wellent scheiden" (chapter IX). Hausen is therefore not meant to emerge as a *jongleur* who merely wishes to dazzle with his ability to play with concepts and values. This chapter does imply, however, that it is rewarding to read below the surface of other Hausen poems. The results obtained may not change the composite view of his work as it now prevails, but it may reveal more clearly Hausen's many-sidedness and thus his stature and complexity as a poet. Hausen, as well as we, will be served by the delineation of the diverse facets in his art.

We do well, therefore, to look at other Hausen poems and, without casting overboard the more generalizing evaluations of his work, seek to detect what precisely Hausen is saying, how he is saying it, and what the possible implications are from within the quasi-real situations he creates in his individual lyrics. Throughout the discussion we keep in mind that Hausen was a man as intelligent as the best of us. Only in this way, it seems to me, can this gifted poet reach across the centuries and communicate with us meaningfully.

This approach suggests that we may come to understand Hausen better if we read and regard him as a poet in his own right—as we read and regard a poet such as Eichendorff, even though he, too, is a member of a movement to which the histories of literature have long ago attached a label. The thesis at stake in the above argument suggests that we may better understand Hausen if we examine the poems individually and attempt to read them on the poet's terms.

II. MICH MÜET DEICH VON DER LIEBEN QUAM

43, 1   I   1   Mich müet deich von der lieben quam   4 C
                     so verre hin. des muoz ich wunt
                     beliben: dest mir ungesunt.
                     ouch solte mich wol helfen daz
      5   5   daz ich ir ie was undertan.
                     sit ichs began,
                     so enkunde ich nie den staeten muot
                     gewenden rehte gar von ir,
                     wan si daz beste gerne tuot.

     10   II   10   Ez waere ein wünneclichiu zit,   4 B, 18 C
                     der nu bi friunden möhte sin.
                     ich waene an mir wol werde schin
                     daz ich von der gescheiden bin
                     die ich erkos für elliu wip.
     15   15   ir schoener lip
                     der wart ze sorgen mir geborn.
                     den ougen min muoz dicke schaden
                     daz si so rehte habent erkorn.

        III   Waer si mir in der maze liep,   5 B, 19 C
     20   20   so wurde es umb daz scheiden rat;
                     wan ez mir also niht enstat
                     daz ich mich ir getroesten müge;
                     ouch sol si min vergezzen niet.
                     wan do ich schiet

25   25 und ich si jungest ane sach,
             ze fröiden muose ich urlop nemen;
             daz mir da vor e nie geschach.

As late as 1961 it was suggested that "Ich muoz von schulden sin unfro" and "Mich müet deich von der lieben quam" form "ein einheitliches Lied."[1] The same view had earlier been advanced by Maurer.[2] But the three strophes under "Ich muoz von schulden sin unfro" seem to attain perfect unity and integrity;[3] the Aeneas-Dido reference constitutes the heart of the lyric and the problem to be unraveled. When it has been solved, when the "surprise" of the *double entendre* has been sprung, the lyric is at an end. Schönbach states it pithily: "Das Lied ist hier aus."[4] The larger composite envisioned by Maurer and Schröder, by way of contrast, amounts to a set of strophes without a trustworthy "plan" to lend it cohesion.

To clinch the matter, we must counter Maurer's and Schröder's reasons in favor of a six-strophe poem by arguing to the contrary purpose. Rather than being redundant by hashing over a point that perhaps is no longer in need of elaboration after the lengthy discussion in the previous chapter, we may use these remarks to bring out features in "Mich müet deich von der lieben quam" that should be mentioned anyway. In the first place, in each lyric the introductory strophe is more or less epic in quality while those that follow are reflective, and in the one case gradually lead to the speaker's proclaimed resolve to remain *staete*, and in the other lapse into past-bound reflections. Second, "Mich müet deich von der lieben quam" alludes to geographical distance between the speaker and a lady; Brinkmann is fully justified in calling it "In der Ferne."[5] "Ich muoz von schulden sin unfro" is not concerned with this kind of separation. Third, in the measure that we give full value to the adjective in "rehte staete" of MF 52,25 (chapter I, p. 15), in the same measure the phrase fails to harmonize with "in der maze liep" of MF 43,19 (see below). Fourth, *if* the two poems are read as belonging together, one of the closing lines in "Mich müet deich von der lieben quam"—"wan do ich schiet"—would refer to the second line of "Ich muoz von schulden sin unfro"—"do ich bi ir was"—and thus would lend the six strophes a circular arrangement. Such a composition would be detrimental to the tone of finality attained in MF 42,27—"diu ist mir von ir güete komen." Fifth, between "rehte staete" of MF 42,25 (projected into the future) and "den staeten muot" of MF 43,7 (with a reference to the past) there exists a clean break in the temporal sense. This would not be a problem since the second set of strophes does display an orientation to a past situation.[6] The discrepancy lies with the tension between the intended "staete pflegen" in the first poem and the attempt to "den staeten muot gewenden" in the second. Clearly, a time lapse would have to be presupposed because the erstwhile intent has collapsed, and hence would turn out to have the strength of a soap bubble, thus destroying or at least detrimentally affecting the very *pointe* of the lyric constituted by that decision.

All this does not deny the similarity of the themes treated in these two lyrics; however, they belong to a realm of limited thematic variations. And nothing prevents the possibility or even likelihood that the two poems were created one shortly after the other. Because of these considerations, we shall discuss "Mich müet deich von der lieben quam" as a separate unit.

Perhaps the most important feature of this lyric is the geographical distance between speaker and lady; it affects the meaning of the various statements, and almost immediately puts the slight epic element of the opening lines to the service of the reflective tone. The number of references to the first person singular is again conspicuous: there are twenty-seven of them fairly evenly distributed over the strophes. Whereas the main thought in each strophe of "Ich muoz von schulden sin unfro" was oriented toward past, present and future respectively, these tenses now occur in each strophe, as do a number of subjunctives. In this sense, "Mich müet deich von der lieben quam" is less tightly organized. For that matter, tightness of organization by whatever means is not an outstanding feature of this lyric.

The opening passage has a repetitive flavor:

> 1 Mich müet deich von der lieben quam
> so verre hin. des muoz ich wunt
> beliben: dest mir ungesunt.
>
> It troubles me that I have come so far from
> my dear one; that leaves me
> wounded; that is harmful to me.

What in "Ich muoz von schulden sin unfro" is conveyed in the first line by means of a reference to the speaker's mental state is here relayed with statements that refer to the speaker's physical condition, though the terms used clearly have a metaphorical ring. Since we are, as yet, totally unaware of the exact nature of the relationship between speaker and lady, these references to his physical state—"wunt beliben," "ungesunt" —may mean anything. Milnes, for instance, colors our awareness in this regard by reminding us that Ovid set an example when he depicted "den Liebenden als 'siech,' 'ungesunt,' weil die Leidenschaft so peinvoll ist."[7] In contrast to this, allusions to the appetites of the flesh are firmly excluded from the elucidation offered by Brinkmann.[8] Whatever their exact value, however, the opening lines stand in contrast to those that follow:

> 4 ouch solte mich wol helfen daz
> daz ich ir ie was undertan.
>
> the fact, however, that I was always
> subservient to her should help me.

And again, we cannot be fully confident about the meaning of these lines. Quite possibly, they imply that the speaker's long-time devotion calls for a reward, whatever its specific nature. In a generalizing statement about *Minnesang* Schmid says: "Hinter allem Geistigen steht schließlich doch der Wunsch nach der Liebeserfüllung, der dem ganzen Minnesang erst seine eigentliche Dynamik gibt."[9] But Langenbucher, equally generalizing, has a totally different point of view: "Minnesang ist überhaupt nicht Liebesdichtung und war nie als solche gemeint. Denn Minne, hohe Minne, ist der zentrale Begriff einer Lebensanschauung, ist eine Philosophie, und als solche Mittelpunkt jener 'höfischen Religion,' wie man die ritterliche Weltanschauung ganz trefflich genannt hat."[10]

These lines—

> 6 sit ichs began,
>   so enkunde ich nie den staeten muot
>   gewenden rehte gar von ir,
>   wan si daz beste gerne tuot.
>
>   since I began this
>   I never could turn my constant mind
>   entirely away from her,
>   for she does what is best gladly.

—could invite the view that "s" of "ichs" (6) refers to the speaker's "ie" (5) having been subservient to the lady, also if we follow Kraus by placing a period after the fifth line. But this "s" may also refer to the lines that follow—"gewenden" (8).[11] In this case it says that from a given moment onward the speaker began the attempt to blot the lady from his mind, but was never entirely successful—"gar" = "completely." Brinkmann favors another possibility, though in doing so he skirts a little problem: "[Der Dichter] konnte von Anbeginn seines Dienstes seinen beständigen Sinn nicht von ihr lösen; denn ihr Handeln erfüllt die höchsten Forderungen und zwar aus innerer Bereitschaft."[12] Brinkmann evidently wants to give the lady all the praise that could possibly come her way. But we are left to wonder whether "rehte gar" (8) indeed means "entirely properly" or whether it means "quite correctly" in the sense of "fully justified." The choice is of some consequence since in the former case the speaker never succeeded *quite* [though he was fully justified and actually tried—apparently repeatedly (cf. "nie" of the eighth line)];[13] in the latter case he could not act with full justification and hence never made an attempt.[14] However that may be, the fact remains that he thought at least of the *possibility* of turning away from the lady, but tried and was unsuccessful, or was not fully justified in doing so and hence refrained. The conclusion seems clear: the passage carries a double meaning, though it must remain a moot question whether the poet meant to be ambiguous, or whether we moderns are no longer sufficiently surefooted when seeking to traverse medieval territory of this kind. At any rate, the lady's qualities as conveyed in the last line of the strophe hold the speaker bound (against his will?), or it constitutes his insight that she will live up to her good repute and will give him his reward in the future. What that reward would amount to is not stated. The realm in which the lady "daz beste gerne tuot" thus becomes all-important, and is (significantly?) left unspecified. However, the speaker's preoccupation as it emerges in the second strophe (see below) suggests perhaps that in his own way of thinking this reward ought to be of a specific kind. Admittedly, this reading stands in contrast to this suggestion: "[Hausens] Lyrik ist ganz dem inneren Erlebnis zugewendet; die Welt als solche bedeutet seiner Dichtung nichts. Hausen ist—aus Anlage, nicht aus Mode—ganz auf Reflexion gestellt."[15] This "Reflexion" calls for a question; it seems to overlook the element of "Spiel," of "performance"; it is "Reflexion" in public and hence the question arises whether it is reflection at all in the common sense of the term.

The fourth line, then, presents an "on the other hand" situation; it conveys the speaker's way of pondering his problem, of seeking a way out of a predicament. Such a mind in such a state is easily given to building castles in the air, and it is therefore not surprising that the following strophe lapses into wishful thinking:

> 10 Ez waere ein wünneclichiu zit,
> der nu bi friunden möhte sin.
>
> It would be a delightful time
> for him who could now be with friends.

Lehfeld finds that "wünneclichiu zit" refers to the spring or summer season.[16] This suggestion conveys at best the fuzziness of the speaker's thought now that he ponders the warm afterglow of enjoyed companionship. There is as yet no compelling reason to understand these lines as relaying the importance of society for its own sake. If we took license to read them this way, they would be consistent with the notion touched upon elsewhere, to the effect that medieval man finds it difficult to be an individual since he must receive his worth through the acclaim of the world around him (see below). As it is, these lines simply seem to indicate the speaker's feeling of loneliness. Brinkmann sees it this way: "Das ist verhüllende Sprechweise des älteren Stils. Der Dichter bekennt seine Sehnsucht nach zugehörigen Menschen, aber nennt sie nur, weil er stillschweigend seine Geliebte in den Kreis der Zugehörigen einschließt."[17]

Brinkmann's statement, incidentally, touches upon the problem arising from the dichotomy between the poet as *Dichter* and the poet as *persona*. The tendency to overlook this difference has with many critics led to the habit of thinking of Hausen's poetry as "Erlebnisdichtung." But in any poetry with references to the first person singular the distinction is of consequence, particularly in *Minnesang*, where we are often aware of an audience. When, as is usual, there is also the preoccupation with a nebulous lady, the relationships between the various "characters" easily become complex, and it is often important whether we view a given passage from the point of view of one character or from that of another. It may even make a difference whether the (present) reader or the (historical) audience is seen as involved in the "performance" of the total poetic product. The matter of *Dichter* over against *persona* will be investigated elsewhere (see chapter XII, pp. 87 ff.) and need not detain us here.

The melancholy pondering of 10 f. causes the speaker to return to the concern with his own state (with which he was already preoccupied in the opening line of the first strophe):

> 12 ich waene an mir wol werde schin
> daz ich von der gescheiden bin
> die ich erkos für elliu wip.

> I believe[18] it will become known by (the sight of) me
> that I am separated from her
> whom I chose before[19] all women.

The C manuscript has a different reading for the twelfth line: "wan siht an mir wol ane strit."[20] Mowatt is tempted to supply "man" for "wan"; "siht" is then the third person singular; if "wan" is retained, "siht" must be an unusual form of second person plural "seht,"[21] and constitute an appeal to the audience. Whether we prefer 4 B or 18 C—the latter emended as suggested by Mowatt, or not—in each strophe there *is* a more or less overt appeal to the audience to take cognizance of the speaker's plight, the effects of which are evidently plainly visible.

Incidentally, Mowatt's interest in the C version stems from his notion that 4 C/18 C/19 C are perhaps not to be read as one poem, and that 4 B/5 B rather than 18 C/19 C are corrupt. With these views, the second of the poems thus formed would have

> wan es mir also niht beschiht
> als si mir gelobet hat
>
> but as it is it will not happen to me
> as she has promised me.

as one of its salient thoughts, thus leaving it up to the reader's imagination what exactly it was the lady promised. The first poem—our present first strophe—would have its thrust in the closing line.

The fourteenth line contains a reference to the past: "erkos." This verb occurs at the very center of the lyric and constitutes the main fact from which everything else derives. In an environment in which passivity and wishful thinking hold sway, the cause of the speaker's problem lies with an active deed on his part in the past. The lack of activity prevailing "now" is the result of that activity, as is the speaker's state—"ungesunt." Clearly he is paying for the choice he has made, and he knows it:

> 15 ir schoener lip
> der wart ze sorgen mir geborn.
>
> her beautiful person
> was born to bring me worries.

In these lines there is a cause-effect relationship established between the subject and "sorgen." As with "von sorgen erloesen" of MF 45,39 in "Ich sage ir nu vil lange zit" (chapter V), "sorgen" may contain "eine verhüllende Umschreibung."[22] If this is indeed the case, it adds something to the value of "ungesunt" (3).

The strophe is brought to an end by a statement which by now is not surprising; it is a restatement of 12 ff.:

> 17 den ougen min muoz dicke schaden
> daz si so rehte habent erkorn.

> my eyes are often affected
> because they selected so well.

This allusion to the speaker's frequent weeping suggests what the critics have defined as a kind of martyrdom for the sake of *hohe Minne*, but it may also suggest the love-starved swain, nothing more and nothing less. In either case, the immediate cause of these tears (explicitly alluded to twice—cf. 12 ff.—and hence begging attention) is emphatically said to be the lady's qualities—see "ir schoener lip" (15). In the second instance, given the adjective accompanying "lip," it would seem possible to translate this noun as "body" rather than as "person."

The second strophe brings to mind a passage in "Ich denke under wilen" (chapter XVII):

52, 3 I 7 mich sehent mange tage   45 B, 47C
              die liute in der gebaere
              als ich niht sorgen habe,
              wan ichs also vertrage.

              many a day people
              see me adopt the demeanor
              as though I have no worries
              for that is the way I bear it.

These lines are interesting. For one thing, the speaker's listeners, it seems, are made aware that he is posing, that he is pretending. For another, the lines have been said to bear testimony to the code that a knight in distress—in this case, because of love[23]—is not allowed to show his difficulties to the world around him.[24] To do so would be akin to allowing lack of *maze* to prevail.

It would seem possible to argue, however, that something other than the welfare of the courtly code is at stake, something much more important. For the conduct touched upon in rather similar fashions in the two passages just cited seems to demand that a person suppress all those feelings which could put a blemish on what may well have been the basic rule by which society of this era lived, *had* to live, in order to maintain itself: "fröide" *must* prevail. The individual who for some reason cannot contribute to it must take his chagrin with him into isolation until he is fit to "play" his part again.[25] Hence joy is much more than the sociability of which Brinkmann speaks; it is not only "eine frohe Seelenlage des einzelnen Menschen"; it is not even only "darüber hinaus das heitere Miteinander eines geselligen Kreises, in dem die Menschen sich gegenseitig zugewandt sind."[26] Instead "fröide" emerges as the prime ingredient with which to *uphold* society, to stay its ever threatening disintegration. For this society to exist it needs *fröide* the way a man needs oxygen. Take it away and you snuff out life. Hence *fröide* is for this society a means toward an end, it is society's defense, and it easily becomes forced, like a mask with a frozen smile. With this, indeed, we see the poet's importance to his society as a bringer of "fröide."[27] Hence in this framework, too, the statement is valid, even if it derives from a different concern: "Ernst ist das Leben und heiter ist die Kunst." Indeed, "die Kunst *muß* heiter sein."

To go one step further, with the above suggestions the question emerges whether perhaps *fröide* is *the* key term in the various literary monuments in the Middle Ages.[28] From this vantage point also, Wechssler seems to tell only half the story, and tell only of characteristics on the surface, when he says this:

> Frohes und wohlgesittetes Weltleben war der Inhalt der höfischen Geselligkeit. Anstatt die Sinnenfreude als sündhaft zu verdammen, veredelte man sie aus derber Lust zu feinem Lebensgenuß. Zum ersten Mal wurde die prinzipielle Verdammung der Welt und des Fleisches aufgehoben. Man entdeckte als neuen Lebenswert die harmonische Ausbildung des ganzen Menschen nach allen seinen Kräften und Anlagen. Man gewann das Bewußtsein von der Würde auch des natürlichen Menschen.[29]

By way of contrast, we would claim with Brinkmann that in *Minnesang* "es immer um menschliches Dasein schlechthin geht."[30] And, in the above sense alone, we can even agree with him that "die Minne stellvertretende Bedeutung hat,"[31] though it makes little difference now whether we speak of *hohe Minne* or love of a more mundane kind being celebrated in this poem. If we must speak of *hohe Minne*, we may do well to remember that along the present line of reasoning it is but subservient to a leading idea.

To put it differently: it is as though the change from erstwhile optimism to ultimate pessimism as it can be readily traced through the literature of the Renaissance—from the concept of the glory that is man's to that of the problematic aspects of his existence—comes about in Hausen's era in a much shorter period of time. It is, indeed, as though optimism (see Wechssler as cited above) is not *followed* but *accompanied* by pessimism, thus confronting the age with a profound dichotomy in man's existence. Brinkmann, from this point of view, is correct when he says that "man das Wesen des Minnesangs durchaus verkennt, wenn man in ihm nichts anders als eine geschichtliche Merkwürdigkeit sieht, ein Zeichen für lebensfremde Verspieltheit, die mit leichter Gebärde über den Ernst des Daseins hinweggeht."[32] For in order to exist, society needs "die leichte Gebärde"; it is but one way amongst several with which to bring *fröide* and thus uphold society. Take *fröide* away and you lay reality bare in all its awesomeness. Hence not "sinnliche Lebenslust ist das Ziel"[33] of courtly society, but rather its attempt to cover up "den tiefen Ernst des Lebens,"[34] and its would-be aim is achieved in the measure that it enhances *fröide*. With this in mind, we can agree with Brinkmann when he finds that regarding *Minnedienst*—not defined in the way he understands it—"eine mächtige Persönlichkeit wie Hausen sich ganz in ihm erfüllte."[35] For Hausen, like the unknown poet of the *Nibelungenlied*,[36] knows all too well that reality must remain covered. Because of the totally different vantage points involved we cite Wechssler for the sake of contrast rather than similarity: "als ideelle Reaktion gegen den Zwang der Realität werden wir den Minnesang am besten begreifen."[37] With "Realität" he means something other than reality as referred to in these paragraphs, where it comes to stand for chaos, destruction, disintegration, awfulness.

It bears pointing out that the suggestions advanced here do not claim to be valid for *Minnesang* at large or even for all the Hausen lyrics. We may wonder, though, whether they are more generally applicable to an important degree. For the above reasoning suggests that Hausen's ambiguities and whatever other poetic devices he employs enable him to serve the principle of *fröide*, not merely as an end in itself, but, on a plane of a different and higher order, as a means to an end. In this sense we are able to appreciate fully what to Wechssler appears as an offensive paradox in *Minnesang*: the poet brings entertainment and hence *fröide* by allowing the speaker to refer to his woes: Wechssler says, "Darin liegt ein Widerspruch, der heute unser Gefühl verletzt."[38]

It follows from the above that in the seventeenth line—"den ougen min muoz dicke schaden"—the speaker's eyes testify to his having shed tears in isolation in order not to violate the first rule of polite society. Thus informing his audience of his lack of *maze*, he claims to have adhered to the rule that *fröide* must prevail. Indeed, his tears become a device with which to entertain and hence bring *fröide*; therefore, for such is the logical paradox, they become a weapon with which to keep reality at bay.

That there is indeed lack of *maze* becomes evident in the third strophe:

> 19 Waer si mir in der maze liep,[39]
> so wurde es umb daz scheiden rat;
> wan ez mir also niht enstat[40]
> daz ich mich ir getroesten müge;
>
> If I loved her moderately,
> there would be a solution to this separation;
> but as it is, I am not in a position
> to console myself regarding her.

These lines serve on more than one level—at least from the modern reader's point of view. On the one hand they indicate that if "such and such" were the case, the speaker could forget his lady—"sich ir getroesten"; on the other hand, "sich getroesten" with a genitive carries the value of "to console oneself regarding someone (or something)," and thus leaves open the question about the exact nature of such solace. Linked with "ir schoener lip" (15), it may be of one kind,[41] but it may also stand there in platonic purity.

Another ambiguity lies with "also" of 21; it may refer to the lady's *not* being "in der maze liep" (italics added) to the speaker, in which case "sich getroesten ir" may stand for "to forget her," "console myself regarding her (elsewhere?)." But "also" may equally well refer to the state of separation prevailing—"scheiden" of the twentieth line. In the former case, it would accord with the fact that the speaker at least *thought* of forgetting his lady (see above); in the latter case, nothing prevents us from wondering whether the speaker refers to a relationship, now ended because of the geographical distance, in which he had the joys coming a man's way who loved happily.[42] The latter notion would gain in plausibility from the following line and lead to the most natural explanation of "ouch" occurring in it:

> 23 ouch sol si min vergezzen niet.
>
>   she should not forget me either.

In contrast to its counterpart in the third line, "ouch" must be rendered as "also": for the very same reason that I am not able to forget her, she should not forget me.

Ambiguity marks the rest of the strophe as well:

> 24 wan do ich schiet
>   und ich si jungest ane sach,
>   ze fröiden muose ich urlop nemen;
>   daz mir da vor e nie geschach.
>
>   for when I departed
>   and saw her for the last time
>   I had to take leave of joys;
>   that never happened to me before.

Evidently, the speaker either took leave from the lady with whom he therefore had personal contact, or he took leave from the environment in which she blossoms. Depending on which of these possibilities we prefer, we can either say that *fröide* may go as far as alluding to the joys of love, or it refers to the joys of beholding the lady; there seems to be no possibility of arguing in favor of one reading exclusively, though this is not to say that Hausen was vague because he *wanted* to be ambiguous.

Baumgarten, who cannot be suspected of sympathizing with the multiple possibilities suggested here, has this to say:

> Wenn . . . Müllenhoff die Worte "ze fröiden muose ich urlop nemen" so zu verstehen scheint, als meinte der Dichter, durch den Abschied von der Geliebten wäre er von aller Freude geschieden, so würde dies nur möglich sein, wenn dastände "zer fröide"; denn nur dies könnte bedeuten von der Freude überhaupt oder von aller Freude; "ze fröiden" aber heißt von gewissen, zwar nicht näher bezeichneten, durch den Zusammenhang aber nicht bestimmte Freuden.[43]

We could accept this argument if it were not for the fact that Baumgarten then speaks of the joys "die das freundliche Entgegenkommen, mit dem die Dame diesmal den Dichter auszeichnete, diesem bereitete."[44]

Whatever our way of reading, on either level the closing line tells us that the speaker has been in the habit of receiving joys. Insofar as the reference to the physical aspect in "ungesunt" (3) and the statement "ir schoener lip/ der wart ze sorgen mir geborn" (15 f.; see above) seem to make the notion of abstract, platonic love questionable, the counterargument hinges on the view that the speaker is forced to keep things platonic (against his wishes?); the "present" situation may not be platonic in intent, but it has to be in actual fact because of the separation.

Along the line of reasoning expounded here, "lieben" (1) is in harmony with either possibility since this substantive adjective suggests *Liebe* as much as *Minne*, and nothing prevents either from being *staete* in the sense of "echt," true.

III. AN DER GENADE AL MIN FRÖIDE STAT

43, 28   I   1   An der genade al min fröide stat,   5 C
                     da enmac mir gewerren noch huote noch nit.
   30   I   mich enhilfet dienest noch friunde rat,
                     und daz si mir ist liep sam min selbes lip.
               5   mir erwendet ir hulde nieman wan si selbe,
                     si tuot mir alleine swaz kumbers ich trage:
                     waz sold ich danne von merkaeren klagen,
   35   nu ich ir huote also lützel engelde?

        II   Mangen herzen von huote ist we,   6 C
              10   unde jent ez si in ein angstlichiu not:
                     so engert daz mine aller richheit niht me
                     wan müese ez si liden unz an minen tot.
44, 1   wer möhte han groze fröide ane kumber?
                     nach solher swaere rang ich alle zit:
              15   done mahte ich leider niht komen in den nit.
                     des hat gelücke getan an mir wunder.

     5   III   Einer swaere muoz ich leider aenic sin,   7 C
                     die doch erfürhtet vil manc saelic man:
                     unbetwungen von huote ist daz herze min.
              20   mir ist leit daz ich von ir den fride ie gewan;
                     wand ich wolde die not iemer güetliche liden,
   10   hete ich von schulden verdienet den haz.
                     nit umb ir minne daz taete mir baz
                     danne ich si beide sus muoz lan beliben.

The opening line:

     1 An der genade al min fröide stat,

     All my joy depends on grace.

is a poetic statement in any idiom. It stands there like an axiom, proclaiming a self-evident truth that each should make his own. Wechssler reminds us that "genade" carries judicial and ecclesiastical connotations. His insight leads him to suggest: "Nachdem einmal im Frauenkult die Herrin gleichsam zu göttlichem Rang erhoben war, lag es nahe, von ihr auch die gratia Dei zu erwarten. So wurde die Gnade vom feudalen Rechtsbegriff in den kirchlichen hinübergespielt."[1] From the ecclesiastical sphere, we must assume, the concept entered the domain of poetry. Committed to a particular way of reading this poetry, Brinkmann states: "Alle Aussagen des Dichters über sein Verhältnis zur Minne und zum Leben (so gar zu Gott) sind in die eine Aus-sage über sein Verhältnis zur Frau hineingelegt."[2] Whatever the ultimate reaction to this view, the reader readily agrees that "genade" has something to do with rapprochement; it evokes notions that center around the receiving of bliss, and the only question is in which realm of life it is applied, and how far it will go, or is expected to go.

Because of the lofty connotations accompanying the opening line, the second comes as a surprise:

> 2 da enmac mir gewerren noch huote noch nit.
>
> neither watchfulness nor envy can deter me from that.

Even in a poem which has as one of its main characteristics the antithetical statement, and is prone to present the reader with dialectical twists of thought, we are totally unprepared for this one, and we quickly must make our adjustment now that it turns out that there is nothing left of the judicial or ecclesiastical sphere to intrude upon the value of the opening line; it is thoroughly "secularized" by the immediately following reference to "huote" and "nit." Brinkmann, too, makes an adjustment: "Der ritterliche Mensch lebt nicht in einem behüteten Dasein; er ist gewohnt, durch Gefahr und Feind zu reiten."[3]

Now, the manuscript has this:

> da en mag mir gewerren weder huote noch kip
>
> neither watchfulness nor lack of cooperation can deter me from that.

If we abide by Kraus' and Brinkmann's emendation we are taking it for granted that "huote" and "nit," both of which basically tell the same tale—that is to say, if we have Kraus' and Brinkmann's views in mind that it is the "nit" of the guardians—will constitute the central motif in the lyric now that it is found to be emphatically indicated by means of the repetitive device. And, it is true, no effective counterargument seems available with which to gainsay the view that "kip" is the product of a later day than Hausen's and stems from some scribe's dabbling with the text as it had been handed down. However, Hausen's exact words are a matter of conjecture, and the scribe's emendation, if it was one, is no less plausible than any other as far as making sense is concerned. It can be argued, then, that we lose nothing if we return to the manuscript. Indeed, we seem to gain something. At least, the use of "kip" is appealing, not so much because it rhymes with "lip" (4)—this desire to have the rhymes neat may be too modern a concern[4]—but because "kip" is not redundant with respect to "huote" and because it helps contrive a set of contrasts and balances:

> 3 mich enhilfet dienest noch friunde rat,
> und daz si mir ist liep sam min selbes lip.[5]
>
> neither service nor the counsel of friends helps me,
> nor that she is as dear to me as my own life.

Now we have an arrangement in which "friunde rat" and "dienest" balance with "huote" and "kip" respectively, so that the activity of the guardians and the uncooperative attitude of the lady[6] are posed over against the counsel of friends and the speaker's own service. The speaker's problem as well as his environment's way of affecting it thus come into play from the very outset.

The third and fourth lines, then, tell us that "genade" is not forthcoming, and whatever the further development may be, we understand from these lines also that the task of the guardians is to protect the lady against the speaker, that she *wants* that protection—though with her effective "kip" she is hardly in need of it. The speaker's coming statements regarding the function of the guardians are therefore tantamount to tilting against windmills, to gesticulating in a vacuum. Though the lady stands at the core of his dilemma, he "forgets" her and thus skirts his real problem.[7] We therefore deal with a lyric in which the emphasis lies on the artful manipulation of concepts rather than the mulling over of a "real" experience, which not only Brinkmann but many other critics consider the basis for this lyric. Seibold, for instance, writes: "Das Besondere in Hausens Stellung zur huote war, daß er sie nicht nur anerkannte, sondern sogar ausdrücklich lobte, wenn hierbei vielleicht auch persönliche Erlebnismomente ausschlagend mitwirkten; denn es war mehr als erstaunlich, daß ein Diener und Verherrlicher der Minne sich in solcher Weise für eine der Liebeserfüllung feindliche Einrichtung einsetzte."[8] Precisely, it is "mehr als erstaunlich," it is impossible (see below). Citing these lines—

50, 27	noch bezzer ist daz ich si mide dan si ane huote waere;	38 B, 40 C

it is still better that I avoid her
than her being without guardians;

—Seibold states: "Allerdings blieb ihm in der Praxis anscheinend die Gelegenheit erspart, die Probe auf diese Theorie zu machen, oder es war vielmehr so, daß die huote, die man seiner Geliebten angedeihen ließ, sich gegen ihn nicht richtete, weil die Liebe nur einseitig war und von der Dame nicht erwidert wurde."[9]

Brinkmann states: "Der Dichter [bejaht] die Fremdheit, die Huote hervorruft, indem sie sich zwischen den Mann und die Frau stellt."[10] But if it is read as reflecting a true-to-life situation the lyric as a whole fails to support the notion that the speaker approves and affirms the function of the guardians. This readiness to equate the poet with the speaker pulls the entire frame of poetic reference awry and wreaks havoc with the endeavor to approach this poem, any poem, on the basis of its own assumptions. According to Brinkmann, every sentence must be taken as coming from the poet's deep interior,[11] from his innermost fund of insights derived from actual experiences. Explications are therefore doomed to be tortuous because they must follow every single twist of the poet's mind as it reveals itself in autobiographical-antithetical statements. Witness the following: "Es kommt in diesem Liede freilich nicht auf die Veränderung[12] in der Stellung der Frau an, sondern auf die seelische Erfahrung, die dem Manne dabei wird. Hausen genügt nicht die selbstverständliche

Erfüllung der Gemeinsamkeit, die 'freude' heißen würde, sondern *er will den Schmerz*, der ansagt, daß das Gefühl auf Grenzen und Widerstand stößt"[13] (italics added). Korn epitomizes the same orientation and thought when he speaks of "die schmerzlich gefühlte *ideelle Notwendigkeit* des immerwährenden Fernseins von der Geliebten, da sonst die hohe Minne zerbrechen müßte"[14] (italics added).

Meanwhile, what in the first line initially sounded like a coming eulogy on "genade" we now know to be something else. These lines state it explicitly:

> 5 mir erwendet ir hulde nieman wan si selbe,
> si tuot mir alleine swaz kumbers ich trage:
>
> only she herself withholds her acknowledgment from me,
> she alone causes me the pain I must bear.

This is the manuscript version:

> mir erwendet ir hulde nieman wan ir melde
> si tuot mir alleine den kumber den ich muos tragen
>
> only her betrayal withholds her acknowledgment from me,
> it/she alone causes me the pain I must bear.

The Kraus emendation, it is clear, gets rid of the manuscript's indictment of the lady; the rationale behind this change is similar to that causing the change of the lady's "kip" in the second line into the guardians' "nit." The orientation behind this emendation process does not seem to stem so much from the justified concern to render obscure lines intelligible as from the determination to have the poem say what it ought to be saying; by changing a key term here and there the lady is rendered impeccable, and thus conforms to the image of her role in the value system of *hohe Minne*. But as Mowatt reminds us in an understatement: "Here Hausen seems to be asserting that the real obstacle is the lady herself."[15] If we adhere to the manuscript's version—"ir melde"—Mowatt's reminder is clearly borne out; the fact that "si" of the following line is now ambiguous since it may refer to the lady directly or to her "melde" is little cause for concern since so far we have encountered ample evidence that Hausen uses ambiguity to lend spice to poetry. It is therefore surprising that Mowatt, who tends to defend (ably) the manuscripts against various types of emendations that seek to "improve" Hausen's poetry for one reason or another, has nothing to say this time about the advocated changes. Is it that Mowatt, too, in his own way seeks to maintain, even against the facts of the manuscripts, the image of the lady on the pedestal?[16]

The following lines testify also to the soundness of Mowatt's view that the lady is the true obstacle in this lyric:

> 7 waz sold ich danne von merkaeren klagen,
> nu ich ir huote also lützel engelde?

> why then should I complain about the guardians,
> now that they do not concern themselves with me?

The last line could also have the value "now that I am not at all the subject of their activity." In either case, these lines tell us that the guardians have no reason to exercise any form of "nit"; there is no necessity for it—see also "unbetwungen von huote ist daz herze min" (19).

We gain from Brinkmann's insight "daß dieses Gedicht seine Festigkeit vornehmlich durch die Substantive erhält."[17] The key nouns are used in such a way as to draw the three strophes closer together. Whereas some of these nouns occur in the first strophe—"huote," "fröide," "kumber"—and others in the third—"huote," "not," "swaere"—they are all found in the second strophe, which thus becomes the *pièce de résistance* in the lyric:

> 9 Mangen herzen von huote ist we,
> unde jent ez si in ein angstlichiu not:
> so engert daz mine aller richheit niht me
> wan müese ez si liden unz an minen tot.
> wer möhte han groze fröide ane kumber?
> nach solher swaere rang ich alle zit:
> done mahte ich leider niht komen in den nit.
> des hat gelücke getan an mir wunder.
>
> Many a heart is beset by watchfulness
> and says it is in dire distress;
> but of all riches mine desires only
> that I would bear it until my death.
> who would have great joy without sorrow?
> after such burden I strove all my time;
> yet, unfortunately, I am unable to incur envy.
> here fortune has performed miracles for me.

It is this amassing of nouns clamoring for attention that makes the strophe interesting, for it brings out even more clearly than the first and third strophes a kind of tension between these evocative terms and the speaker's marked tendency to hover around the subject of his concern. Though this pull is detectable also if we read the lyric with Kraus' emendations in mind, it becomes more clearly evident with the manuscript reading; the latter contains terms more startling than the emended version. This does not only apply to "kip" and "melde" of the first stanza, but also to the nouns in the closing line of the second.

About this last line as found in *Des Minnesangs Frühling* Sanders states: "Für diese eigenwillige Prägung findet sich keine Parallele, sofern man nicht auf den Gott der vorhöfischen Dichtung zurückgreifen will, der uns oft als 'wunderaere' erscheint. Trotzdem, was kann eine transzendente, dem Willen des Menschen sich entziehende, aber objektiv zu seinem Besten handelnden Schicksalsmacht zu dieser Zeit anders sein als die göttliche Vorsehung?"[18] The reaction to this suggestion can be unequi-

ocal: it was not Hausen (as represented by the manuscript) who reached back to precourtly periods, but it was Kraus who did—that is to say, Kraus as understood by Sanders. For the force alluded to in "gelüke" as found in the manuscript

> des hat gelüke vil getan an mir tumber
>
> fate has done that to me, simpleton

does *not* objectively act for man's good—as seen by the speaker (see below)—and there is nothing here of "göttliche Vorsehung"; "gelüke" refers to fate in the most secular manner possible. Indeed, the use of this term provides a clue regarding the "value" of this strophe, and hence of the lyric as a whole.[19] And "tumber," awkward though its nominative form may be, rather than "wunder" is meaningful. We must acknowledge that the line as found in the manuscript very plainly tells us something about the speaker's own view of his situation, and consequently about himself. It so happens that his self-revelation harmonizes perfectly with the self-delineation of the speakers in several other Hausen poems. With this, it should be stated that Kraus may have a point when he says: "Die Zahl der Änderungen [in diesem Gedicht] (18 in 24 Versen) wird manchem zu groß erscheinen."[20]

At its half-way point the strophe has the line that signals a turn in the development of the motifs touched upon: "wer möhte han groze fröide ane kumber?"[21] The natural answer would be "Why, everybody of course!" but no such answer is intended. The rhetorical question disregards the (many) lucky ones who do enjoy "gröze fröide ane kumber," and veers instead toward rationalizing on the speaker's own, less fortunate state. From his viewpoint it is unreasonable, things being what they are, even to think of the possibility of having "gröze fröide ane kumber," and so he sets out to cover his wound with a piece of verbal (and entertaining) plaster.[22] Whether this philosophizing is equatable with entertaining patter under the guise of "Reflexion" is a question that touches upon the depth of this lyric. This much, at any rate, seems certain: "An der genade al min fröide stat" is not a poem in which the speaker leads himself through a school of learning for the sake of arriving at an insight with immutable and compelling verity. Instead we are dealing with a lyric which aims at entertainment, and thus at bringing "fröide." In this manner, "tumber" (16) may not refer to a person who has no experience, but to one who is incapable of learning from such an experience.

Brinkmann says about this poem that "eine neue Kunst des erwägenden, zugespitzten Sprechens im Schluß ihre Bewährung [besteht]."[23] This is precisely the case and it follows that in actuality the answer to the centrally located question *would* be in the affirmative—"everybody of course"—that consequently the successful pursuit of love constitutes the pinnacle of all things desirable in love. And a statement like this is puzzling: "Die anderen, die den Weg zur Frau mit Blick und Wort bewachen, empfindet der Liebende, der den Eingang in das Heiligtum sucht, als Feind,"[24] not because it is not true, but because it contradicts Brinkmann's own statement as cited above, to the effect that the speaker "die Fremdheit [bejaht], die Huote hervorruft,"[25] and because the alleged search for "den Eingang in das Heiligtum" gives the poem an entirely unwarranted metaphysical twist. The third strophe, like strophes I and II, fails to support the trend of Brinkmann's argument:

> 17 Einer swaere muoz ich leider aenic sin,
> die doch erfürhtet vil manc saelic man:
> unbetwungen von huote ist daz herze min.
> mir ist leit daz ich von ir den fride ie gewan;
> wand ich wolde die not iemer güetliche liden,
> hete ich von schulden verdienet den haz.
> nit umb ir minne daz taete mir baz
> danne ich si beide sus muoz lan beliben.
>
> Unfortunately I must do without one affliction,
> though many a happy man fears it;
> my heart is free from guardians;
> I am sorry I ever gained peace from them;
> for I would always bear such distress without
>   complaining,
> if I had earned hatred with good cause.
> envy because of her love would serve me better
> than remaining as I do without either.

This strophe "tells it like it is," even though it still engages in the same "Kunst des erwägenden, zugespitzten Sprechens"[26] as the preceding strophes; "leider" (17) and the lyric's closing lines "give the show away."

Schmid says: "Wenn in diesem Gedicht der Ritter klagt, er würde lieber als die Unerbitterlichkeit der Dame der Merker 'nit umb ir minne' erdulden, so kann damit nur die Liebeserfüllung gemeint sein, da sich wohl kaum der Neid gegen eine geistige Minne wenden würde."[27] There is no contradiction involved when we accept this statement together with the metaphor according to which the speaker "den Eingang in das Heiligtum sucht."

With Brinkmann's view of a development being observable in Hausen's lyrics and his conviction that we therefore can learn from them how the poet arrives gradually at an insight, a philosophy of love to be called *hohe Minne*, he has good reason to call this poem "Umwertung." But with "kip" and "melde" attributed to the lady, things take on a quite different color, and it would seem that the cerebral quality saturating this poem draws emphatic attention to the manipulative dexterity displayed throughout. And it belies the notion of an "experience" celebrated, as it defies any attempt to put it in a reliably chronological order with other Hausen lyrics. At best we can only guess and wonder on the basis of a given poem, based on the artistry that went into its composition, whether a particular lyric is likely to be an early or a late one. And if we wish to venture a guess, we still run the risk that a "good" poem, by whatever standards and criteria we apply, could have been written at an early, inspired moment, or a "bad" one at a later, lackluster hour.

IV. DIU SÜEZEN WORT HANT MIR GETAN

44, 13   I   1 Diu süezen wort hant mir getan,   8 C
                 diu ir die besten algemeine
   15   sprechent, daz ich niene kan
                 gedenken wan an si aleine.
                   5 min ander angest der ist kleine,
                 wan der den ich von ir han.
                 got weiz wol daz ich nie gewan
   20   in al der werlt so liebe enkeine.
                 des sol si mich geniezen lan.

       II   10 Swes got an güete und an getat   9 C
                 noch ie dekeiner frowen gunde,
                 des gihe ich im daz er daz hat
   25   an ir geworht als er wol kunde.
                 waz danne, und arne i'z under stunden?
                 15 min herze es dicke hohe stat.
                 noch möhte es alles werden rat,
                 wolden si die grozen sunde
   30   geriuwen dies an mir begat.

       III   Swaz got an fröiden lat betagen,   10 C
                 20 dazn kan er mir an ir niet meren,
                 wan alse ich ir min angest sage,
                 daz kan si leider wol verkeren.
   35   ein hartez herze kan siz leren,
                 dazs also lihte mac vertragen
                 25 so grozez wüefen unde klagen
                 deich lide umbe ir hulde sere
                 die ich niemer mac getragen.

The opening statement has been said to relay the blossoming of love from afar in the framework of *hohe Minne*, because the lady is lauded by the molders of public opinion:

     1 Diu süezen wort hant mir getan,
        diu ir die besten algemeine
        sprechent, daz ich niene kan
        gedenken wan an si aleine.

        The sweet words which the best people
        generally speak about her

> have affected me so that
> I can think of her only.

This is the opinion of Brinkmann, who adds: "Aus der Ferne strahlt nur der Ruhm eines leuchtenden Gestirns; jeder Schritt in ihre Nähe ist ein Schritt ins menschliche Dasein."[1] However, nothing prevents the notion that public opinion, though important, has merely enhanced the feeling which was there to begin with. This good repute enhances the lady's desirability. The phenomenon is not all that startling and not exclusively typical of *Minnesang*. It corresponds to the basic human need to meet with approval of one's important choices and decisions in life. This must have been true particularly for an era of which the literature testifies again and again that such abstract goods as honor came a man's way primarily through the acclaim of others. Honor could come to a man or could be taken away from him simply by his environment saying that he had it, or did not have it.[2] Viewed in this way, love upon hearsay may have been readily plausible to the medieval mind and something natural within any framework of thinking, whether that of *niedere Minne*, *echte Minne*, or whatever type of love we should wish to consider. There is therefore no reason to look upon love from afar and before first sight or upon hearsay as a characteristic of *hohe Minne* exclusively.

Without wishing to detract anything from the above suggestion, which has implications so far-flung as to demand wider and closer investigation, we may say that "Diu süezen wort hant mir getan" does not, Brinkmann notwithstanding, allude as a matter of course to love before first sight. In fact, there is reason to think the opposite (see below). For the moment we can only say that "gedenken" (4) is not equatable with loving (in any fashion).[3] The verb signifies at best the speaker's *readiness* to do so, and thus conforms to the notions touched upon above.

We learn from the following lines that the speaker's state of mind as relayed in the first statement comes with "angest":

> 5 min ander angest der ist kleine,
> wan der den ich von ir han.
>
> my other worry is small
> compared to that I have from her.

The fifth line may well be a litotes carrying the value "none at all" ("I have no worries whatsoever save the one I have because of her"); and this anguish seems to derive from the speaker's "gedenken" (4). Pondering matters, does he perhaps come to the conclusion that with the proclaimed qualities of the lady he should deem himself to be incapable of gaining her favor? Or do these lines not at all convey a lack of self-confidence, and must we look for an explanation such as Brinkmann offers? He states: "Angest meint nicht . . . ein Gefühl der Angst, sondern eine Situation des Menschen, bei der es auf Tod und Leben geht. In solche Situation hat ihn die Frau gebracht, und nur von ihr aus droht ihm Gefahr. Die Gefahr liegt im Übermaß der Liebe."[4] Does Brinkmann come close to putting an unequivocal meaning to the closing line of the strophe?

> 7   got weiz wol daz ich nie gewan
>   in al der werlt so liebe⁵ enkeine.
>   des sol si mich geniezen lan.
>
> God knows that I never loved
> anyone so much in the world.
> she should let me enjoy that.

Fischer, translating freely, renders the closing line this way: "Drum führ sie mich zum Glück die Bahn!"⁶ According to Frank it has the value of "Das soll sie mir zugute halten (lohnen)."⁷ The former translation is only slightly less informative than the latter as to the possible connotations that may come with this line. Milnes, for instance, could argue from his point of view that the line fits into a much more earthly environment than Brinkmann envisions.⁸

The second strophe suggests that we are not dealing with love from afar; the speaker seems to know the lady:

> 10 Swes got an güete und an getat
>   noch ie dekeiner frowen gunde,
>   des gihe ich im daz er daz hat
>   an ir geworht als er wol kunde.
>
> Whatever God granted in goodness and beauty
> to any woman, I must admit
> that he has endowed her with it
> as he well was able.

The emphatic quality of these lines can hardly stem from the opinion of others, no matter how reliable their judgment is thought to be. Love thus did not stem from the praise of "die besten algemeine," but was enhanced by it. This is not to deny that the lady is without blemish; that, in fact, is precisely the reason why anyone can readily join the chorus in her praise. For as Schönbach reminds us: " 'güete' und 'getan' zusammen machen erst einen Menschen glücklich: pulchritudo corporis und bonitas animae fügen sich zusammen zu beatitudo."⁹ Whether we have license to interpret this insight as a sign of religious or mystical influences working behind this line of poetry is a different matter; on other occasions, too, Hausen turns out to be quite capable of severing completely the umbilical cord between an erstwhile religious or mystical tenet and the actual value with which he imbues a line of poetry seemingly derived from such a tenet.¹⁰

There is a surprising development after these lines; it comes in the form of a rhetorical question; the manuscript delivers it in these words:

> was danne und arnez under stunde
> min herze es dike hohe stat
>
> what then if it is affected on occasion?
> my heart is often raised high because of it.

Says Kraus: "Das apokoinou . . . ist in der Lyrik kaum je zu finden, auch würde der Konjunktiv bedeuten 'möge es mein Herz arnen,' während hier der Sinn sein müßte 'wenn es auch mein Herz entgelten muß,' und schließlich ist der Gegensatz von 'ich' und 'herz' sehr geistreich."[11] On the basis of this rationale he rewrites:

> 14 waz danne, und arne i'z under stunden?
> min herze es dicke hohe stat.

One may wonder, however, whether Kraus' "Gegensatz von 'ich' und 'herz' " is at least in part motivated by his awareness that this contrast is found elsewhere in Hausen's poetry.[12] Besides, the original line may be more "geistreich" than Kraus' emendation: the use of the verb "arnen" has wit; it refers to the speaker's heart "harvesting grief," and the following line returns with a neat twist to the normally desirable result of "arnen" ("to reap the benefit") by referring to the effect such "arnen" has on the heart, thereby presenting the speaker as subject to the oscillation between high hopes and low spirits that we encounter in several other Hausen lyrics. If we also consider that there seems nothing wrong with reading the fourteenth line as "möge es mein Herz arnen," we lose nothing if we return to the reading provided by the manuscript: the speaker—or rather, his heart—alternates between despair and high spirits, a common phenomenon at any time and place in love poetry, and the equivalent of alternate paling and flushing of a swain's cheeks or any other conventionally relayed oscillation between optimism and pessimism. This oscillation is punctuated by the time elements "under stunde" and "dike."

As the strophe's closing statement indicates, the speaker's high feelings derive from an envisioned state of grace; again we cite the manuscript:

> noch möhte es alles werden rat
> wolden si die grozen wunde
> erbarmen die si an mir begat
>
> everything could still be well,
> if the great wounds which she inflicts
> on me would cause her pity.

"Wunden *begat* man nicht,"[13] says Kraus, and he changes to "sunde geriuwen." Brinkmann objects to this,[14] and Kraus himself does not want to be dogmatic: "Scheint dies und die umlautlose Form 'sunde' zu kühn, so könnte man wohl . . . an 'wunder' denken."[15] Since the manuscript's "wunde" are only factual as metaphor— as "sunde" would be—there seems to be no compelling need to follow Kraus' attempt at improvement. Nor is it necessary to follow Korn: "Inmitten der bewegtesten Klagen stehen die zuversichtlichen Worte von ihrem Erbarmen. Wenn irgendwo die Anknüpfung des Minneethos an die tiefen Gedanken der Mystik gerechtfertigt ist, dann hier."[16] For there is nothing "zuversichtlich" about the speaker's subjunctive statement (his optimistic mood has an "if" situation as its flimsy basis), and there are no mystical allusions to be found in it, neither with "sunde geriuwen" nor "wunde erbarmen"; *if* there were, they would have been so "secularized" as to be totally valueless coins within the mystical realm. Korn's is a case of *Systemzwang* for the sake of a leading idea, Korn's idea, that up to this point in our readings fails to stand in any close and obvious relationship to Hausen's poetry.

The third strophe has caused difficulties; we cite the manuscript again:

> Swes got an frowen aller tagen
> das enkan mir an ir nieman gemeren
> wan alse ich ir muos min angest sagen
> das kan si leider wol verkeren

And it is true, the nineteenth line does present a problem since there seems to be no way of accounting for the genitive "aller." Emendations have therefore been mandatory. Kraus, for instance, changes "aller tagen" into "lat betagen." Mowatt agrees that some such change is needed but he sees no justification for Kraus' emending "frowen" into "fröiden."[17] Brinkmann switches to "swes got an fröiden alle tage" which he translates as "was Gott an Freuden schenkt," on the basis of the assumption that "an" is the preterite of "gönnen" rather than a preposition.[18] Other commentators have advanced other solutions.[19] Without claiming to have the only correct emendation we suggest turning "aller" into "alle" which then modifies "frowen," and to take "tagen" as in infinitive ("to bring to light") with the auxiliary "kan" (20) serving two infinitives. We thus get this:

> Whatever God can bring forth in all women,
> cannot be improved in her in my eyes,
> unless I must tell her my anguish;
> she can unfortunately change that.

Now 19 f. are intelligible with only one slight emendation.

The above suggestion does not imply that the following lines are very clear. As understood here, 21 f. constitute an antithesis to 19 f.—joy versus anguish—and the balsam envisioned in the strophe's opening lines is counterpointed by the fear that the lady may change this positive value (cultivated by mere wishful thinking) *if* he were to tell her of his anguish; for then she might (unfortunately) change his high opinion of her into despair, presumably by firmly rejecting her pleading suitor (see the following lines): here again is the notion of the daunted lover. This reading seems mandatory because of the occurrence of "leider" (22); hence this term makes unavoidable that "daz" of the same line refers to lines 19 f. Incidentally, 21 tells us that the lady does not know of the speaker's anguish. This lack of awareness on her part affects the way in which we read the following passage:

> 23 ein hartez herze kan siz leren,
> dazs also lihte mac vertragen
> so grozez wüefen unde klagen
> deich lide umbe ir hulde sere
> die ich niemer mac getragen.

> a hard heart may teach her
> that she can so easily bear
> such great woe and lament
> which I suffer with pain for the sake of her favor,
> which I shall never be able to bear.

Since the lady knows nothing, these lines lack all force. Stated in a moment of pessimism, they provide a counterweight to the fifteenth line: "min herze es dicke hohe stat." In this manner, the mind tortures itself by vacillating between hope and despair; the speaker suffers all the pangs of love before he knows he must bear them because the lady has definitely rejected him. As yet there is no indication that she has done so, and the question of her making a statement to that effect never arises. This, indeed, is the daunted lover, preferring to remain in the limbo of indecision by not confronting the lady of his choice with his problem. Incidentally, the passage does not say that the lady *has* a hard heart.

A word is to be said about the references to God in this poem. They have been interpreted as bearing testimony to the depth of Hausen's faith.[20] But though Hausen's was perhaps a devout age,[21] there are some exceptions to be found in it, such as Gottfried von Strassburg,[22] or the unknown poet of the *Nibelungenlied*.[23] Besides, such general devoutness, if true, would not mean that Hausen's references to the deity should be taken in a literal rather than a literary sense. The following discussions of various other Hausen lyrics indicate that the occurrences of God's name do not constitute proof of piety.

It does not occur to us to think of someone like John Donne as a tortured lover, except in the sense that the speaker in some of his poems is projected as such. The historical facts pertaining to his personal life may suggest something else again, even though the problem of love was undoubtedly of consequence to him—as it is to all of us. Something very similar, I suggest, was the case with Hausen who, for all we know, had the most tranquil of love lives, *if* he wanted and had one at all. Becker sees it differently: "Hausen ist der erste, der die romanische Form des Frauendienstes in Deutschland nicht bloß *im Leben* übte, sondern auch nach Art der Provenzalen in seinem Dichten abspiegelte" [italics added].[24] The close interrelationship between *Leben* and *Dichten* which Becker and other critics assume,[25] is not tenable. Since we know so comparatively little about Hausen's private life, the distinction between his poetry on the one hand and his personal sphere on the other is mandatory.

V. ICH SAGE IR NU VIL LANGE ZIT

45, 19 I 1 Ich sage ir nu vil lange zit   13 C
20   wie sere si min herze twinget.
    als ungeloubic ist ir lip
    daz si der zwivel dar uf dringet
    5 daz si hat alselhen nit
    den ze rehte ein saelic wip
25   niemer rehte vollebringet,
    ·daz si dem ungelonet lat
    der si vor al der werlte hat.

  II 10 Nieman sol mir daz verslan,   14 C
    sine möhte mich vor eime jare
30   von sorgen wol erloeset han,
    ob ez der schoenen wille ware.
    ouch half mir dicke ein lieber wan:
    15 swanne si min ougen san,
    daz was ein fröide für die sware,
35   alleine wil sis glouben niet
    daz si min ouge gerne siet.

45, 1 III Gelebte ich noch die lieben zit   11 C
    20 daz ich daz lant solt aber schouwen,
    dar inne al min fröide lit
    nu lange an einer schoenen frouwen,
5   so gesaehe minen lip
    niemer weder man noch wip
    25 getruren noch gewinnen rouwen.
    mich duhte nu vil mangez guot,
    da von e swaere was min muot.

10 IV Ich wande ir e vil verre sin   12 C
    da ich nu vil nahe ware.
    30 alrerste hat daz herze min
    von der frömde groze sware.
    ez tuot wol sine triuwe schin.
15   waere ich iender umb den Rin,
    so friesche ich lihte ein ander mare,
    35 des ich doch leider nie vernam
    sit daz ich über die berge quam.

These strophes have caused problems. Ipsen, for instance, is of the view that they do not belong together.[1] Brinkmann divides them into his numbers X and XI, and calls them "Die Unglaubliche" and "Heimweh" respectively.[2] Maurer sees the strophes as forming a unit.[3] Kraus cites an array of additional opinions.[4] The present discussion is based on the opinion that the order as presented above makes for a four-strophe arrangement of which the plot line is perfectly smooth.

The introductory statement seems clear enough:

> 1 Ich sage ir nu vil lange zit
> wie sere si min herze twinget.
>
> I have been telling her for a long time now
> how much she has been affecting my heart.

Because of the sequential order he has in mind Brinkmann has little choice but to find "nu vil lange zit" "eine übertreibende Formel."[5] But with the tendency of many a speaker in the Hausen poems to leave his lady uninformed, we cannot be fully confident that "sagen" must be taken literally. After all, this "sagen" may be similar to "sagen" in "Ich denke under wilen," where the verb becomes equatable with "arranging my thoughts" (see chapter XVII, p. 118). Brinkmann sees no problem here: "Die Frau vernimmt, aber glaubt nicht,"[6] and thus provides an example of the tendency on the part of the lady in Hausen's poetry not to trust her suitor's *staete*[7] — what else could she be disbelieving about?

The rest of the strophe forms one long sentence, chaining one dependent clause to another, thus creating the illusion of moving further and further away from reality. The main clause contains the reference to the lady's alleged disbelief in the speaker's proclaimed feelings:

> 3 als ungeloubic ist ir lip
> daz si der zwivel dar uf dringet
> daz si hat alselhen nit
> den ze rehte ein saelic wip
> niemer rehte vollebringet,
> daz si dem ungelonet lat
> der si vor al der werlte hat.

For reasons perhaps similar to those lying behind the emendation of "kip" and "melde" in "An der genade al min fröide stat" into "nit" and "selbe" respectively (see chapter III, p. 28), Kraus arrives at this reading by emending the manuscript; the latter reads:

> als ungeloubic ist ir nit
> das si der zwivel dar us bringet
> das si hat als selhen kip

Jungbluth sympathizes with Kraus' view, but goes further: "Die Reimreihen ... verraten deutlich den Bearbeiter.[8] 'nit' kann ... keinesfalls richtig sein, da dieser

Begriff zumindest im älteren Minnesang und gerade auch bei Hausen ausschließlich auf die Einstellung der Merker und nicht auf die Gesinnung der Dame dem Ritter gegenüber bezogen zu werden pflegt; das richtige Wort wird vielmehr 'strit' gewesen sein."[9] Mowatt, too, seems to feel uncomfortable with the manuscript's version; at any rate, he is silent about Kraus' change and thus refrains from his habit of defending the manuscripts against emendations. However, in view of the fact that in "An der genade al min fröide stat" we found good reason to retain "kip" over against the changes suggested for that poem (see chapter III, p. 28), it would seem that in "Ich sage ir nu vil lange zit," too, the term can be kept. Whatever Hausen said or did not say remains guess work, however intelligent, and if we can understand from a manuscript what a poem says, it might be more consistent to leave it alone. With these considerations, "nit" as occurring in the manuscript's third line seems as reliable a term as any other, and nothing is gained by emending it;[10] we find indication elsewhere that "nit"—meant as "anger" by a speaker who projects himself as being overly suspicious, or even paranoic—can readily be imputed to the lady in Hausen's lyrics. Similarly, "kip" seems to be perfectly acceptable, if we translate is as "lack of cooperation" and interpret it as the speaker's myopic and self-centered assumption which is not necessarily supported by the lady's demeanor. Such inferences on the part of the speaker occur rather frequently in Hausen's poetry.

There have been other emendations made in this passage. Brinkmann is suspicious of "rehte" in the seventh line and changes it into "mere."[11] Jungbluth objects and speaks of a "Schlimmbesserung": "Weder Brinkmann noch F. Maurer, der sich ihm anschließt, haben erkannt, daß hier ein geistreiches Wortspiel vorliegt: 'ze rehte ein saelic wip'—und das ist die Geliebte!—wird nie in der Lage sein, 'rehte' den 'strit' durchzuführen und den erbetenen Lohn zu verweigern; ein schelmischer, auch selbstgewisser Appell an die schöne Widerspenstige, mit verschmitzter Miene vorgetragen—ein echtes Hausenstück."[12] Jungbluth is persuasive, though we discount his suggestion about "strit" as the closing term for the fifth line, and take "Appell" as part of a fictitious plot without having to conclude from it that the lady knows anything.

Brinkmann interprets "zwivel" (4) as "Widerpart der staete."[13] To be sure, the criticism thus leveled at the lady is watered down through the process of placing it in a dependent clause to another dependent clause. By the time we read that "ein saelic wip" should reward the speaker for his devotion, we have moved some distance away from the reason for her aloofness, which the speaker calls unmotivated anyway (see esp. 32), and from her alleged annoyance resulting from her disbelief in his commitment to her. The situation is not unlike that of the lady in "Ich muoz von schulden sin unfro," who refuses to play the Dido role over against the speaker's alleged Aeneas behavior (see chapter I).

As already stated, it is a moot question whether the speaker is correct in detecting "nit" and "kip" in the lady's bearing toward him. We shall become accustomed to the fact that Hausen's speakers seldom inform their ladies of the feelings nourished for them, with the result that the laments are voiced in a vacuum and the ladies remain unaware of them. This is perfectly possible also in "Ich sage ir nu vil lange zit," for the opening line may very well be a similar gesture—spoken to an audience and making a statement with a metaphorical ring to it. On the other hand, if in this particular instance the lady is assumed to be aware, her "nit" and "kip" stem from her doubt about the speaker's *staete*.[14]

With these terms from the manuscript re-introduced into the text, the second part of the first strophe translates this way:

> her anger is so incredible
> that lack of belief brings her to the point
> of displaying such lack of cooperation
> —which a blessed woman can never show
> righteously without justification—
> that she leaves him unrewarded
> who esteems her above all the world.

With the above evaluation, too, because of the ambiguities encountered in it resulting from the question as to whether the lady is informed, this strophe is "ein echtes Hausenstück"[15] if we assume that the poet deliberately remained vague.

The introductory statement of the second strophe amounts to wishful thinking, employing the subjunctive mood. This wishdream has therefore nothing to do with "reality" as it is seen and depicted by the speaker in the first strophe:

> 10 Nieman sol mir daz verstan[16]
> sine möhte mich vor eime jare
> von sorgen wol erloeset han,
> ob es der schoenen wille ware.

> Nobody should deny me this:[17]
> she could have set me free of
> my troubles a year ago
> if that had been the will of the beauteous one.

That "vor eime jare" is a more specific time element than "vil lange zit" of the lyric's opening line. There is some tension between this greater degree of preciseness in time and the speaker's apparently "forgetting" that the lady's demeanor is motivated either by her not knowing anything (that is to say, demeanor as he interprets it), or by her disbelief in his sincerity.

This reflection on a past situation causes the speaker to be somewhat imprecise in his delivery; the link by means of "ouch" with the following sentence hence acquires a wavering value. The ambiguity thus resulting is enhanced by "wan":

> 14 ouch half mir dicke ein lieber wan:
> swanne si min ougen san,
> daz was ein fröide für die sware.

Kraus states about 14: "Der Doppelpunkt, den Vogt von Schönbach statt Lachmanns Punkt übernimmt, scheint mir nicht richtig: ihr Anblick ist kein 'wan,' sondern eine Tatsache."[18] Perhaps Kraus is saying that "wan" is an actual belief, as contrasted with an unjustified one. He seems correct in view of the "fröide" which the speaker experienced. But there is also the likely possibility that a "wan" crept through the speaker's mind whenever he beheld the lady. In this sense, there is the fact that "wan" is a thing of the past when the speaker was indeed hoping—for something specific? For all we know, he knows better now since it has begun to dawn upon him that his erstwhile hope or belief was vain and to no avail. "Furthermore" may therefore be a more felicitous term for "ouch" than "also" or "nevertheless"; it is neutral and fits in with either reading of these lines, no matter whether judged from the "present" point of view, or from that of the "past" one:[19]

> furthermore a sweet illusion often helped me:
> whenever my eyes saw her,
> it was solace to my sorrow.

Ambiguity may mark also the closing statement of the strophe:

> 17 alleine wil sis glouben niet
> daz si min ouge gerne siet.
>
> but she does not want to believe
> that my eye is glad to see her.

or, less likely perhaps:

> that she is glad to see my eye.

Either reading is possible. In the latter case we are dealing with an ironic statement: the lady herself does not believe, does not *wish* to believe (in view of her doubt about the speaker's sincerity) that she appreciates his eye beholding her beauty. In the former case these lines simply state that she does not believe in his delight in seeing her. Though this is the more likely reading, it is also repetitive in view of the preceding lines, and the wording is flat.[20]

Schmid sees these lines from a different perspective: "Freilich können wir nicht wissen, ob diese heimliche Liebe nicht ihrerseits ein 'wan' ist. Die Erforschung des Minnesangs wird unendlich durch die sich immer wieder stellende Realitätsfrage erschwert."[21] The reaction to this view is clear from the approach used in these pages: everything is make-believe.

The third strophe is in its entirety a wishdream: "this and that" would happen if "such and such" were the case. The strophe consists of two sentences of the same lengths as those forming the first stanza, but they now come in reverse order; first there is a seven-line statement:

> 19 Gelebte ich noch die lieben zit
> daz ich daz lant solt aber schouwen,
> dar inne al min fröide lit
> nu lange an einer schoenen frouwen,
> so gesaehe minen lip
> niemer weder man noch wip
> getruren noch gewinnen rouwen.

> If I experienced the moment again
> when I should see the land
> in which all my joy has been
> with a beautiful woman for a long time now,
> then neither man nor woman
> would ever see me lament again
> or incur grief.

and then comes the two-line sentence:

> 26 mich duhte nu vil mangez guot,
> da von e swaere was min muot.
>
> I would think many things good now
> that formerly weighed heavily on my mind.

Evidently, the speaker is incapable of confronting the basic matter at stake: the lady's lack of belief in his sincerity—a possible inference against which he never defends himself—or the fact that she knows nothing. He can only make an elaborate statement to the effect that suffering in the lady's presence now seems preferable to suffering far away from her.

The fourth strophe continues the mood pervading the third:

> 28 Ich wande ir e vil verre sin
> da ich nu vil nahe ware.
>
> Formerly I fancied to be far away from her,
> whereas now I would be very near.

The thought is a repetition of the closing statement of the third strophe and has a similar meaning, except that its effect now relies on an antithetical statement playing with the concept of geographical and personal distance over against proximity to or distance from the lady in an abstract or intellectual sense. In the third strophe the contrast was evoked by "guot" (26) versus "swaere" (27) and a reverse order of the time elements: "nu" (26) versus "e" (27); now it is "e" (28) versus "nu" (29).

The following lines:

> 30 alrerste hat daz herze min
> von der frömde groze sware.
>
> only now my heart feels (truly)
> great sorrow because of the distance.

refers ambiguously to both the geographical separation and the lady's aloofness as the real and more serious cause of the speaker's troubles, and the following line:

> 32 ez tuot wol sine triuwe schin.
>
> it clearly shows its steadfastness.

gives the lie to the lady's reason for displaying "nit" and "kip." Of course, the experience of the heart being inward, it does not prove anything to *her*, and it fails to go to the root of the speaker's problem, unless somehow the "whole man" would manage to convey this heartfelt fact to the lady. The geographical situation does not make this likely to happen.

The following statement expresses the hope that *if* the speaker were back at the Rhine (and *if* he could convince the lady of his *staete*), he might hear a tale other than that of her "nit" and "kip":

> 33 waere ich iender umb den Rin,
> so friesche ich lihte ein ander mare,
>
> if I were anywhere in the region of the Rhine,
> I might hear a different tale,

Stated in the subjunctive mood, the "hope" expressed here lacks strength. Geography prevents the speaker from seeking to turn the lady's disbelief and consequent "nit" and "kip" into belief, or from simply telling her how he feels. Hence the closing lines have no force either:

> 34 des ich doch leider nie vernam
> sit daz ich über die berge quam.
>
> which unfortunately I never heard
> since I crossed the mountains.

The closing line is our first encounter with a statement with some biographical value embedded in it. As used here, however, it is poetic in value and serves to indicate the distance between lady and speaker. The reference to the Rhine does not necessarily constitute an accolade to Hausen's homeland, as Wechssler suggests.[22] Instead we may say that it is used to play out the conceit inherent in the contrast between geographical over against personal distance.

It should be pointed out that "iender" (33) occurs in a dependent clause and has the value of "somewhere," "anywhere"; it is positive in its connotations. The negative value of the line in which it occurs stems from the subjunctive verb form. This fact renders questionable the manner in which the critics have evaluated "iender" in "Wafena, wie hat mich Minne gelazen," where its meaning is of major consequence to the meaning of the passage in which it occurs and therefore to the meaning of the lyric as a whole (see chapter VI, p. 51).

On first reading, the exact relationship between the first two strophes and those that follow seems obscure. Nothing prevents us, however, from reading the first two as having been written with a "backward" look, whereas the third and fourth are preoccupied with the speaker's "present" state, in which he can do no more than ponder in the subjunctive mood. The interrelationship between these pairs of strophes is thus similar to that found to be prevailing between the first two strophes of "Mich müet deich von der lieben quam" and those that follow them as the third and fourth strophes (see chapter II).

VI. WAFENA, WIE HAT MICH MINNE GELAZEN

52, 37   I   1. Wafena, wie hat mich Minne gelazen!   15 C
             diu mich betwanc daz ich lie min gemüete
53, 1   an solhen wan der mich wol mac verwazen,
             ez ensi daz ich müeze geniezen ir güete,
         5   von der ich bin   also dicke ane sin.
    4   mich duhte ein gewin,   und wolte diu guote
             wizzen die not diu mir wont in mim muote.

         II Wafen, waz habe ich getan so zuneren   16 C
             daz mir diu guote niht gruozes engunde?
         10 sus kan si mir wol daz herze verseren.
    10   deich in der werlt bezzer wip iender funde,
             seht dest min wan.   Da für so wil ichz han,
             und dienen nochdan   mit triuwen der guoten,
             diu mich da bliuwet vil sere ane ruoten.

    15   III 15 Waz mac daz sin daz diu werlt heizet minne,   43 B, 45 C
             unde ez mir tuot also we zaller stunde
             unde ez mir nimt also vil miner sinne?
             in wande niht daz es iemen erfunde.
             getorste ich es jen   daz ichz hete gesen
    20   20 des mir ist geschen   also vil herzesere,
             so wolte ich gelouben dar an iemer mere.

         IV Minne, got müeze mich an dir gerechen!   44 B, 46 C
             wie vil du mim herzen der fröiden erwendest!
    25   und möhte ich dir din krumbez ouge uz gestechen,
             25 des het ich reht, wan du vil lützel endest
             an mir solhe not   so mir din lip gebot.
             und waerest du tot,   so duhte ich mich riche.
             sus muoz ich von dir leben betwungenliche.

After "Min herze und min lip diu wellent scheiden" (chapter IX), more attention has been paid to this lyric than to any other of Hausen's *oeuvre*. Brinkmann discards the fourth stanza as "unecht."[1] So does Singer,[2] together with a number of other commentators. The closing strophe of "Min herze und min lip diu wellent scheiden" has suffered the same fate, and for similar reasons: in each case the closing strophe has been thought to be unacceptable in part because of its lack of finesse in courtly terminology.

"Wafena, wie hat mich minne[3] gelazen" is not the easiest of the Hausen poems.

47

As we shall argue, ambiguities and double readings lie at the root of the problems involved. The following discussion will seek to suggest also that if anywhere, then here, the order followed by Kraus—this poem comes immediately after "Sich möhte wiser man verwüeten" (chapter XVI)—is eminently sensible since the one can readily be perused as a sequence to the other.

> 1 Wafena, wie hat mich minne gelazen!
> diu mich betwanc daz ich lie min gemüete
> an solhen wan der mich wol mac verwazen,
> ez ensi daz ich müeze geniezen ir güete,
> von der ich bin also dicke ane sin.

> Alas, how love has left me!
> which compelled me to direct my mind
> toward such hope as may well devastate me;
> unless I should enjoy her goodness
> which so often drives me out of my mind.

In a manner of speaking, the opening line contains the entire story. "Wafena" is more than an expression of grief. This is the call for help of a man who is in dire straits. Baumbarten speaks of "erregte Stimmung."[4] According to Becker "erklärt man die vermehrte Klage in diesem Lied am leichtesten, wenn man annimmt, daß der Dichter in der Ferne weilt."[5] Kraus' "wehe" does not quite cover the value of the Middle High German term as used here.[6] Similarly, his "wie hat mich Minne im Stich gelassen" seems to lose something; besides, it assumes that in the past the speaker has been more fortunate than he is now; this notion contradicts some of the salient lines in the lyric (see below). Schönbach's "in welche Lage hat die Minne mich gebracht"[7] appears to be a more accurate rendering; for by reading the line in close conjunction with "verwazen" (3), and by taking it in the sense of "left behind" after having been ransacked, we can see "verheert" as an adequate modern equivalent to depict the situation suggested. However, Schönbach himself thinks that "verwazen" is too general a term, and he opts for "vertwazen, das heißt, dumm, blöde machen."[8] It would seem, though, that "verwazen" fits in with the martial imagery employed in these lines. Furthermore, and this is perhaps of greater consequence, "verwazen" enhances the quality of precarious oscillation of "wan" as false hope or belief, or as justified hope or belief (see below).[9] Isbăşescu sees "Minne" als "Unheil bringende Macht, als Allegorie."[10]

The effect created by spasms of optimism alternating with lapses of pessimism emphasizes the degenerative process to which the speaker has fallen victim. That is also the reason why "verwazen" stands in juxtaposition to "geniezen ir güete" of the following line. It is an either-or situation of long standing—"von der ich bin *also dicke* ane sin" (italics added)—the suspended outcome of which would enervate any man and leave him limp. This juxtaposition, because "verwazen" suggests that the speaker is physically affected, or rather, the imagery used has such overtones, may imply that "ir güete geniezen" would cure his ailments; indeed, the strophe states this unequivocally.

Because of the temptation to think during the reading of this poem of the lyric preceding it in *Des Minnesangs Frühling* (with its allusion to a soul riding the highroad to hell and the lady's function being that of a catalyst bringing about the dichotomy and ever widening distance between God's will and the speaker's will—see the discussion of "Sich möhte wiser man verwüeten" in chapter XVI), "güete geniezen" is at best ambiguous because it may express the speaker's thoughts of fulfillment.[11]

That such gratification is no more than a figment of the mind is not only indicated by the ambiguous value of "wan" (3), but becomes evident also in a more realistic thought embedded in the strophe's closing statement, showing that the speaker roams a never-never land:

> 6 mich duhte ein gewin, und wolte diu guote
> wizzen die not diu mir wont in mim muote.
>
> I should think it a gain if the good person
> were willing to take cognizance of my plight.

Brinkmann deduces from this that "Mitteilungen dem ritterlichen Liede keineswegs fern lagen."[12] Lehfeld suggests that "die Verse 53,2 und 53,5/6 mehr Hoffnung auf Erhörung als ernsten Willen zum Abbrechen der Werbung [ausdrücken]."[13] The choice between these two views is not a felicitous one from within the present frame of reference, nor does the poem say anything to warrant either one as a plausible option. Instead there is on the one hand mere wishful thinking, as the verbs indicate, and of which the lady does not seem to know anything, while on the other hand there is (forceless) despair.

The deferential reference to the lady as "diu guote" does not need to be cause for surprise; the speaker can readily use it since in a manner of speaking his problem has nothing to do with her; she is a mere catalyst who deserves neither praise nor criticism for what goes on in the deep interior of this victim of love. With the situation couched in these terms, it becomes possible to wonder whether we should attribute a demonic quality to "Minne" as the force that may well turn out to be successful in destroying the speaker—"verwazen" (3). *Minne* pitted against the speaker makes for an unevenly balanced confrontation, and the outcome seems inevitable.

De Boor sees this dispute with personified love as one of several indications that "Hausens Lyrik sich ganz in den Bahnen des hohen Minnesangs bewegt," and that Hausen is thus the first lyricist in this era "dem die tiefste Problematik der hohen Minne bewußt wird."[14] But so far we have encountered nothing that could compel the view of this poetry as anything more or other than love poetry.[15] *If* this is *hohe Minne* exclusively, then it is difficult to see why it should be restricted to the twelfth and thirteenth centuries, since it is of all times and places, depending on the disposition at a given moment of a given poet engaged in the writing of poetry dealing with love, and with a predilection for using a rather limited number of motifs.[16]

The second strophe is reflective:[17]

53, 15 II 8 Waz mac daz sin daz diu werlt heizet minne,   43 B, 45 C
unde ez mir tuot also we zaller stunde
unde ez mir nimt also vil miner sinne?

49

> What could it be that the world calls love,
> and causes me pain continuously,
> and robs me of so much of my senses?

With a natural stress falling on "werlt," we see the contrast between the world's concept of love, which is joyful, and that of the speaker: love robs the latter of his senses, suspends his ability to use his reason,[18] turns him into a slave, and causes him to serve the lady against his better insight (see below). Kraus sees "minne" (8) from the point of view of the world and logically calls it "gegenseitige oder glückliche Liebe."[19] Schmid looks at it from the speaker's point of view and equally logically speaks of "die rein negative Auffassung unerfüllter Liebe, die sich in der [dritten Strophe] ja auf geradezu groteske Weise austollt."[20]

The speaker's question turns out to be rhetorical; he has his own answer ready:

53, 18 II 11 in wande niht daz ez iemen erfunde.   43 B, 45 C
              getorste ich es jen daz ichz hete gesen
              des mir ist geschen also vil herzesere,
              so wolte ich gelouben dar an iemer mere.

> I did not believe that anyone would find out.
> if I could say that I had seen from which
> so much heartache has come my way,
> I would believe in it forevermore.

—in love as joy, that is.

The third strophe is reflective also; the value of "Wafen" now seems to contain nothing of the martial connotations that accompanied the term in the lyric's opening line. Instead the tone is subdued and lends "wafen" a pleading quality. We may imagine the speaker as having been "devastated" now and as capable only of voicing a plea. That quality is also present in the question with which the strophe begins:

53, 7 III 15 Wafen, waz habe ich getan so zuneren   16 C
              daz mir diu guote niht gruozes engunde?

> Alas, what dishonorable thing have I done
> that the good one did not grant me a greeting?

The question seems to suggest that the lady snubbed the speaker, whatever the reason for her behavior. But nothing prevents these lines from meaning, in the frame of poetic verisimilitude evoked, that she did not see him, that it made no difference to her, who knows nothing, whether she greeted him or not, and therefore refrained. If his hypersensitivity drove him to distraction and led him to the suspicious notion that she deliberately looked the other way, then he has a problem indeed. The question, it has been suggested on a different level of evaluation, also turns our attention to an audience.[21]

This is the second time that the lady is referred to as "diu guote." The same designation will be used once again, in 20, and the question is how we must evaluate this repetition. Does it emphatically place the lady beyond reproach and therefore makes it impossible to see "Minne" as synonymous with her? Or does this repetition draw attention to the phrase in order slyly to undermine the assurance that the lady *is* "guot"?

The remaining lines of the strophe are interdependent for their meaning:

53, 9 III 17 sus kan si mir wol daz herze verseren.   16 C
deich in der werlt bezzer wip iender funde,
seht dest min wan. da für so wil ichz han,
und dienen nochdan mit triuwen der guoten
diu mich da bliuwet vil sere ane ruoten.[22]

This passage has caused problems. Kraus substitutes "verseren" for the manuscript's "verkeren." Schönbach translated the original line as having to do with "mich um den Verstand bringen."[23] "To turn my heart away" would seem to be a more logical translation. The development of the lyric as evaluated below makes this reading entirely plausible. Kraus' "*kan* verseren" [italics added], on the other hand, makes little sense after the much stronger "wan der mich wol mac verwazen" of the lyric's third line.

Of consequence is the element of doubt surrounding 18 f. There is, first of all, "wan" (19). Kraus finds this to be identical to "wan" of the third line and to have the value of "justified belief (hope)."[24] But if this equality must indeed be accepted, it should be pointed out that in the third line such belief or hope stands in danger of destroying the speaker by his own account, and hence carries unavoidably the connotation of being false (in retrospect). For that "wan" occurs in a situation which depicts it as stemming from a past event—"betwanc" (2). Hence from the speaker's "present" point of view, his hope or belief as it was in the past turns out to be without justification. Therefore, "wan" of the third line is ambiguous. So, we suggest, is "wan" of the nineteenth line.

Lehfeld views the matter this way and at the same time touches upon the problem of "iender" of the eighteenth line: " 'daß ich in der Welt nirgends eine bessere finde, seht, das glaube ich,' denn 'iender' im abhängigen Satze wird doch stets mit 'nirgends' übersetzt, und ich wüßte nicht, welche Umstände hier zu einer Ausnahme berechtigen sollten."[25] Brinkmann asks: "fühlt der Dichter sich unsicher, daß er sich mit dem hinweisenden 'seht' an die Hörer wendet, das wohl mehr Befestigung sucht, als sicher Geglaubtes anderen bekräftigt?"[26] Schönbach translates thus: "Dafür sehe ich es auch an, ich erkenne es als 'wan' . . . und doch. . . ."[27] The critics have followed Lehfeld's reasoning with respect to "iender" meaning "nirgends." The fact remains, however, that in "Ich sage ir nu vil lange zit," the fifteenth line—"waere ich iender umb den Rin" ("if I were anywhere/somewhere in the region of the Rhine")—is also a dependent clause, but "iender" in that case can only have the value of "somewhere" or "anywhere," not of "nowhere" (see chapter V, p. 46).

And so the problem remains; it is nettlesome because it affects the value of the lyric as a whole and determines the attitude of the speaker toward the basic matter at

stake in it. If we continue casting about for a solution, these possibilities emerge:
a) "iender" is "somewhere"; "wan" is "false belief/hope"; "da für" of 23 stands for "hence," "consequently": It is an erroneous notion of mine that I could find a better woman somewhere (anywhere) else in the world; therefore. . · . .
b) "iender" is "somewhere"; "wan" is "justified belief/hope"; "da für" is "nevertheless": I am certain that I could find a better woman somewhere else in the world; nevertheless. . . .
c) "iender" is "nowhere"; "wan" is "false belief/hope"; "da für" is "nevertheless."
d) "iender" is "nowhere"; "wan" is "correct belief/hope"; "da für" is "therefore."
The last combination represents Lehfeld's evaluation. As for the present line of reasoning: we are confronted with four possible combinations, and find an intelligent choice impossible because of the wavering values of the key terms employed. Having thus to decide that we are dealing with deliberate ambiguity, we find the passage virtually impossible to translate. An attempt yields something like this:

> thus she may well turn my heart away;[28]
> that I would find a better woman somewhere else in the
>   world,
> see, that is my notion.[29]
> hence/nevertheless that is the way I want it,
> and I shall serve the good one faithfully,
> who beats me blue without using a rod.

In this manner, the addition of "nochdan" (24) becomes superfluous;[30] in fact, it destroys what Hausen, I think, intended as a case of deliberate ambiguity since he wanted to have it all the possible ways.

The proclaimed intention to continue service is either against the speaker's own better judgment, or it involves a development in which the taut line of reasoning turns out to be untenable, suddenly snaps, and causes the speaker's reasoning power to break down. This disintegration in his bearing accounts for the uncouth ring of the strophe's closing line. Regarding it, Kraus finds "daß Hausen das Vermögen [fehlt], das Gedachte durch wechselnde Ausdrücke logisch klar darzustellen."[31] Against this view we have Neumann's: "Ich kann nicht finden, daß es hier noch der Sprache an den Vermögen fehle, das Gedachte klar darzustellen. Was Hausen bewußt erfaßt, vermag er zu sagen."[32] And Jungbluth finds that the more keenly we appreciate "Hausens eigenartige Begabung, kluge und hintergründige, schelmische und sehnsuchtsvolle Gedanken in nie affektierte, die zeitbedingte Reimtechnik ausgenommenen formvollendeten Sprache umzusetzen, je deutlicher erkennt man, daß gedankliche Unklarheiten, unbeholfener Ausdruck, rhythmisches Holpern nie und nimmer diesem Manne zur Last gelegt werden können."[33] We may benefit from these three suggestions by combining them into the view that the closing line of the third strophe relays the impression of a speaker so upset (because he is aware of the state in which he finds himself) as to "forget" to maintain a courtly bearing.[34] His lack of finesse in speech conveys the frenzy of his mind; it causes him to drop all façades and self-discipline (*maze*), including that of polished language. Hence a polite and reflective stance is (deliberately) ruptured, and this rupture is subservient to something more important than maintaining a smooth demeanor; it serves to emphasize and draw attention to the psychological state of the speaker, who becomes vehement now:

> 22 Minne, got müeze mich an dir gerechen!
> wie vil du mim herzen der fröiden erwendest!
> und möhte ich dir din krumbez ouge uz gestechen,
> des het ich reht, wan du vil lützel endest
> an mir solhe not, so mir din lip gebot.
> und waerest du tot, so duhte ich mich riche.
> sus muoz ich von dir leben betwungenliche.

Love, God must revenge me against you,
since you expel joys from my heart!
and if I wanted to stab out your squinting eye,
I would be in the right for you do not relieve at all
the distress you inflicted upon me;
and if you were dead I would deem myself rich;
as it is, I must live slavishly because of you.

It is clear: the speaker has sought to remain reasonable and polite, but suddenly he can no longer continue. Another thing becomes evident from the closing strophe as well: the speaker is hungering for the joys of love as the world knows them. The very fact that he must do without them leads him to curse *Minne*. That is to say, he curses love as it allegedly functions in the framework of *hohe Minne*, and he longs for love that comes with rewards. There is nothing courtly about the speaker's thinking here. From this point of view, it would be odd indeed for him to continue couching his thoughts in a language that could be labeled courtly. Uncouth and violent language is the only thing this victim of love has left to vent his despair. After all, we are explicitly told that (courtly) reasoning has been affected: "ez mir nimt also vil miner sinne" (11) shows love's effects on a man who, because of love, must live "betwungenliche" (28).

VII. SI WELNT DEM TODE ENTRUNNEN SIN

53, 31   1 Si welnt dem tode entrunnen sin,   17 C
              die gote erliegent sine vart.
              deswar est der geloube min
              daz si sich übel hant bewart.
           5 swerz kriuze nam und si gespart,
              dem wirt doch got ze jungest schin,
              swann im diu porte ist vor verspart
              die er tuot uf den liuten sin.

This little poem has been thought to stem from a late date.[1] Together with "Min herze den gelouben hat" (chapter X), it stands apart from Hausen's other lyrics in that it does not address itself to some problem pertaining to love. Also, whereas other Hausen compositions are easily envisioned as delivered to an audience, and thus enhance their effectiveness by the roles of speaker and listeners being pitted against each other, it is difficult to think of this strophe as being similarly delivered to a circle of listeners. The strophe immediately testifies to its simplicity of thought and sincerity; its translation:

> They think to have escaped death
> who simulated God's crusade.
> it definitely is my belief
> that they have protected themselves badly.
> whoever took the cross and then refrained,
> to him it will nevertheless become evident at the last
>   day,
> when the door remains closed before him
> which He opens for his people.

Critics dealing with this stanza have mainly preoccupied themselves with emending the text,[2] partly because the content seems so simple and straightforward as to need no clarification. Because it affected the meaning of the entire strophe, Jungluth's was the most important proposal: "Die Furcht vor dem leiblichen Tode hat hier . . . nichts zu suchen. . . . 'dem tode' ist verdächtig und wird als Ergänzung erkannt und durch 'im' (Gott) ersetzt werden müssen."[3] Mowatt opposes this line of reasoning: "It is obvious that this argument is a rationalization of a decision taken on other grounds. The manuscript after all says nothing about 'leiblich' or about 'Furcht.' By inserting these qualifications, Jungbluth invents a distinction between the death which is escaped by taking (and if possible dying for) the Cross, and the death which is avoided by staying safely at home. But Hausen just writes 'dem tode,' and has it both ways."[4]

Mowatt is correct of course; yet, Jungbluth has a point, too; when he speaks of fear, he seems to have in mind fear of God because of fear of eternal punishment.[5] The fear to which he refers is hence not the fear of physical death *per se*, but the fear of what lies beyond it. That is the reason why the speaker puts in the reminder that death (and the following judgment) cannot be escaped, no matter where one is or what one does. At best, death (and judgment) may be postponed for a time—by not going on a crusade, for instance—though this is not a safe procedure; for one thing, "nieman weiz wie nahe im ist der tot,"[6] wherever he is; for another, those who "gote erliegent sine vart" (2) do so at the cost of their spiritual welfare. Of course, by abiding by the text of the manuscript, Mowatt's reading has room for Jungbluth's emphasis as well as for the second, physical, value of "tot." With him, Hausen indeed has it both ways.

In this manner, the strophe elicits the question whether proclaiming one's intention to go on the crusade but not intending to carry it out gathered the pretender not only honor in the eyes of his fellow-men, but occasionally was thought to accrue merit in the eyes of God also, so as to facilitate one's entering into the kingdom of heaven. Hence the speaker's warning that God will gather his own from among those who sought to deceive him. With this in mind, Schönbach's insight into Hausen's knack for paraphrasing (deliberately or inadvertently) ecclesiastical and religious writing in general[7] could have led him readily to refer to the story of Ananias and Sapphira who were punished on the spot for their attempt to deceive the minister of God confronting them.[8] With Mowatt's stance in favor of the manuscript's text, then, "Si welnt dem tode entrunnen sin" shelters perhaps more implications than are apparent at first glance. Like some of the previously discussed lyrics, it depends for its full "value" on the *double entendre* occurring in the opening line. And it stands to reason that "übel" (4) also partakes of this ambiguity; it may mean "badly" in the sense of "poorly" but it may also stand for "evilly." Here, too, Hausen has it both ways.

VIII. SI DARF MICH DES ZIHEN NIET

45, 37   I   1 Si darf mich des zihen niet,   6 B, 20 C
                    ichn hete si von herzen liep.
46, 1   des mohte si die warheit an mir sen,
                    und wil sis jen.
              5 ich quam sin dicke in solhe not,
                    daz ich den liuten guoten morgen bot
5   engegen der naht.
                    ich was so verre an si verdaht
                    daz ich mich underwilent niht versan,
            10 und swer mich gruozte daz ichs niht vernam.

       II   Min herze unsanfte sinen strit   7 B, 21 C
10   lat, den ez nu mange zit
                    haldet wider daz aller beste wip,
                    der ie min lip
            15 muoz dienen swar ich iemer var.
                    ich bin ir holt: swenn ich vor gote getar,
15   so gedenke ich ir.
                    daz ruoche ouch er vergeben mir:
                    ob ich des groze sünde solde han,
            20 zwiu schuof er si so rehte wol getan?

      III   Mit grozen sorgen hat min lip   8 B, 22 C
20   gerungen alle sine zit.
                    ich hate liep daz mir vil nahe gie:
                    dazn liez mich nie
            25 an wisheit keren minen muot.
                    daz was diu minne, diu noch mangen tuot
25   daz selbe klagen.
                    nu wil ich mich an got gehaben:
                    der kan den liuten helfen uzer not.
            30 nieman weiz wie nahe im ist der tot.

      IV   Einer frouwen was ich undertan   9 B, 23 C
30   diu ane lon min dienest nam.
                    von der enspriche ich niht wan allez guot,
                    wan daz ir muot
            35 zunmilte wider mich ist gewesen.
                    vor aller not so wande ich sin genesen,
35   do sich verlie
                    min herze uf genade an sie,

          der ich da leider funden niene han.
    40   nu wil ich dienen dem der lonen kan.

V   Ich quam von minne in kumber groz,   28 B, 24 C
   40   des ich do selten ie genoz.
47, 1   swaz schaden ich da von gewunnen han,
          so friesch nie man
    45   daz ich ir spraeche iht wan guot,
          noch min munt von frouwen niemer tuot
 5   doch klage ich daz
          daz ich so lange gotes vergaz:
          den wil ich immer vor in allen haben,
    50   und in da nach ein holdez herze tragen.

Kraus finds this lyric to be "ein Virtuosenstück allerersten Ranges."[1] Brinkmann places it as number six in the series and calls it "Frauendienst und Gottesdienst."[2] Elsewhere he sees it as a poem in which "Kreuzzug und Minne in der höheren Einheit der religiösen Gedanken verbunden werden."[3] This becomes possible for Brinkmann in part because he sees *Minne* as "des allzu Erdhaften entkleidet." Also for Ehrismann,[4] de Boor[5] and other commentators (Jungbluth excepted), the poem lends itself eminently to expounding the view that Hausen overcame the deep antithesis between "herze" and "lip," and arrived at a gradualistic outlook in which he places God above *Minne* while managing to give the latter its due also. Over against these views stands that of Jungbluth; elucidating "Min herze und min lip diu wellent scheiden," he finds that each of Hausen's "herze-lip" lyrics constitutes a love poem *par excellence*, that is to say, that the poet confronts the problem of *Minne* but ultimately seeks the solution within the earthly as opposed to the religious realm.[6] Wechssler could be cited to bring tangential support to Jungbluth's view:

Die Kreuzlieder zeigen nur nicht, wie der Frauenkult dem Sänger seine Religion bedeutete; sie beweisen . . . auch, daß die kirchliche Religion ihre Macht und Wirkung auf die Kreise . . . verloren hatte. Nur ein äußerliches Christentum war in diesen Gemütern noch lebendig. . . . Dies und nichts weiters kann man daraus schließen, daß manche Vertreter der neuen Weltanschauung so tun, als ließe sich Frauenminne und Gottesminne ohne Schwierigkeit vereinigen. Der tatsächliche Gegensatz war ihnen doch wohl ohne Zweifel bekannt; aber es scheint fast, daß sie ihn nicht merken wollten.[7]

For Schmid, *Minne* in these strophes "ist das psychologische Phänomen, das Reinmar mit 'herzeliebe' wiedergeben würde."[8] Sayce speaks of the great virtuosity in the use of echoing rhymes.[9] The first strophe is bound this way to all others and all the rhymes in the third strophe are paralleled in the preceding or following strophes. Kraus investigates these rhymes fully.[10]

The first strophe does not touch upon any religious motif—in contrast to the strophes that follow. At least part of the explanation for this may lie in the fact that the first strophe presents a kind of balance sheet referring to a past situation when the problem of *Gottesdienst* had not yet become acute.

> 1 Si darf mich des zihen niet,
> ichn hete si von herzen liep,[11]
> des mohte si die warheit an mir sen,
> und wil sis jen.
>
> She cannot reproach me
> with not loving her with all my heart;
> she could see the truth of that
> if she were willing to acknowledge it.

For once we have a poem that begins with a reference to a lady, though as usual the strophes abound in references to the first person singular, and the lady herself seems of less consequence than the effect she has had and continues to have on the speaker. There is no indication that she actually did reproach him with not loving her sufficiently, and we can only surmise that she did if we argue that preceding poems have made this matter clear, that is, that the Hausen lyrics are interrelated in a particular order, and thus give us information from one poem to the next.[12]

The fourth line has been understood in various ways. Schönbach follows the more common way of understanding: "Wofern sie's überhaupt zugestehen will."[13] Colleville translates: "voudra-t-elle le reconnaître?"[14] The former particularly seems to take it for granted that the lady knows of the speaker's condition, but as the following remarks seek to make evident, it is entirely possible that this lyric merely constructs windmills in order then to do battle against them: line 3 tells us that the lady *could* see the veracity of the speaker's claim in his face *if* she deigned to look at him.

> 5 ich quam sin dicke in solhe not,
> daz ich den liuten guoten morgen bot
> engegen der naht.
> ich was so verre an si verdaht
> daz ich mich underwilent niht versan,
> und swer mich gruozte daz ichs niht vernam.
>
> because of that I often ended up in such distress
> that I offered the people good morning
> toward evening;
> I was so lost in thought of her
> that at times I did not pay heed
> and did not hear whoever greeted me.

Whereas the strophe rings psychologically true, we cannot be unequivocally certain that we grasp its meaning. On the one hand the passage depicts a situation by means of conventional topoi;[15] on the other, the speaker displays characteristics that lead Kolb to say: "Die Minne beraubt den, der sich ihr zuwendet, eines Teils seiner seelischen Kräfte."[16] Kolb intends his statement to have a particular ring having to do with *hohe Minne*. But his insight lends itself to a different line of reasoning, for it can be used to suggest that the speaker creates his own hell by fancying the mere possibility that the object of his devotion accuses him of loving her insufficiently. He has fallen victim to something like paranoia, for there is no indication whatsoever that she actually did or will accuse him. Indeed, she may not even be aware of his feeling towards her. In this manner, the strophe starts out on a plane that has little bearing on the relationship (or rather the lack of relationship) prevailing between them. His first statement barely stops short of accusing her. Such is the amazing ability of victims of paranoia to turn the tables on their alleged tormentors. This much is certain: the speaker is deprived of the proper functioning of his senses.[17] So was Hamlet, and we remember that his mental disintegration, while regarded as a vice, was a source of amusement to Dr. Johnson's contemporaries. This raises the question whether the first strophe of "Si darf mich des zihen niet" does not aim perhaps at registering a comical effect. The question is all the more warranted since the improper functioning of the speaker's senses is presented as an affliction of the past; the "present" situation as depicted in the following strophes seems to be different. The first strophe thus would indulge in self-irony to which the speaker can subject himself since, as he seems to see it, the situation has changed. In actual fact, however, the "past" problem is carried over into the present, as is indicated by the blending of the present and past verb forms that occur in the strophe. What happened then may happen again.

There is another matter. It touches upon the medieval view that passion (that is to say, according to the medieval definition) is sinful because it prevents a person from exercising rational control, thus leading him to violate the tenet that man in view of his reasoning power is created in the image of God. The implications of this view of passion will be discussed elsewhere (see chapter XVI, p. 113) and need no elaboration here. Meanwhile, the notion of a love-seduced mind lends additional color to the opening strophe of "Si darf mich des zihen niet."

Wechssler has a totally different view: "Die Sehnsucht nach der Gottheit entrückt den mystisch Liebenden der jeweiligen Umwelt.... Die deutschen Minnesänger gebrauchen für dieses Entrücktsein die treffende Bezeichnung 'verdaht.' Das ist das zweite Stadium des mystischen Denken."[18] And later he states: "nur wenige ... Motive sind an sich spezifisch mystisch. Bestimmt kann man das nur von den Vorstellungen des Entrücktsein und Verzückung behaupten.... In der Verbindung mit den echt mystischen Motiven wurden auch die andern ins Mystische transponiert."[19] Many commentators have advanced similar views. But it seems possible to argue that the transposition of which Wechssler speaks in this particular poem went into the opposite direction, as suggested here: the mind becomes unhinged through passion rather than through mystically colored processes. This is all the more plausible if we take into account the generally prevailing opinion regarding Hausen's gradualistic view of "Gott und Welt." This gradualism is found first in the writing of the scholastics. These same schoolmen also elaborated on passion as sin.[20]

A general remark about the second strophe applies to all those that follow: in each, the opening lines allude to the lady in order then to drop her virtually out of sight; this is not a very "mystical" procedure. In this sense the lyric is more repetitious than any other Hausen poem. The "progress" comes about through the speaker's gradual turning toward God; we see careful balancing acts in which the merits of serving a lady are weighed against the merits of loving or at least serving God. Each successive strophe delimits the speaker's devotion of the lady a little more precisely.

> 11 Min herze unsanfte sinen strit
> lat, den ez nu mange zit
> haldet wider daz aller beste wip,
> der ie min lip
> 15 muoz dienen swar ich iemer var.
> ich bin ir holt; swenn ich vor gote getar,
> so gedenke ich ir.
> daz ruoche ouch er vergeben mir:
> ob ich des groze sünde solde han,
> zwiu schuof er si so rehte wol getan?
>
> My heart has difficulty ceasing the struggle
> it has waged for a long time now
> against the best of all women,
> whom I must serve wherever I go.
> I love her. whenever I dare before God
> I think of her;
> may he deign to forgive me for that;
> if I committed a sin because of that,
> why did he create her so beautiful?

Wentzlaff-Eggebert's elucidation focuses on the second part of this strophe, and comes to this conclusion: "Maßvolle Liebe steht nicht im Gegensatz zu den Forderungen Gottes; er selbst hat den Grund zur Minne damit gelegt, daß er die Geliebte so schön geschaffen hat."[21] It would seem, however, that love—which, incidentally, seems to be motivated by the lady's physical beauty rather than anything more abstract, such as "güete"—is not "maßvoll" if it deprives the lover "eines Teils seiner seelischen Kräfte."[22] Vogt does not commit himself and paraphrases the sixteenth line as "soweit er sich dessen vor Gott getraut,"[23] but his wording, to say the least, suggests that in his view the speaker's argument is not based on the safest of grounds. This is Brinkmann's view: "Soll das wirklich eine Einschränkung sein? Hausen kann doch nur meinen, daß er seine Liebe selbst vor Gott zu vertreten wagt."[24] Prior to this he finds that "das fast wie Trotz [klingt],"[25] and elsewhere he suggests that the speaker does not actually have to feel guilty since God created beauty which thus was elevated into the metaphysical sphere.[26] With these views prevailing, it is disconcerting to remember that a similar statement was made by Adam when he indecorously told God that the woman whom the deity himself had created for him enticed him into violating the divine command.[27] If Adam's is a case of absurd and warped logic, what, then, is the speaker's? The conclusion seems fair: the closing argument of this strophe is at best ambiguous, and it actually may blend irony with lack of decorum before God.

On a different plane, of course, the strophe conveys the speaker's awareness that he has suffered all too long and should realize the futility of his endeavor ("exercised" in a vacuum in so far as the lady may know nothing). It should be pointed out, however, that these lines indicate the difficulty coming the speaker's way when he wishes to abide by a decision he has (apparently) just made: to leave the lady. For difficult though it is, he decides to stop his attempts to persuade her—in a vacuum—and the result of such a decision can have one unequivocal result only: total abandonment. The reason why this decision is not clearly stated lies with the "faulty" chronological order in which the various considerations are brought forward. Indeed, we may wish to read the strophes as bringing testimony that the erstwhile confusion of the senses (as encountered in the first strophe) is still with the speaker; there is a rambling quality about the way he reasons.

The above evaluation suggests, then, that the opening lines of the second strophe hint at the speaker's having made up his mind. The actual turning point in the development of the thought process involved does not come until the third strophe; the key phrase is situated in the center of the poem (25):

```
21  Mit grozen sorgen hat min lip
    gerungen alle sine zit.
    ich hate liep daz mir vil nahe gie:[28]
    dazn liez mich nie
25  an wisheit keren minen muot.
    daz was diu minne, diu noch mangen tuot
    daz selbe klagen.
    nu wil ich mich an got gehaben:[29]
    der kan den liuten helfen uzer not.
    nieman weiz wie nahe im ist der tot.
```

With many worries I have
struggled all my life;
I loved what was very dear to me.
that never allowed me
to turn my mind to wisdom;
that was love which still causes
many a man the same lament.
now I wish to serve God;
he can help people out of distress.
nobody knows how close he is to death.

Wechssler finds that the opening statement "noch alte und neue Anschauung vereinigt. Hier bedeutet 'min lip' soviel wie 'mein Lieb,' d.h. 'ich.' "[30] Kraus and other commentators (Mowatt excepted) have rewritten the key sentence which in the manuscripts reads this way:

```
    das verlie mich nie
    an wisheit kerte ich minen muot
```

     that never left me;
     I turned my mind to wisdom.

Mowatt states: "The manuscript's version of lines 23–27 would . . . be roughly translatable as: 'I had a source of happiness to which I was much attached. It never abandoned me so that I could turn my mind to more lasting things. And the cause of all this was *minne*, which afflicts many a man in the same grievous way.' "[31] It is clear that with Mowatt the speaker's inability to turn to wisdom stems from his adherence to *Minne*.

  In contrast to this elucidation, it could be argued that the wording as transmitted by the manuscripts places 24–25 in juxtaposition to each other in order to convey that something began to happen ("an wisheit kerte ich minen muot") while something else continued ("das verlie mich nie"): the decision to turn the mind to wisdom stems from the speaker's awareness that he continues to be under the sway of love and realizes the folly of such victimization. Hence "wisheit" has nothing to do with *Minne* or the lady, but with something else, something belonging to a different—and opposing—order. With this reading, "das" (24) as found in the manuscripts may refer to "liep haben" of the preceding line, but behind that lies the immediate awareness of the connection between this "liep haben"[32] and "mit sorgen ringen" of the strophe's opening line. In this way, "an wisheit kerte ich minen muot" (25) stands in contrast to the lines preceding and following. And "daz" (26) does not refer to "wisheit" or the entire line in which it occurs, but to 24: "das verlie mich nie." Nothing prevents this "daz" from introducing a thought of this nature: it was the kind of love that causes many another man the same lament. Line 25 is thus turned into an interjected statement, and prepares us for what follows in the fourth and fifth strophes; it regales us with a twist of thought of the kind that we have encountered elsewhere in Hausen's poetry.

  With this way of reading it is possible to agree with Schmid that "Minne" (26) is "Verliebtheit."[33] The lines 28 f. are a repeat of 24, and the reasonableness of the decision lying at the base of "an wisheit kerte ich minen muot" is supported by the reminder in the strophe's closing line that man's end may come unexpectedly. The thought issuing into this self-reminder runs from the specifically personal "wil ich" (28) to man's condition in general—"den liuten" (29). Hence Bartsch would seem to view the closing lines too narrowly when he surmises from them that the lyric was written during a crusade.[34] Instead it can be suggested that they indicate the speaker's awareness that it is high time to think of the welfare of his soul, a welfare which is not at all served by the lady or *Minne*. On the contrary, there is nothing of the religious quality about her effect on the speaker that Mowatt and the other critics speak about. She must be seen as drawing him away from God ("wisheit") or as preventing him from heeding the divine in the way he should. That the speaker is aware of this "earthly" quality is already indicated in the second strophe; it compelled him to forego "sinen strit wider daz aller beste wip," however difficult it was to do so.[35] It follows from these considerations that "not" (29) is totally different from "not" of the fifth line; the one pertains to the threat of perdition, the other to unrequited love.

  Brinkmann has clearly seen that the poem could end here[36] because a station has been reached, and an important one at that. He also has made it clear, however, that the two remaining strophes belong with the three discussed so far, and from the point of view presented in these pages his reasoning receives added support: the "degrading" of the lady is continued, the reasonableness of turning to God receives further argumentation, and the give and take regarding the lady's positive and negative attributes is traced further.[37]

> 31 Einer frouwen was ich undertan
> diu ane lon min dienest man.
> von der enspriche ich niht wan allez guot,
> wan daz ir muot
> zunmilte wider mich ist gewesen.
> vor aller not so wande ich sin genesen,
> do sich verlie
> min herze uf genade an sie,
> der ich da leider funden niene han.
> nu wil ich dienen dem der lonen kan.

> I served a lady
> who accepted my service without reward.
> I speak nothing but good of her,
> except that her disposition
> towards me has been too ungenerous.
> I thought to be cured of all distress
> when I entrusted my heart
> to her for grace;
> which, however, I have unfortunately never found.
> now I want to serve him who knows how to reward.

By the sound of it, the speaker decides to turn to God *faute de mieux*. It is therefore difficult to think of a way of reasoning more pragmatic than that coming to the fore in this and the previous strophes. To be sure, the speaker seeks to divest himself of earthly concerns in order to turn to religious values. But this shows on the one hand precisely the difference between the realms in which the lady and God are operative; she is of earth, God is of heaven. On the other hand, the reasons for this turning to God are dubious in quality. "Mit Gott läßt sich besser markten als mit der Frau," and the prognoses for the future are better with him than with her. In this manner, it is unlikely that we are dealing in this lyric with the speaker's preoccupation with a deeply religious problem; language, tone, and thought-process speak against it. Instead it could be argued that ambiguity and irony prevail with regard to the lady: under the guise of praise she is criticized. Wechssler has a different view because he works within a different frame of poetic reference by placing a connection between the stuff of poetry and the stuff of life. Referring to 39—"der ich da leider funden niene han"—he says that many poets thought it wise "ausdrücklich zu betonen, daß sie keine Liebesgunst empfangen . . . haben. Besonders ehrlich waren darin die Deutschen; sie konnten sonst von ihrem Publikum, dem die höfische Sitte des

Frauendienstes nicht immer ganz geläufig sein mochte, leicht mißverstanden werden."[38] From the stance taken in these pages—poetry as pure fiction—the speaker's lament refers to the lady's failure to bring him "genade" (38). Milnes could have suggested that this "genade" is of a specific kind;[39] from his point of view there is no connection whatsoever between the lady's "genade" and God's; he has a point, whether or not we accept his suggestion that "genade" is of a specific kind.

The closing strophe continues the gradual turning to God for succor and, corresponding to the turning of the "I" to "den liuten" in 26 f., the reference to one lady shifts to that of women in general; this development is also of consequence.

> 41 Ich quam von minne in kumber groz,
> des ich doch selten ie genoz.
> swaz schaden ich da von gewunnen han,
> so friesch nie man
> 45 daz ich ir spraeche iht wan guot,
> noch min munt von frouwen niemer tuot
> doch klage ich daz
> daz ich so lange gotes vergaz:
> den wil ich iemer vor in allen haben,[40]
> und in da nach ein holdez herze tragen.

> Because of love I became greatly distressed,
> which, however, I never enjoyed.
> whatever harm I have incurred from that,
> nobody will hear me
> speak anything but good of her,
> as my mouth ever does about women.
> but I lament having
> forgotten God for so long;
> I shall hold him above them all forever,
> and thereafter bear them a loving heart.

Schmid says of "minne" of 41 that "hier mag von der totalen oder bereits der negativen Minne die Rede sein."[41] However that may be, this strophe, too, suggests what the preceding ones have told us: not love of God but unrequited love of a lady is the reason for the speaker's decision to turn to the deity. He makes the second best choice because the first has turned out to be unrewarding and hence serves no purpose. This choice ultimately derives from his decision to "play it safe." The statement that he "so lange gotes vergaz" is therefore not an insight deriving from contrition but from attrition, not from love of God but from fear of eternal punishment (which could come the speaker's way if he continued to hope for the lady's "lon"). The line "den wil ich iemer vor in allen haben" is hence as much a declaration of rational and prudent purpose as of deeply felt conviction, if not more so.

It is interesting that 46—"noch min munt von frouwen niemer tuot"—leaves room for the question whether the speaker does in fact *think* ill of the ladies.[42] It is also noteworthy that the C manuscript has in the closing line "im" rather than "in," thus stating that the speaker will hold God before all women and only bear *him* a devoted heart; this amounts to a complete turning away from women and whatever they have to offer (the individual lady is not even mentioned). In this way, the generally held view that the speaker remains faithful to the concept of *Frauendienst* according to the canons of *hohe Minne* must be emphatically denied. Instead the lyric tells us of the speaker's rationalized intent to forsake love of women entirely and bask henceforth in the light of divine love. This declaration of purpose finds its counterpart in "Min herze und min lip diu wellent scheiden" (chapter IX), where it is found that carrying out such a purpose is not an easy matter.

The reading here presented suggests, then, no matter whether we use the closing line of B or C, that the alleged synthesis of *Frauendienst* and *Gottesdienst* is nowhere to be found in this lyric. Instead we are dealing with a speaker who plays with concepts, mutually illuminates them and (ironically?) balances them, the one against the other. These strophes do not bear testimony to Hausen's devoutness.

IX. MIN HERZE UND MIN LIP DIU WELLENT SCHEIDEN

47, 9	I	1	Min herze und min lip diu wellent scheiden,	10 B, 25 C
10			diu mit ein ander varnt nu mange zit.	
			der lip wil gerne vehten an die heiden:	
			so hat iedoch daz herze erwelt ein wip	
		5	vor al der werlt. daz müet mich iemer sit,	
			daz si ein ander niene volgent beide.	
15			mir habent diu ougen vil getan ze leide.	
			got eine müeze scheiden noch den strit.	
	II		Ich wande ledic sin vol solher swaere,	24 B, 27 C
		10	do ich daz kriuze in gotes ere nam.	
			ez waere ouch reht deiz herze als e da waere,	
20			wan daz sin staetekeit im sin verban.	
			ich solte sin ze rehte ein lebendic man,	
			ob ez den tumben willen sin verbaere.	
		15	nu sihe ich wol daz im ist gar unmaere	
			wie ez mir an dem ende süle ergan.	
25	III		Sit ich dich, herze, niht wol mac erwenden,	11 B, 26 C
			dun wellest mich vil trureclichen lan,	
			so bite ich got daz er dich ruoche senden	

                    20 an eine stat da man dich wol enpfa.
                        owe wie sol ez armen dir ergan!
        30   wie torstest eine an solhe not ernenden?
                        wer sol dir dine sorge helfen enden
                        mit solhen triuwen als ich han getan?

                IV 25   Nieman darf mir wenden daz zunstaete,   25 B, 28 C
                        ob ich die hazze diech da minnet e.
        35   swie vil ich si geflehet oder gebaete,
                        so tuot si rehte als ob sis niht verste.
                        mich dunket wie min wort geliche ge
                    30 als ez der summer vor ir oren taete.
        48, 1   ich waere ein gouch, ob ich ir tumpheit haete
                        für guot: ez engeschiht mir niemer me.

More discussions have centered on this one lyric than on all other Hausen poems combined. Hence the literature on it is so ample (and often contradictory) as to make it seem unrewarding to add anything to it in an attempt to cast some additional light.[1] But the effort must be made, if only to support the view that the manner of perusal advocated in these chapters yields new possibilities of evaluation.

The first lines tell us that there are three "characters": the heart, the body and—above these two—the speaker:

> 1 Min herze und min lip diu wellent scheiden,
> diu mit ein ander varnt nu mange zit.
>
> My heart and my body want to separate,
> which have been together now for a long time.

The former two, we must assume, together make up something like the whole man, but not *quite*, for the speaker cannot be the whole man also, but must instead represent a component part, the reasoning mind, we may say.[2] This mind presides over the decomposition about to take place. It has little control left, and "presiding" cannot hide the failure of retaining hegemony over the parts that are about to veer off into different directions. This multi-directional pull is not surprising: it is a metaphorical way of conveying a common human experience when a man finds himself beset with a problem. The surprise, if there is any at all, lies with the fact that not the heart but the body is said to be capable of what we should be allowed to call spiritual devotion:

> 3 der lip wil gerne vehten an die heiden:
>
> the body wants to fight against the paynim.

But there is a problem here insofar as "gerne vehten" may not be too different from what Panzer calls "Kampfwut" when he discusses the tendency of the various characters in the *Nibelungenlied* to throw themselves into battle at the very moment the mind has become unhinged.[3]

> 4 so hat iedoch daz herze erwelt ein wip[4]
>   vor al der werlt. daz müet mich iemer sit,
>   daz si ein ander niene volgent beide.[5]
>
> but the heart has chosen a woman
> before all the world; that has afflicted me ever since,
> that the two no longer agree with each other.

In these lines it is perhaps of consequence that the speaker's expressed concern (as contrasted to a possibly implied one) does not lie with love *per se* (whether love of a lady or love of God), but with the threat of separation of the parts "diu mit ein ander varnt nu lange zit" (see below).

For a moment there is reference to an additional component part: the speaker accuses the eyes which are said to be the cause of suffering:

> 7 mir habent diu ougen vil getan ze leide.
>   got eine müeze scheiden noch den strit.
>
> my eyes have caused me much suffering.
> God alone must decide the struggle.

As Schönbach reminds us: "Die Vorstellung von der Schädlichkeit der Augen geht von der Asketik aus, welche die Thätigkeit der Augen als gefährlich erachtet, weil die Sinnenlüste vornehmlich durch das Auge auf den Menschen eindringen."[6] On the basis of the way in which Schönbach words this—"Sinnenlüste"—love is not as a matter of course to be identified with *hohe Minne*. However that may be, the mind has lost control and its natural function is reduced to the "inactive" insight that God alone is able to decide the outcome of the confrontation. On the one hand, this poem thus uses a motif related to one that was common in medieval literature (that of the body versus the soul); on the other hand, it is interesting that a similar motif can be found in the work of the early German sonneteers.[7]

Throughout the first strophe there is no explicit indication that the speaker (the mind) agrees with one or the other of the factions opposing each other. We know only that the function of the eyes is the essence of the problem's cause. This does not mean, however, that the mind automatically favors the choice of the body over against that of the heart. Particularly if we think in terms of the former's eagerness to do battle ("Kampfwut"—see above), there is reason to think that "Husen does not anywhere in this poem equate 'min lip' with 'ich.' "[8] It nevertheless *is* true that the speaker can take the body's choice for granted so that they can work together, though not because they are of the same opinion for identical reasons. With the harmony between them thus emerging as a possibly "accidental" harmony, the mind can focus attention on the recalcitrant heart:[9]

> 9 Sit ich dich, herze, niht wol mac erwenden,   11 B, 26 C
>   dun wellest mich vil trureclichen lan,[10]

> so bite ich got daz er dich ruoche senden
> an eine stat da man dich wol enpfa.
>
> Since, heart, I am not able to dissuade you,
> (and) you wish to leave me in sadness,
> I pray to God that he may deign to send you
> to a place where you will be well received.

In addition to all that has been said about these lines, to the effect that the speaker gives up in despair and wishes the heart all the best in its endeavor to attain its would-be goal, there seems to be another reading possible. For one thing, Mowatt states this:

> Jungbluth understands [lines 3 f. of strophe II] as a request to God to resolve the conflict by assigning the heart to a successful *Minnedienst*. But such an interpretation ignores the whole tone and structure of the stanza. The first four verses express reluctant resignation in the face of the heart's determination: "Alright, then, if that's the way you want it, may God give you success!" But the next two lines express great doubt about the whole project.... The appeal to God merely mentions what the heart *needs*, which is then at once contrasted with what it is likely to *get*. The poet paints a depressing picture of *Minnedienst*.[11]

And, it is true, the outbreak into exclamations and questions that need no answer in the following lines:

> 13 owe wie sol ez armen dir ergan!
>   wie torstest eine an solhe not ernenden?
>   wer sol dir dine sorge helfen enden
>   mit solhen triuwen als ich han getan?
>
>   alas, how will you poor one fare?
>   how could you face such distress all alone?
>   who will help you end your sorrow
>   with the faithfulness that I have displayed?

seems to support Mowatt's view. With this reading, however, the prayer mentioned in the eleventh line lacks sincerity; indeed, in view of an earlier argument—"got eine müeze scheiden noch den strit" (8)—it becomes tinged with irony and nullifies completely the immediately convincing sincerity of the first strophe's closing line. This, in turn, reduces us to the conclusion that the speaker's concern with the soul's welfare (see below) should not be taken too seriously. Though it seems possible to argue this way, and thus to cast doubt on the sincerity of Hausen's religious orientation, the possibility must be rejected for *aesthetic* reasons: it would undo the entire framework of poetic reference in which the lyric moves; that is to say, for the sake of the poem's verisimilitude of "plot" and for the sake of its internal integrity we must be able to take the sincerity of the eleventh line seriously.[12] We are able to do this by deciding that the prayer mentioned in this line aims at God's compelling the heart away from love and towards the crusade. To be sure, the crusade has not yet been mentioned, but is is already part of our awareness because of the third line: "der lip wil gerne vehten an die heiden." Thus seen, the strophe's first four lines do *not* express "*reluctant resignation* in the face of the heart's determination" (italics added), but are a repeat of the eighth line—"got eine müeze scheiden noch den strit" (in favor of the speaker rather than the heart): since *I*, the mind, can do nothing, I pray that *God* may compel you to follow the right way, which is the way I have chosen.

In this manner, the above passage is perfectly meaningful and without any obscurities whatsoever: the mind has decided to take the cross, thus taking the heart away from what Mowatt calls "temptation"[13] but what in actual fact may be called love paving the road of doom—cf. "solhe not" (14).[14] In this way, the mind's question of the strophe under discussion—"wer sol dir dine sorge helfen enden/ mit solhen triuwen als ich han getan?" (15 f.)—may be seen as an indication that it put a (potential) end to the heart's unavoidable plight by faithfully—"mit triuwen"— taking care of its true welfare, and thus of the would-be "whole" ("lebendic") man, by the decision to go on the crusade. This suggests that the mind (still) has a little confidence in its ability to deal with the situation confronting it; its semblance of superiority shines through when it addresses the heart as "armen dir" (13). The speaker becomes reflective now:

> 17 Ich wande ledic sin von solher swaere,   24 B, 27 C
> do ich daz kriuze ... nam.
>
> I thought I would be without such problems
> when I took the cross. ...

These lines leave open the possibility that the mind was not yet aware at the moment it decided in favor of the cross that it was about to be confronted with the problem which it faces "now": The body "then" is not as a matter of course to be identified as an integral part of the speaker. The two working together and taking each other for granted did not turn out to be a possibility until the moment the mind decided, found the body eager to go along with that decision, but was confronted by the heart's recalcitrance.

There is no indication that the speaker has set out on the crusade.[15] It is a plan not yet carried out. Indeed, the question arises as to who in this state of affairs will carry the victory: the heart which is devoted to a lady, the body which "wil gerne vehten an die heiden," or the would-be mediator between these two. The latter must ponder how to bring harmony or, failing that, how to force a decision in a situation where the heart's devotion is complete but goes in an undesirable direction (from the mind's point of view), while the body's choice is the desirable one but may stem from less than pure reasons.

In view of the tenor of the strophe's closing line, this may also be of consequence: Mowatt makes a distinction when he indicates that "in gotes ere" may mean "to the glory of God" but may also stand for "in the fear of God." Of course, this suggestion goes beyond the immediate text, questions the reason of the speaker's decision to take the cross, and seems warranted in view of the tenor of lines 21 and 24 f. (see below).

> 17 Ich wande ledic sin von solher swaere,
> do ich daz kriuze in gotes ere nam.

Says Mowatt: "The poem forces no choice but it is true that the poet at this point is more concerned with his state of mind than with the ultimate consequence of his action."[16] Nevertheless, we still have reason to wonder about the true nature of the speaker's motivation to go on the crusade. This, in turn, evokes wonder about the purity of the devotional spirit which this lyric has generally been thought to display. For along the present line of reasoning it turns out that fear rather than love of God may have caused the speaker to decide to take the cross.

The following lines as they occur in the manuscripts have bothered the critics:

> ez were ouch reht das es also were
> wan das min stetekeit mir sin verban
>
> it would be right that it were so,
> if it were not for the fact that my steadfastness made
>   that impossible for me.

Ludwig offers an explanation by referring "also" to the *staete* of the heart; the fact that the heart itself is not mentioned he explains as "Auslassungsfehler . . . als Hipographie auf Distanz."[17] Kraus emends drastically to acquire something desirable:[18]

> 19 ez waere ouch reht deiz herze als e da waere
> wan daz sin staetekeit im sin verban.
>
> it would be right that the heart were there as before,
> except that its steadfastness forbade it.

Mowatt offers this as a way out on the basis provided by the manuscripts: "Not the lady, but the whole concept of service to a lady as a way of life is condemned measured against the completely different set of values of the crusade, or of service to God."[19] Mowatt is thus in a position to see "ez" (19) as referring to the state of affairs mentioned in the seventeenth line: it would be right if indeed I were without problems. Equating "min staetekeit" with "dem tumben willen sin" of 22 (which refers to the heart's recalcitrance), he then suggests: "There is no inconsistency if 'ich' is taken to include heart and body. . . . They are different ways of referring to the same state of affairs."[20] With this view, the following lines would follow logically:

> 21 ich solte sin ze rehte ein lebendic man,
> ob ez den tumben willen sin verbaere.
>
> I would be truly a living man
> if it would forego its stubborn will.

Mowatt, it seems, could have made his point more telling by making the most of his own distinction between "to the glory of God" and "in the fear of God"—"in gotes ere." Arguing that the speaker's decision to go on the crusade was perhaps not so much an act of devotion as a prudent decision dictated by the policy of looking ahead for the sake of the soul's welfare, Mowatt could have claimed that the speaker himself (the mind) was not without devotion to the lady, though not quite as ardent as the heart with its "tumben willen." To a degree, then, the mind would be involved in the heart's desire to stay with the lady, and "min staetekeit" (with respect to her) would not only be the *staete* of the heart, but also of the mind. The speaker, in other words, would not be *quite* as opposed to loving the lady as it would seem to be at first glance.

However all this is ultimately to be evaluated, there seems to be another reading possible, one that may be more simple and hence preferable. This reading sees "staetekeit" as an ideal not only in the realm of love, but as desirable also in other realms of life, including that of religious tenets and values.[21] Whereas "ez" of the manuscript's nineteenth line still refers to the seventeenth line—"ledic sin von solher swaere"—"min staetekeit" now refers to the mind's steadfastness regarding its decision to go on the crusade. Hence "staetekeit" does *not* equate with "den tumben willen" of the heart, but stands in juxtaposition to it: it would be correct if I were without problems, but my steadfastness (with respect to my decision to go on the crusade) made that impossible. In this way, the use of "lebendic" (21) retains all the connotations and spiritual values associated with that term: I would be a truly living man, because I would be a whole man, if my heart would forego its stubborn will. With this, nothing prevents "tumb" from meaning "inexperienced" rather than "stubborn" or even "stupid" since from the mind's point of view the heart is indeed in error because it lacks experience in matters pertaining to the crusade, God, or the question of the soul's salvation.

The question still stands whether the speaker's steadfastness stems from his fear of God or from his love of God. Perhaps the distinction has its true home in the subtleties of early Baroque dogmatics[22] and is of no consequence in a medieval value system. If this is the case, there is, as Mowatt has already told us, little difference from a theological point of view between "in the fear of God" and "to the glory of God," and the whole matter can best be dropped. However, since we are dealing with a case where "in gotes ere" has entered the realm of poetry, the question *is* of value, whether we can find an answer to it or not: the phrase, if rendered as "in the fear of God," blemishes the antithetical and juxtapositional values which we detect when we think of two types of love opposing each other. Instead we have a kind of love (represented by the heart) and a kind of fear (represented by the mind).

The following statement is lucid:

> 23 nu sihe ich wol daz im ist gar unmaere
> wie ez mir an dem ende süle ergan.
>
> now I clearly see that it does not care
> how things will fare with me in the end.

Not only do these lines tell of the heart's indifference to what will happen to the would-be "whole," would-be "lebendic" man, they also indicate that the soul's welfare is indeed at stake. Says Mowatt, who uses the statement with a somewhat different slant of meaning: "A Crusade should be sovereign against death, but not when undertaken in this half-hearted frame of mind."[23]

The reading here advocated casts an interesting sidelight on the theological implications it harbors. The decision to go on the crusade "in gotes ere," though perhaps issuing from attrition rather than contrition, seems to be regarded by the speaker as sufficient to purchase the commodity desired: the soul's eternal welfare.[24]

Besides, we are now ready, contrary to the views of many,[25] to suggest that MF 47,33 is intended as an integral part of the lyric, regardless of whether or not it should be thought of as having been added at a later date. For now the outburst of the fourth strophe may be seen as the inevitable result of the speaker's awareness that love of a lady is a dangerous trap and threatens to be an inescapable one now that the speaker is confronted by the recalcitrance of a heart so stubborn. There is, therefore, nothing left of the concerned but superior tone to which we were sensitive in 13: "owe wie sol ez *armen dir* ergan!" (italics added):

> 25 Nieman darf mich wenden daz zustaete
> ob ich die hazze diech da minnet e.[26]
> swie vil ich si geflehet oder gebaete,
> so tuot si rehte als ob sis niht verste.
> mich dunket wie min wort geliche ge
> als ez der sumer von triere taete.[27]

> Nobody need blame me for inconstancy
> if I hate her whom I formerly loved.
> however much I pleaded or entreated,
> she does exactly as if she does not understand.
> it seems my words fare in the same manner
> in which the "sumer von triere" did.

If we read this strophe as referring to a situation anterior to the one delineated in strophes I, II, and III, there is no need whatsoever to think that the heart has become one with the speaker; that would undo the danger of *threatening* "decomposition" on which the effect of the entire arrangement depends. Rather, the speaker is still the mind (incorporating the body, or rather, taking its position for granted). The fourth strophe thus clearly indicates that the speaker, too,[28] once loved the lady, but for reasons indicated in the discussion of the preceding strophes decided to take the cross. Having attempted to free itself from the bondage such love entails, it now flails out in bitterness and sounds as if deranged, as if unhinged from the rest of the "whole" man —cf. "Kampfwut" as mentioned above. It is this being torn that accounts for the speaker's total loss of courtly bearing which it could be expected to display towards a recalcitrant lady even in the direst circumstances.[29]

A would-be "lebendic" man is thus confronted with his own, total disintegration: the heart is driven to follow its "tumben willen," the body "wil gerne vehten an die heiden," and the mind has lost its proper function and hence all chances of bringing about an acceptably reasoned solution. It is therefore small wonder that the speaker's last statement amounts to a negative appraisal of the lady:

> 31 ich waere ein gouch ob ich ir tumpheit haete
> für guot: ez engeschiht mir niemer me.

I would be a fool if I took her dumbness for
lief: it never will happen to me again.

There are a few further comments to be made about this poem. For one thing, in view of the mind's state in the end as evaluated just now, there is irony in the reference to itself as a "gouch" in the subjunctive mood; if it could still function properly, the mind might gain the insight that it already *is* a "gouch." For another thing, and this on a totally different level of evaluation, if we should read "Min herze und min lip diu wellent scheiden" in conjunction with other Hausen lyrics, it might be tempting to argue that the situation developed is the result of a tenacious misunderstanding between the lady and the speaker. From the Aeneas-Dido reference in "Ich muoz von schulden sin unfro" (chapter I) onward there have been several occasions when the lady was projected as doubting her suitor's reliability and *staete*. The one reading of the Aeneas-Dido riddle vindicated the lady and agreed with her reasons for not trusting the speaker. The motif has recurred since then and could perhaps be used to claim that in "Min herze und min lip diu wellent scheiden," too, the lady is *staete* in her lack of belief—cf. "niht verste" (28)—which the speaker calls "tumpheit" (31). With this, given the speaker's tenacity in entreating her (cf. 27: "swie ich si geflehet oder gebaete"), she would emerge as being the same individual throughout the poems, and the long-range effect would be one of misunderstanding warping all along what in the speaker's mind is not warped—or so he has been claiming. The whole matter is of course hypothetical and the attempt to read the poems as a sequence in a particular order is abortive because there are no reliable criteria by which to establish such an order.

And this, too, must be said: the "solution" of this lyric as it comes to us in the fourth strophe lies with values pertaining to love rather than religion. This lays bare a problem: whereas the speaker decided for the crusade and hence for God, in the end his concern centers on his bereavement rather than the deity: religious values are brought in but then abandoned, or at least "forgotten," and the mind can only flail out against fateful love. In doing this, it does not turn to *hohe Minne* values or even to values coming with love of any kind. The language is uncourtly, the speaker turns his back on *staete*, forsakes *Minne* and *Minnedienst*. We deal in the end with a speaker who is bereft of everything; no solace of any kind comes his way, neither from the realm of *Frauendienst* nor from that of religious values. The alleged endeavor to harmonize *Frauendienst* and *Gottesdienst* is not successful.[30] Indeed, there seems to be no good reason to think that such an attempt is made.

To put it differently: it seems strange to think of these four strophes as constituting a crusade song. Its central theme is not the speaker's religious devotion, but his fear of threatening decomposition and his concern with his soul's welfare.[31] This is not even a matter in which the spirit is willing but the flesh is weak, or vice versa. It is instead, a situation in which both the heart and the mind are losers. And particularly if the decision to take the cross stems from fear of God, the crusade fails to be a positive choice between two desires, but is only a means of escaping a dilemma. Bitterness rather than peace is the final note struck, and the would-be "lebendic" man loses on both counts, that of love as well as that of service to God, now that the erstwhile decision to take the cross degenerates into a diatribe against the lady. Indeed, this poem could be called *Disintegration* or *Zerfall*.

X. MIN HERZE DEN GELOUBEN HAT

48, 3   I   1 Min herze den gelouben hat,   26 B, 29 C
               solt iemer man beliben sin
     5   durch liebe od durch der Minnen rat,
               so waere ich noch alumbe den Rin;
            5 wan mir daz scheiden nahe gat,
               deich tet von lieben friunden min.
               swiez doch dar umbe mir ergat,
    10   got herre, uf die genade din
               so wil ich dir bevelhen die
            10 die ich durch dinen willen lie.

         II   Ich gunde es guoten frouwen niet   27 B, 30 C
               daz iemer mere quaeme der tac
    15   dazs ir deheinen heten liep
    18   der gotes verte also erschrac.
    17   15 wie kunde in der gedienen iet?
    16   wan ez waere ir eren slac!
               dar zuo send ich in disiu liet,
    20   und warnes als ich beste mac.
               gesaes min ouge niemer me,
            20 mir taete iedoch ir laster we.

Lehfeld speaks of "ein tief empfundenes Lied, das eine friedlich-sehnsüchtige Stimmung atmet."[1] Wentzlaff-Eggebert thinks that Hausen "ohne die Erfahrung weiblicher triuwe auf die Fahrt gezogen [ist]."[2] It is one of the few Hausen lyrics where the "I" does not stand at the center of attention. Instead thoughtful and concerned objectivity prevails, and the poem is imbued with immediately convincing sincerity.

          1 Min herze den gelouben hat,
            solt iemer man beliben sin
            durch liebe od durch minnen[3] rat,[4]
            so waere ich noch alumbe den Rin;

74

> My heart believes that,
> if ever a man should have stayed behind
> because of love or love's counsel,
> I would still be in the Rhine region;

In view of the "herze-lip" dichotomy encountered in the previous discussion, it is interesting to note that it is the heart, as contrasted to the mind-speaker, which is said to have this belief. This does not mean that Brinkmann must be supported when he gives matters a somewhat metaphysical twist by finding that his lyric "mit dem Glauben des Herzens [beginnt]: es ist also ein Glaube, der tief im Inneren wurzelt."[5] After all, there is no indication that "gloube" is to be identified with faith in the normal sense of the term—as Brinkmann suggests. As used here, it is no more than "notion," "view": "my heart is of the opinion." In fact, the passage leaves open the possibility that the mind-speaker is of a different opinion. The difference with "Min herze und min lip diu wellent scheiden" lies in the fact that the heart in that poem wanted to go its own stubborn way, whereas this time it is merely of the view that *if* ever anyone had the right to stay home for the sake of love, it would be the speaker; but he went.

> 5 wan mir daz scheiden nahe gat,
>   deich tet von lieben friunden min.
>
>   for I am greatly affected by the departure
>   I took from my dear friends.

With the view implicit in the first part of the strophe that all honorable men are on the crusade, it would seem logical that "friunden" of the sixth line refers to the ladies left behind. The speaker's concern pertains to their honor, as becomes evident in the second strophe. Before that we have the heartfelt wish pronounced in the second part of the first strophe:

> 7 swiez doch dar umbe mir ergat,
>   got herre, uf die genade din
>   so wil ich dir bevelhen die
>   die ich durch dinen willen lie.
>
>   whatever will happen to me,
>   Lord God, to your grace
>   I wish to commend those
>   whom I left for your sake.

That "dar umbe" (7) seems to refer to the two lines preceding: whatever happens to me as a result of the fact that I had to take leave from dear friends. And again, it is a moot point whether the references focus on "taking leave" because having to go on a (dangerous) crusade, or on "taking leave from dear friends" and hence having to suffer anguish because of separation. Whatever the exact connotation, the strophe ends with a warm wish. Since the lyric celebrates women in general rather than a single lady, this poem has something in common with "Ich muoz von schulden sin unfro" (chapter I) insofar as one reading of it prompted a similar concern with womanhood in general, albeit on a different plane of argumentation and with a concern seemingly less colored by devoutness.

Insofar as the first strophe leaves room for the possibility of thinking of the speaker in terms of the *miles christianus*, the second strophe turns out to be somewhat of a disappointment. Unless we read this strophe Brinkmann's way,[6] the speaker's concern, though lofty, is exclusively of a secular nature: good women sacrifice their honor if they deign to involve themselves with those who did not go on the crusade:[7]

> 11 Ich gunde es guoten frouwen niet
> daz iemer mere quaeme der tac
> dazs ir deheinen heten liep[8]
> —wan ez waere ir eren slac!
> wie kunde in der gedienen iet?—[9]
> der gotes verte also erschrac.
>
> I would not wish for good women
> that the day would ever come
> that they would love anyone of those
> —for it would be a blow to their honor;
> how could he ever serve them?—
> who became frightened in this way of God's crusade.

Evidently, the speaker does not at all agree with the heart's "glouben"; he identifies anyone who stayed behind for reasons pertaining to love as one who "gotes verte also *erschrac*" (italics added). Clearly, "became frightened" may be too strong a term to render the value of the verb; "refrained from the crusade for such a reason" seems a more accurate way of rendering its value. In this manner, the second interjected statement (15) tells us that the straggler for love's sake is no longer worthy of such love. He becomes the victim of his own action. If we allow ourselves to read these lines in conjunction with "Min herze und min lip diu wellent scheiden" as delineated in chapter IX, we see how close the speaker of "Min herze den gelouben hat" has come to falling victim to love in precisely the same way. Somehow he has struggled to the point where the mind could prevail over the heart.[10]

It is the speaker's concern for the ladies' honor that compels him to send them his "liet";

> 17 dar zuo send ich in disiu liet,
> und warnes als ich beste mac.[11]
>
> therefore I send them these verses
> and warn them as best I can;

and he concludes with this afterthought:

> 19 gesaes min ougen niemer me,
> mir taete iedoch ir laster we.

>   if I never saw them again,
>   their dishonor would nevertheless pain me.

Wentzlaff-Eggebert understands the closing line to say that the speaker, though uncertain of his return, nevertheless "die Ehre des Standes zu wahren [sucht]."[12] He is probably correct, for otherwise "ir laster" would have to stand for "their slander" and refer to the possibly malicious gossip (about the speaker) on the part of those who stayed behind—"si" (19) would then have to refer to the gossipers rather than the ladies. Such an interpretation would detract from the lyric's heartfelt sincerity and lend an egocentric color to the speaker's delivery.

In addition, this poem seems to be a counterpart to "Si welnt dem tode entrunnen sin" (chapter VII). The possibility of one lyric being a pendant to the other is enhanced by the fact that each constitutes a warning; in one, this warning concerns the ladies, in the other those who "welnt dem tode entrunnen sin." Brinkmann brings out this interdependence by calling one "Warnung an die Frauen" and the other "Warnung an die Ritter."

XI. IN MINEM TROUME ICH SACH

48, 23	1 In minem troume ich sach ein harte schoene wip	29 B, 31 C
25	die naht unz an den tach: do erwachete min lip.	

	5 do wart si leider mir benomen,
	  daz ich enweiz wa si si,
	  von der mir fröide solte komen.	

30	daz taten mir diu ougen min: der wolte ich ane sin.	

The theme of this stanza is of all times and places. Wechssler[1] and Kolb[2] have pointed out passages in medieval literature, German and other, showing the popularity of the dream motif. We are likely to have read variations of it, some elaborate, some simple. Whatever the way it is presented, however, it is dualistic when used for a poem written in the first person singular; a private experience—or rather, what is presented as such—enters the public domain. This domain is represented by an audience if the poem is recited or sung, or by readers. In either case audience or reader reacts in whatever fashion is deemed suitable for the occasion. Since "In minem troume ich sach" deals with what seems to be an unsophisticated treatment of the dream motif, and on the axiom that a poem be understood on the basis of it own assumption, we read it in the manner in which it is composed. The acquiescence into which we thus lull ourselves does not mean that we cannot ask questions. On the contrary, asking questions is very much part of acquiescent but inquisitive reading. Similarly, nothing prevents us from seeking to be on the alert for whatever implications we may encounter in the simple, perhaps deceptively simple, statements[3] in which the dream is told, and from asking questions about such implications as well.

The opening line:

> 1 In minem troume ich sach
>
> In my dream I saw

is indicative of the speaker's state of mind. His continued preoccupation with his experience causes a slip in delivery; instead of saying objectively "in a dream" he begins with the subjective "in my dream," thus raising his experience to a higher plane of significance than the audience or reader may be willing to take for granted. Only a dream of some consequence may warrant this egocentric delivery. With it, the speaker projects himself as introvertedly riveting the mind's eye on the experience he has had and on whatever lies beyond it.

The second line could hardly be vaguer:

> 2 ein harte schoene wip
>
> a very beautiful woman.

When we then find out that the dream dealt with her all night long

> 3 die naht unz an den tach:

we wonder why we hear nothing specific about her; it is as if she is of little consequence in her own right, as if she is only important as a representative of her sex.[4] On a different plane, this lack of identity has been interpreted as stemming from the speaker's determination to retain the lady's incognito,[5] thus supplying a touch of realism to an event that otherwise is hazy and—as far as the reader is concerned—at least twice removed from whatever kind of quasi-reality is thought to be prevailing.

Brinkmann has pointed out that the third line, because of its epic ring, is reminiscent of "die heimische Tradition"[6] (as contrasted to that of Provence). Ittenbach is of the same opinion: "Bei Friedrich von Hausen tritt die Aufbauform der alten Dichtung noch klar zutage."[7] The epic element is indeed pronounced here, at least when compared to the content of Hausen's poetry in general. But whereas Ittenbach reasons that this strophe is one of Hausen's early poems and as such still stands close to the homeland tradition, Brinkmann argues that in his later lyrics, of which he sees "In minem troume ich sach" as an example, Hausen *returns* to the homeland tradition. It is strange, however, to have to think that Hausen, a twelfth century member of international society, should have fallen prey to this kind of chauvinism.

The following passage tells us that the speaker awoke:

> 4 do erwachete min lip.
> do wart si leider mir benomen,
> daz ich enweiz wa si si,
> von der mir fröide solte komen.
>
> then I awoke,
> then she was unfortunately taken from me,
> so that I do not know where she is
> from whom joy was to come to me.

Schönbach is not happy with the fourth line and proposes "do erwachet(e) erst (=endlich) min lip."[8] Kraus does not like this change, nor the one suggested by Bartsch. He finds that " 'erst' sich mit dem folgenden in Widerspruch befindet: es wäre nur am Platze, wenn es sich um einen Angsttraum handeln würde. Bartsch setzt: 'do wart erwaht min lip,' was aber zu gewalttätig klingt und nur für ein vorzeitiges Aufwecken passen würde. Man bleibt also am besten bei der Überlieferung."[9] This sound advice does not prevent the passage from having a stubborn ring. The passive of the fifth line may not be the most natural—because it is also too forceful—in this state of affairs; a false passive, if available, would serve the purpose better. And "daz ich enweiz wa si si"[10] demands a suspense of disbelief[11] because it does not make much sense in terms of a connection between a plausible cause (taken away) and an equally plausible effect (not knowing where she is).

In the reading outlined so far, "fröide" (7) lends itself to an interpretation which sees this strophe as celebrating some of the ingredients of love of a specific sort. Kolb, for instance, reads this strophe in terms of the "Last des Schicksals, das den höfischen Sänger [zur Minne] bestimmte,"[12] and this *Minne* is then defined in such a way as to equate with *hohe Minne*.

There is a vehement tone in the closing line:

> 8 daz taten mir diu ougen min:
> der wolte ich ane sin.
>
> my eyes did that to me;
> would I were without them.

This vehemence is somewhat surprising in view of the dreamlike stance which the speaker is generally thought to take and retain until the end. Several critics have read these lines as the speaker's cursing his eyes because he opened them upon awakening, thus ending the dream.[13] This comes with the notion that no woman was present before the dream. So, for instance, but with a particular twist, Kraus, when he approvingly cites Jellinek's view: "Der Dichter sah im Traume eine ihm vorher unbekannte Frau und verwünscht nun seine Augen, weil sie, indem sie sich öffneten, dem Traum ein Ende machten."[14] In actual fact, of course, eyes open *after* awakening. Cause and effect are reversed in Jellinek's view, unless he would take "opening of eyes" to be a metaphor for awakening or would favor the view that the speaker is daydreaming (in the night, of course)—Jellinek does not do either. If we take the closing lines at face value, we must indeed surmise that to be without eyes does not prevent anyone from dreaming in the way Jellinek fancies—"über eine ihm vorher unbekannte Frau"—but it would prevent dreaming motivated by prior seeing. Thus, "daz" of the eighth line would refer to 4 f. Incidentally, it is interesting to note that Jellinek's way of reading could come close to suggesting that "fröide" of the seventh line is the joy of the senses about to be satisfied (in the dream), but this does not correspond to his interpretation of poems of this genre.

Brinkmann's opinion differs from Jellinek's. Drawing conclusions from the way in which he orders and interrelates Hausen's poems, he says: "Es ist keine große Unbekannte, von der [der Dichter] träumt,[15] sondern die Schöne des zehnten, elften und zwölften Liedes."[16] Baumgarten takes a stand between Jellinek and Brinkmann: the woman was unknown to the poet but "immerhin kann er wohl vor dem Traum die Dame wirklich gesehen haben."[17]

Now, it seems perfectly fair to wonder whether the fourth line can only be translated as "then I awoke." A literal rendering would yield "then my person (body) awoke," and immediately we seem to have gained something since the line reminds us now that the mind did not need awakening. It has been active all along—"die naht unz an den tach." We thus have an example of the tendency of the speakers in Hausen's lyrics to "decompose" themselves into various "actors," in this case the mind and the body (and the eyes). Baumgarten sees this decomposition as a sign of an early poem,[18] though it occurs throughout Hausen's work, and Brinkmann uses it as an additional argument in favor of the strophe's late date of composition.[19]

Furthermore, and this is the crux of the matter, whereas the use of "lîp" in lieu of the personal pronoun is common in Middle High German, the reader may wonder whether at times it is used deliberately, in such a way as to suggest a second level of meaning.[20] In the present case, speaking of the body awakening, or of life becoming awake, in a situation involving a dream of a specific kind, the verb might be metaphorical in value[21] and serve to allude to the stirring of the dreaming man's sensual appetite. With this way of reading, the following lines convey the outcome of the dream: then she was taken away from me (in my dream), so that I do not know where she went, from whom joy was (about) to come to me (in my dream).[22] Dreams like that tend to end that way; they are not the most agreeable. Such a dream, in fact, can easily leave the dreamer exhausted and give him the sensation that it lasted a long time—"die naht unz an den tach."

In order to clinch the matter, we cite Brinkmann now, whose way of phrasing serves as well as any other to convey the interpretation commonly given to the latter part of the strophe, but whose wording helps us to put things more precisely: "Der Tag nimmt wie im Tagelied die Gegenwart der Frau, die ihm so ins Unbekannte entrückt wird."[23] The difference with the dawn song is of course that in the latter the man is usually urged to leave the woman—the situation is more or less reversed—and we might benefit from indicating this difference by giving "In minem troume ich sach" the title "Nachtlied," if indeed this little nine-line item may be called "Lied."

Such a night song is "safer" than the dawn song in that the speaker does not run the risk of blemishing his honor through discovery; for that matter, he does not risk anything. But it is also less rewarding; indeed, it is not rewarding at all. For in this reading the closing lines show the woman to be more perhaps than a mere figment of the imagination on the part of a lovesick man in sleep. She exists, for all we know, and the speaker has actually seen her. Now he wishes he had not, for the sight of her stirred him, and there is nothing left but yearning—or wasted energy. This time, the strophe does not clearly indicate when the dream comes to an end. Instead there is the abrupt break between what was about to be (in the dream)—"von der mir fröide solte komen"—and the speaker's wish to be rid of his eyes.

In this connection, Jungbluth has an intriguing suggestion to make when he opts for getting rid of the last line: " 'der wolte ich ane sin' verdient . . . motivisch keinen Glauben und ist aus guten Gründen im Manuskript ohne Parallele: denn zwar sind die Augen (das Sehen!) so oft die Schuldigen an der leidvollen Lage der jeweiligen Sprecher, aber doch auch der Quell maßloser Freuden, und es wäre widersinnig sich ihrer beraubt zu wünschen."[24] Of course the speaker's wish is "wider die Sinne" but to say so is a *non sequitur*. Since the dream has a disagreeable ending, the abruptness of the ill-wish fits neatly into the "plot" of the strophe. Without eyes, the speaker would not have seen the woman who therefore would not have visited him in his dream. In this reading also, "daz" of the eighth line does not refer to "do erwachete min lip" but to the experience of seeing the woman; this experience carried everything else in its wake.

The reading here suggested, while different from the traditional one, is not far-fetched if we proceed without the benefits—or impediments—of concepts stemming from the view what this strophe should amount to within the frame of *Minnesang* as a whole.[25] For one thing, reading the strophe as an independent unit does not demand any forcing of the line; it merely asks for the close scrutiny that Hausen requires elsewhere by virtue of his cerebral, dialectical and often ambiguous procedure. Then, too, as has been stated above, the established way of reading has led to various values being read out of some of these lines; the present argument simply suggests an additional one to be detectable in the fourth line.

"In minem troume ich sach," then, has its ambiguities and serves various levels of meaning simultaneously. Hence if we allow ourselves to think once again of the speaker's audience, we now see that its reaction is less simple than we envisioned. In fact, (mere) reaction will not do. The demand, it turns out, is for active participation which consists in the endeavor to stay abreast of the implications flowing from the *double entendre* found in "do erwachete min lip" and consequently in the lines following. We thus are led to the conclusion that a statement like this is strange: "Wir haben durchaus keinen Grund, daran zu zweifeln, daß sich Hausens Lieder auf wirkliche Verhältnisse beziehen."[26] This belief allows Baumgarten to be one critic among many who steadfastly identifies the poet as *Dichter* with the poet as *persona*. It may be more pertinent to say instead that a sophisticated poet plays a sophisticated game with a sophisticated audience.

With this conclusion we must wonder whether "In minem troume ich sach" is indeed one of Hausen's later poems; if it is, it must be for reasons totally other than those advanced by Brinkmann, when he speaks of Hausen's deliberately returning to the tradition of his homeland (see above). For the *double entendre* on which the lyric's effect hinges brings to mind a number of considerations presented by Wechssler whom we must cite at some length.

Wilhelm Scherer hat einmal gesagt, nichts sei so schwierig für den Literarhistoriker als nach Jahrhunderten festzustellen, was zur Zeit der Abfassung komisch oder humoristisch gewirkt habe. Bei vielen Provenzalen ... komme ich nicht über den Eindruck des leicht Scherzhaften, oft sogar Ironischen hinweg. ... Wir müssen fragen: wurden die Lieder als Ernst oder Scherz vorgetragen und aufgenommen? ... War man gerührt und ergriffen, vielleicht gar erschüttert? Oder freute man sich des geistreichen Gedankenspiels? ... In seiner Heimat wenigstens scheint das Minnelied eine feine und stille Heiterkeit in sich getragen und beim Publikum ausgelöst zu haben. Anders in Deutschland. Dort wurde der eigentliche Minnesang in seinem Wesen vielleicht nicht überall richtig verstanden, nach allem Anschein aber mit jener Gründlichkeit und tiefen Ernsthaftigkeit aufgenommen, die noch Frau von Stael den Deutschen nachrühmt. Hier scheint die fremde Gedankenwelt und die neue, schwierige Technik eher als eine ernste und würdige Arbeit, denn als heitere Kunst betrachtet worden zu sein.[27]

"In minem troume ich sach," I think, suggests with many other Hausen lyrics that the poet did understand correctly "den eigentlichen Minnesang in seinem Wesen"—as understood by Wechssler in the above passage. In view of the "deep" meaning which the critics have imbued into this lyric, a question emerges: who, then, has been deprived of a correct understanding? This question is a disconcerting one if "In minem troume ich sach" is to be seen not merely as an isolated phenomenon, but as representative of other Hausen poems as well. Beyond that looms large the equally disconcerting fact that Hausen has generally been regarded as a typical representative of the poets celebrating *hohe Minne*.

XII. DEICH VON DER GUOTEN SCHIET

48, 32	I	1	Deich von der guoten schiet	30 B, 32 C
			und ich zir niht ensprach	
			also mir waere liep,	
35			des lide ich ungemach.	
		5	daz liez ich durch die diet	
			von der mir nit geschach.	
49, 1			ich wünsche ir anders niet,	
			wan der die helle brach,	
			der füege ir we unt ach.	
	II	10	'Si waenent hüeten min	31 B, 33 C
5			die sin doch niht bestat,	

```
                    und tuont ir niden schin;
                    daz wenic si vervat.
                    si möhten e den Rin
                 15 gekeren in den Pfat,
    10              e ich mich iemer sin
                    getroste, swiez ergat,
                    der mir gedienet hat.'
```

Ittenbach thinks this to be a rather early poem;[1] so does de Boor.[2] Brinkmann places it as number sixteen in his collection and calls it "Abwehr der Huote: Zweistimmig."[3] Elsewhere he suggests that a trip to Italy or a crusade "[den Dichter] aus dem Kreise geliebter Menschen [rief]."[4] An indirect argument in favor of Ittenbach's view is given by Lehfeld: "Bei den älteren Dichtern haben die Klagen und das Liebesleid ihren Grund in der huote und dem nit, von Hausen ab aber in der Verweigerung der Geliebten."[5]

A man speaks the first strophe; it consists of two compound sentences, the first a lament, the second an ill-wish. A woman speaks the second strophe; it consists of two sentences also, which together constitute a defiant acknowledgement of her *staete*. Typical of the *Wechsel*, the stanzas do not form a dialogue. Instead, without reference to distance or proximity between the speakers, each addresses an imagined audience or nobody at all. In either case they may be envisioned as declaiming their private thoughts and feelings regarding the matter at stake. In "Deich von der guoten schiet" the speaker's concern pertains to the "diet" or "hüeter," those nebulous and angry or envious guardians whose function, assigned or self-assumed, it is to waylay any attempt on the part of would-be lovers to meet each other under private circumstances.[6]

The implausible aspect evoked in the *Wechsel*—one stanza addressing itself to the theme elaborated also in the second but failing to form a dialogue with it—may be responsible for some of the interpretations advanced for "Deich von der guoten schiet." They vary, even though the situation suggested seems simple and self-explanatory, especially when we consider that Hausen had able predecessors to emulate or improve upon in the exercise of the genre.[7]

The first strophe begins in the same egocentric way as does many another Hausen lyric, thus leaving the audience, if there is assumed to be one, guessing about the lady who evidently occupies the speaker's mind:

```
    1 Deich von der guoten schiet
      und ich zir niht ensprach
      also mir waere liep,
      des lide ich ungemach.⁸
```

When I separated from the good woman
and did not speak to her
as I should like to,
that caused me discomfort.

Korn reads from this passage that " 'ungemach' noch auf die übelwollenden Mitmenschen zurückgeführt [wird]."[9] The reader may wonder whether that "ungemach" is of the mind, or whether it is of a somewhat different nature (see below).

There is something recalcitrant about the first strophe insofar as the reason given for the separation remains obscure. This is the B manuscript:

> 5 das lies ich durch die valschen diet
> von der mir nie geschach
> dehainer slahte liep
>
> I refrained because of the guardians
> from whom I never experienced
> anything kind.

This round-about statement is anemic, and it evokes the notion of a speaker who is plaintive because he feels petulant; it seems also insufficient insofar as it does not explain why exactly the speaker should feel deterred from retaining a coveted relationship.

The C manuscript has this:

> daz lies ich durch die valschen diet
> von der mir nie lieb beschach
>
> I refrained because of the guardians
> from whom I never experienced anything kind.

Kraus prefers this version—it has at least the virtue of being briefer—but he changes "nie lieb" into "nit," thus acquiring a more forceful statement. It could be argued, however, that the bloodlessness encountered in each of the manuscripts fits in with the mood permeating the entire strophe (see below).

Because of the speaker's decision to be circumspect, we must surmise that the "diet" can do harm, perhaps to one's honor.[10] We can gather only that the speaker's concern is more for his own sake than the lady's;[11] this apparent egocentricity leads him to curse his nebulous enemies. In B he does it this way:

> wan der die helle brach,
> der füege in ungemach
>
> unless he who harrowed hell
> would cause them discomfort.

Incidentally, if this "ungemach" is to be thought of as the discomfort suffered in hell (see below), is both mental and physical, perhaps "ungemach" (4) suffered by the speaker should also be read as being both mental and physical.

The C manuscript has this:

> ich wünsche ir anders niet
> wan der die helle brach
> der füege ir we und ach

> I wish them nothing else
> than that he who harrowed hell
> would cause them pain and misfortune.

It is not easy to decide which of the manuscripts we should follow. Though their "messages" are roughly the same, their attitudes seem to differ, the one in C being more explicit and more forceful. Then, too, it is questionable that Hausen would use in one and the same strophe a "gemach" rhyme twice.

Whatever our choice in the matter, the claim that this stanza exemplifies how "der Einklang mit der Welt zerbrochen [ist]," and that "der Raum, bei Dietmar noch verbunden, nun trennt,"[12] is something of a *non sequitur* since this *Wechsel*, any *Wechsel*, presupposes spatial dimensions between the speakers.

In "der die helle brach" we have an example of a device common enough to have received a designation; it is an antonomasia[13] and not indicative of a flippant attitude in regard to religious tenets or sacred matters in general. Instead the phrase, now that it has entered the realm of poetry, serves to tell us something about the "diet," at least as far as the speaker's view of them is concerned: like the denizens of hell, they may be thought of as being beyond redemption and utterly reprehensible. This may have something to with the fact that the stanza refers to "diet," whereas the second strophe alludes to the "hüeter" (see below).

Those "diet" must be of consequence, otherwise there is no explaining the speaker's combining his vehement curse with complete passivity. For this strophe does strike a passive pose (particularly in the B manuscript) despite Ittenbach's view that "die Sprache der Frauenstrophe ebenso entschieden, stolz und rücksichtslos ist wie die der Männerstrophe."[14] Brinkmann suggests that what we call passivity issues from the speaker's doubt regarding the lady's feeling towards him,[15] and that his courtliness commands that he leave it up to the lady to put her (public) stamp of approval on the relationship. At any rate, this suggestion concedes the role of an audience which in effect becomes a "character" now that it is allowed to be a retarding element in the development of the "plot."[16] All this, however, derives from notions based on data lying beyond the immediate scope of the *Wechsel* at hand.

In the second strophe the woman takes a defiant stand against the meddling "hüeter":

> 10 Si waenent hüeten min
> di sin doch niht bestat,
> und tuont ir niden schin;

Says Mowatt:

Editors accept C here; ... the only difficulty is with "sin" (a genitive). This, as the subject of the verb, would normally be in the nominative, but there are also examples where the negative verb produces a genitive subject.... It looks as if the scribe of B experienced doubts, and was moved to substitute "si" for "sin," thus introducing a nominative, but unfortunately feminine subject for "bestat." In the face of all this confusion, it seems possible that this was not one of Hausen's happier turns of phrase.[17]

Since "sin" cannot stand for "Verstand," we are left with this attempt at translation:

> They think to guard me,
> though it is not their concern,
> and show their envy;

There is no indication to whom the "hüeter" turn their sentiments; they are merely said to show them, presumably to the speaker of the first strophe as a sole individual or to would-be intimates of the lady in general.

As with the first strophe, there is a lack of smoothness also in the second. To say that the show of envy or anger will not avail the "hüeter" leads us to expect a declaration of the lady's determination to continue seeing her suitor. But she makes a hyperbolic and emphatic statement instead to the effect that she will not forget him who has served her:

> 13 daz wenic si vervat.
> si möhten e den Rin
> gekeren in den Pfat,
> e ich mich iemer sin
> getroste, swiez ergat,
> der mir gedienet hat.'
>
> that avails them not.
> they are more likely
> to lead the Rhine into the Po
> before I ever forget the man
> who has served me,
> come what may.

As though the "hüeter" are the guardians of the mind!

At best, then, the lady's words must be assumed to bypass the thought of the possibly long period during which the guardians may be active. Only with this assumption is the reason to call her determination not ever to forget the man the logical outcome of her declamation. In this manner, we may find that "e ich mich iemer sin/ getroste" is more than merely "forget"; it has the value of "proclaim *staete*," of "never give up," and beyond that carries the concomitant value of her wishing and being eager to reward her suitor, come what may. And the mood of the lyric is such as to leave no doubt regarding the ultimate intent of the speakers: they aim at the consummation of their relationship. As in the older *Wechsel*, the lady comes closer than her friend to giving explicit expression to this intent.

Brinkmann, for one, reads differently: "Die Frau spielt mit Unmöglichkeiten.... Er genießt seinen Triumph, wenn er die Frau zum Schluß die Anerkennung seiner Leistung aussprechen läßt (in einem Relativsatz)."[18] This view seems to stem from Brinkmann's habit of identifying the poet as *Dichter* with the poet as *persona*, that is, the speaker of the first strophe. The result is a curious pulling awry of the lady's words.

There is still the question as to what the "diet" amount to. Schönbach states: "MF 48,36 haben BC 'valschen' eingesetzt. Für Hausen bedeutete somit 'diet' an sich schon schlechte Leute."[19] And it is true, though both manuscripts have "valschen," it does not fit metrically; hence we may have to assume that "diet" was to the scribes more neutral in value than it was to Hausen, and that they inserted the adjective in order to convey the reprehensibility of their activity—that is, reprehensibility from the speaker's point of view. At any rate, "diet" or "valschen diet" fits in with the view that they are, as seen by the speaker, fit candidates for perpetual sojourn in Satan's realm (see above). The lady, by way of contrast rather than similarity, does not go beyond alluding to "hüeter" and their anger or envy. It may well be that he speaks of "diet" because he thinks of hired help, whereas she knows better and is aware that "hüeter" comprises (voluntary or paid) help as well as (anxious) relatives or at least "Standesgenossen."[20] After all, the guardians affect these two speakers differently; she is protected—against her will, to be sure—against him.[21]

Schönbach's claim that "Nicht die berufsmäßigen Hüeter gemeint sind, sondern neidische Standesgenossen *des Dichters*"[22] [italics added], constitutes another case of equating the poet as *Dichter* with the poet as *persona*, and that, as we take the opportunity to point out, is a view with sometimes devastating results. For "Deich von der guoten schiet" lends itself well to dealing with this manner of evaluation applied to Hausen's poetry; it could be called the biographical method. It leads to some contradictory claims, particularly if combined with an attempt to stand up for the *Liederbüchleintheorie* as advanced by Müllenhoff,[23] and as defended, "refined," and otherwise supported or dealt with by Becker,[24] Baumgarten[25] and others, who tenaciously identify the speakers in these lyrics with the poet, and are bent on seeing the lyrics as interrelated in a specific order.

In connection with the *Liederbüchleintheorie*, then, Becker states this: "[Baumgarten] faßt . . . die Frauenstrophen richtig auf. Er schließt aus MF 49,4 . . . nicht. . . . daß die Frau dem Dichter günstig war, sondern nur, daß dieser auf ihre Gunst hoffte."[26] If we then turn to Baumgarten to see whether the unbelievable must be believed, we find this:

[Die Bemerkung], daß MF 48, 32 den Dichter schon ziemlich in der Liebe fortgeschritten zeige, ist nur durch die Frauenstrophe MF 49, 4 begründet. Die Frauenstrophen aber müssen, wie ich glaube, bei einer chronologischen Bestimmung gänzlich ausgeschlossen werden, weil sie nicht von der Dame selbst kommen, sondern nur der Einbildung des Dichters entsprungen sind, der der Geliebten das in den Mund legt, was er von ihr vernehmen möchte. Muß man aber aus diesem Grunde . . . die Frauenstrophen zunächst wirklich ausschließen, so bleibt vom zweiten Liede allein die erste Strophe übrig, in der nur erhalten ist, daß der Dichter mit der Dame zusammengetroffen sei, aber der Leute wegen ihr nicht gesagt habe, was er auf dem Herzen hatte. Wenn er gerade dies hervorhebt, so liegt es wenigstens mit Berücksichtigung [von "In minem troume ich sach"] nahe, an eine Liebeserklärung zu denken und dadurch die Annahme des Anfangs eines Liebesdienstes bestätigt zu finden. Wenn aber dann im dritten Liede . . . der Dichter . . . auf eine schon lange Zeit der Liebe hinweist, so scheint dies schlecht für den Anfang eines Liebesverhältnis zu passen.[27]

So it continues. Baumgarten's is the best argument to date against the biographical interpretation of the Hausen lyrics. Though it is small wonder that the critics came to pronounce doom over the *Liederbüchleintheorie*, the biographical approach is still with us, and its natural end may come only gradually, if ever.[28]

Meanwhile, given the uncertain values to be attributed to "diet" and "hüeter," we must conclude that "Deich von der guoten schiet" leaves us with questions unanswered. One thing is reasonably evident, however: there is little connection between this *Wechsel* as evaluated in these pages and the philosophy of *hohe Minne*.

XIII. MIR IST DAZ HERZE WUNT

49, 13   I   1 Mir ist daz herze wunt   32 B, 34 C
                und siech gewesen nu vil lange
   15   (deis reht: wan ez ist tump),
                sitz eine frowen erst bekande,—
             5 der keiser ist in allen landen,
                kust er si zeiner stunt
                an ir vil roten munt,
   20   er jaehe ez waere im wol ergangen.

         II   Sit ich daz herze han   33 B, 35 C
            10 verlazen an der besten eine,
                des sol ich lon enpfan
                von der selben diech da meine.
   25   swie selten ich ez ir bescheine,
                so bin ichz doch der man
            15 der ir baz heiles gan
                dan in der werlte lebe deheine.

         III   Wer möhte mir den muot   34 B, 36 C
   30   getroesten, wan ein schoene frouwe,
                diu minem herzen tuot
            20 leit diu nieman kan beschouwen?
                dur not so lide ich solhen rouwen,
                wan sichz ze hohe huop.
   35   wirt mir diu Minne unguot,
                so sol ir niemer man voltrouwen.

As is the case with several of the previously discussed lyrics, with "Mir ist daz herze wunt," too, the very "plot" is at stake if we read it as an independent unit. A semblance of objectivity prevails in the opening lines in that the "whole man" reports on the state of his heart:

1 Mir ist daz herze wunt
und siech gewesen nu vil lange

My heart has been hurt
and ill now for a long time.

To the modern reader these lines may be of little consequence as far as their value as imagery is concerned, but they may have throbbed with vitality in Hausen's own day. At any rate, the image must have been closer to the business of living than it seems to us now. "Dem ritterlichen Menschen lag es nahe, die Gefährdung seines Lebens als Verwundung zu sehen."[1] Brinkmann's claim rings true; but this is not the case when his biographically slanted understanding of Hausen's poetry leads him to this semi-metaphysical twist: "Die Frau hat ihn verwundet und nur sie vermag ihn zu heilen. . . . Wenn alles Menschliche Ruhe findet, versagt sich dem Dichter der Schlaf."[2] This statement is then followed by a discussion so deep and so serious and so preoccupied with working out a grave problem—culminating in *Frauendienst* versus *Gottesdienst*—that we may well hesitate to view this lyric as written in a lighter and more playful mood. But since deliberate ambiguity comes to the fore as a leading poetic device in previously discussed lyrics (and is evident also in those that follow), there is as yet no compelling need to think of Hausen as exclusively the deep ponderer and as one who struggles with a philosophy of love. Indeed, so far there have been no unequivocal signs pointing in that direction. Instead Hausen has revealed himself as a poetic poet rather than a systematically philosophizing one, and he should be read accordingly until we encounter clear evidence to the contrary.

The quasi-objectivity of the speaker in the opening statement allows the interjection of a deprecation of the heart's experience and consequent wisdom:

3 (deis reht: wan ez ist tump),

that is true for it is foolish.

For the moment it seems fair to translate "tump" as "foolish"; in view of "nu vil lange" the term can hardly have the value of "inexperienced."

The first statement is brought to an end with

4 sitz eine frowen erst bekande,

ever since it knew a lady.

With the heart for its subject, "bekande" cannot mean "acknowledged" in the sense of "conveyed"; it simply tells the story of a wounded heart that continues to be ailing because it is in the bonds of love. Whereas it is clear that the speaker has little sympathy with the heart—"ez ist tump"—there is no evidence that the lady is aware of its feeling toward her. Hence the entire lament remains private and becomes "ein schönes Weinen" without consequence. At the same time, the function of the audience is important in this lyric, as is particularly indicated by the rhetorical question in the third strophe and the "moral" indignation against *Minne* at the end (see below).

In this way, the lyric becomes a tug of war between the private and the not so private, between failure to inform the lady and the emphatic display of feeling in public. Since the speaker's *staete* is kept private, the following sentence comes as a surprise:

> 5 der keiser ist in allen landen,
> kust er si zeiner stunt
> an ir vil roten munt,
> er jaehe ez waere im wol ergangen.
>
> he who is emperor of all lands,
> if he kissed her at one moment
> on her very red mouth,
> he would say he had done well.

The passage constitutes a counterweight to the heart's being found "tump," since the lady is now said to be such as to have potentially the same effect on the emperor as she has had on the speaker. Hence if the latter's heart is "tump," this would also be true for the emperor's, and consequently, we may infer, for the heart of anyone who came to kiss "den vil roten munt."[3] It is easy to agree with Brinkmann that this passage "an einem möglichen Fall die erotische Schönheit der Frau vergegenwärtigen [soll],"[4] though we discount his claim that the lyric was recited in the emperor's presence.[5] This may have been true, of course, but not more so than if the same claim were made for any other Hausen lyric.

The first sentence of the second strophe states:

> 9 Sit ich daz herze han
> verlazen an der besten eine,
> des sol ich lon enpfan
> von der selben diech da meine.
>
> Since I have entrusted my heart
> to one of the best,
> I should be rewarded by
> the very person whom I mean.

Brinkmann suggests: "Dieses Lied packt (drohend oder beschwörend?) die Minne bei ihrer Ehre, die von ihr verlangt, daß sie einem Liebenden wie ihm nicht ihre Güte versagt."[6] Says Schönbach: "Die zugrunde liegende Anschauung ist dem Leben entnommen; ein Höriger wird von seinem Herren gegen Entgelt ausgeglichen. Diese Auffassung wird durch MF 50,11 und 50,15 bestätigt."[7] This intra-lyrical "proof," incidentally, is thought to be compelling also by Baumgarten,[8] Becker,[9] and many others. Mowatt is of a different opinion regarding the acceptability of this procedure[10]—correctly so from the present point of view. Besides, Schönbach's argument is circular since MF 50,11—"ich han von kinde an sie verlan"—is an expression that should not be taken as an autobiographical statement,[11] and the subject in MF 50,15 —"min herze ist ir ingesinde"—turns the phrase into a metaphor. In addition, even *if* we accepted Schönbach's implication that the line of communication is still open between a line of poetry and the aspects of daily life that gave inspiration for such a line, there would be some questions left unanswered. Who in this passage is "der Hörige?" The heart? And who is "der Herr?" That must be the speaker! What sort of "lon" does this speaker want or expect? The fact that it is the speaker, as contrasted to the heart, who is to receive this reward may insinuate anything.

The eleventh line—"des sol ich lon enpfan"—is affected by "nu vil lange" of the second line.[12] It is an "ought to" of long standing but never realized—entirely due to the fact that the lady has never been told anything? The second sentence gives explicit evidence of this failure to communicate:

> 13 swie selten ich ez ir bescheine,
> so bin ichz doch der man
> der ir baz heiles gan[13]
> dan in der werlte lebe deheine.
>
> though I never show it to her,
> I am nevertheless the man
> who grants her better happiness
> than anyone else in the world.

Baumgarten interprets the thirteenth line as an indication "daß diese Lieder nicht sehr schnell einander folgten";[14] he must be of the opinion that the line does *not* constitute a litotes and hence does not carry the meaning "never" for "selten."

The connection between the two sentences forming the second strophe is not clear, and we wonder why "lon enpfan" of the eleventh line should by any logic lead to the speaker's statement about "heiles gan." Indeed, the strophe makes little sense in any frame of reference; even if in a particular sphere love called for a reward, such a claim would become empty of meaning when love is never brought to the attention of the lady involved.

The third strophe is addressed to the audience whose reaction to the question

> 17 Wer möhte mir den muot
> getroesten, wan eine schoene frouwe,
> diu minem herzen tuot
> leit diu nieman kan beschouwen?
>
> who could console me but
> a beautiful lady
> who brings woe to my heart
> that nobody can fathom?

is generally thought to be an emphatic "no one!" though Touber poses a question:

"Ist hier die Antwort wirklich 'niemand' oder vielleicht 'die Minne?'"[15] Says Brinkmann: "Diese rhetorische Frage ist zugleich ein Anruf an die Frau."[16] Even a generous amount of suspension of disbelief fails to make this suggestion a viable notion, unless we follow Brinkmann and place the closest possible connection between (entertaining) poetry and (actual) life. Schönbach asks about "beschouwen": "soll es einfach heißen 'erkennen,' 'sehen,' nicht: 'besichtigen,' um zu pflegen, zu heilen?"[17] Whatever one's reaction to this question—Kraus does not like it[18]—the fact remains that this line in particular represents the essence of the tug of war between the private and the public spheres, and the reader receives no indications as to where he might receive an answer to the question.

The *Abgesang* of this strophe falls into two separate statements which are not closely connected but stand side-by-side. The only link between them is a to-be-assumed thought process which skips one or two in-between stations to start from

> 21 dur not so lide ich solhen rouwen,
> wan sichz ze hohe huop.
>
> of necessity I suffer such grief
> for it (my heart) raised itself too high.

and to arrive at

> 23 wirt mir diu minne[19] unguot,
> so sol ir niemer man voltrouwen.
>
> if love becomes unkind to me,
> no man should ever trust it.

Whereas Becker detects here the emphasis on "die Noth der hohen Minne,"[20] Arnold interprets this section as revealing "unmaze," and he finds that "der hohe Mut in der Beherrschung des ungezügelten Lebensdranges [beruht]."[21] Götz states: "Noch unerfüllte Liebe bringt 'riuwe' . . . , eine Liebe, die unerfüllt bleiben muß, weil die Geliebte zu vornehm ist."[22] Brinkmann suggests: "Das Gedicht endet mit dem Ausblick, der einer verhüllten Drohung gleicht: wenn die Minne sich mir unfreundlich zeigt, dann soll man ihr überhaupt kein Vertrauen schenken."[23] Neunteufel wonders: "Ist hier nicht an ein verstecktes Bild zu denken? Die Dame in der Kürnberger Strophe sagt vom Falken 'er hup such uf vil hohe,' und Reinmar von Hagenau singt später: 'Min herze hevet sich ze spiel . . . als der valke tuot und der ere enswie.' "[24] Regarding "man" of the closing line Mowatt points out that it can be substantive as well as pronominal—"man" as well as "one."[25]

The final sentence resists close scrutiny. No matter whether "Minne" is taken as love, as Venus,[26] or as the lady to whom the speaker is referring,[27] the future tense is startling after more than two strophes filled with laments regarding love's alleged recalcitrance—alleged, since "minne" has not had an opportunity to hold sway over an uninformed lady.

In this way, the lyric leaves us with questions, and pulls us in several directions simultaneously. Brinkmann seems to be of the same opinion, though perhaps for

different reasons: "Das Lied verrät nichts von der geistigen Energie, die das dritte Gedicht—"Ich lobe got der siner güete" (chapter XV)—durchdrang und zur geschlossenen, wenn auch vielgliederigen Einheit formte. . . . Die Einheit des Gesamtliedes überzeugt nicht. Liegt es daran, daß ['Mir ist daz herze wunt'] mehr aus dem Gefühl entsprang, während ['Ich lobe got der siner güete'] aus dem Geiste empfangen war?"[28] Perhaps Brinkmann's problem stems from the fact that he, too, thinks that the lady does not know of the speaker's travail.[29]

We must also face Isbăşescu's claim; interpreting "Minne" as "unheilbringende Macht, als Allegorie," he speaks of "Vertiefung and Vergeistigung des Minnebegriffs."[30] With this, we must wonder whether we have missed something vital and retrace our steps to seek answers to some of the questions left open.

Why, for instance, would the emperor speak as indicated if he were to kiss the lady's "vil roten munt?" Is it the ultimate accolade given to the lady in this poem? And if so, does it lead to the conclusion that she is worthy indeed, so worthy, in fact, that even he, the emperor, could not go further than a kiss? Or is the lady merely worthwhile? One thing seems certain: in the emperor's case, if his heart is palpitating, it may be palpitating for very mundane reasons.

In this connection it may be good to cite the first stanza as it occurs in the C manuscript.

> Mir sint die sinne wunt
> und siech gewesen von vil banden;
> das ist in rehte kunt,
> sit si ein frowen erst bekanden
> der keiser ist in allen landen
> kust er si zeiner stunt
> an ir vil roten munt
> er hete sin iemer frome ze sinen handen

We cite Mowatt now: "The choice between 'herze' B and 'sinne' C is a choice between clichés. The 'tumbez herze' of the third line in B is also a cliché, but does not really fit in with the following line, since 'tumpheit' is ordinarily the result of ignorance rather than experience. The version in C makes reasonable sense but editors have preferred B, perhaps because C is so unsatisfactory in the last line of the stanza."[31]

If we translate these lines, we get something like this:

> My senses have been wounded
> and are sick of many bonds.
> that is properly known
> ever since they committed themselves to a lady.
> he who is emperor of all lands,
> if he kissed her once
> on her very red mouth
> he would be able to feel good whenever he wanted to.

Clearly, C simply states in the closing line what it seems to state: the lady's red mouth would be available to the emperor whenever he would wish it. Why this reading should be unsatisfactory is not clear. Admittedly, the irony emerging here is something totally different from the (more delicate) ambiguity that may lie embedded in "er jaehe ez waere im wol ergangen" as preferred by the commentators (see above), but that is no reason why it should be discarded outright. After all, the irony is not all that different from the one which Mowatt detects in the occurrence of "ungerne" of MF 50,25 (see chapter XV, pp. 103). On the one hand we have a lady who, according to Mowatt's reading, likes to listen to what other men have to say to her, and on the other hand, we have a lady who likes to be kissed by the emperor. Imperial kisses, she may find, are for various reasons, all hinging on their imperial quality, preferable to the kisses of others, particularly the ones that fail to come her way from a non-communicative speaker.

We could add to these considerations by asking about the exact meaning of "lon enpfan." And what is the exact nature of "bas heiles gan," and of "getroesten?" Brinkmann interprets this "heiles gan" as meaning that the speaker wishes the lady all the best,[32] but it is not clear why this should be emphasized in a particular way by the addition of "dan in der werlte lebe deheine." Perhaps we should remember that "heil" may mean a number of things (simultaneously), such as "good fortune," or "happiness." It may be that the quaint emphasis contains a boast related to the speaker's ability to grant the lady "heil" of a specific kind.

With this, it is not difficult to suggest that "getroeste" is perhaps more than "bring solace" in a platonic fashion; Götz sees "trost" as possible "Liebeserfüllung"[33] and though he does not bring "getroeste wan eine schoene frowe" as an example there is little to prevent the line from carrying this meaning, especially in view of "lon enpfan" of the eleventh line. Schönbach may be making the same suggestion, but in that case he puts it in a circumspect metaphor: "Nur die Hand, die Wunden schlägt, kann auch heilen."[34]

Regarding "sichz ze hohe huop" we can only say that it does not seem to issue from a difference in social standing between lady and speaker. If that were the case, it would be unrealistic on the speaker's part to come forth with his "moral indignation" of the closing lines. Instead we may surmise that "sichz ze hohe huop" refers to the speaker's heart going too far in its wishes and having the gall to envision an outcome so fulfilling as to leave nothing to be desired.

That "moral" of the closing statement tells the audience that love is not to be trusted if it is not good to the speaker. This is irony if we consider that "Minne" is envisioned as coming to the speaker from a lady who knows nothing, so that love will have no opportunity of becoming effective in either a positive or negative way. This contradicts the notion that anything positive comes the speaker's way through his private sufferings—unless we must think that a self-educating aim lies behind the speaker's delivery. There is no indication that we should think so.

XIV. ICH SIHE WOL DAZ GOT WUNDER KAN

49, 37 I 1 Ich sihe wol daz got wunder kan 35 B, 37 C
     von schoene würken uzer wibe.
50, 1   daz ist an ir wol schin getan:
     wan er vergaz niht an ir libe.
    5 den kumber den ich des erlide,
     den wil ich iemer gerne han,
5   zediu daz ich mit ir belibe
     und al min wille süle ergan.
     min frowe sehe waz si des tuo:
    10 da stat dehein scheiden zuo.

   II Si gedenke niht deich si der man 36 B, 38 C
10   der si ze kurzen wilen minne.
     ich han von kinde an si verlan
     daz herze min und al die sinne.
    15 ich wart an ir nie valsches inne,
     sit ich si so liep gewan.
15   min herze ist ir ingesinde,
     und wil ouch staete an ir bestan.
     min frowe sehe waz si des tuo:
    20 da stat dehein scheiden zuo.

There is no reason to attribute a deeply religious feeling to this poem merely because it credits the deity with the ability to endow women with beauty:

  1 Ich sihe wol daz got wunder kan
   von schoene würken uzer wibe.

  I see clearly that God can work
  miracles of beauty with women.

Schönbach sees these lines as a reflection of "deus mirabilia fecit," which occurs some twenty times in the Psalms.[1] "She" is proclaimed to be a perfect example of that:

  3 daz ist an ir wol schin getan:
   wan er vergaz niht an ir libe.

  she makes that perfectly evident,
  for he forgot nothing on her body.

Wechssler points out that "weil die kirchlichen Gelehrten alle leibliche Schönheit als Symbol und Beweis einer schönen Seele und zugleich als Unterpfand der Gottähnlichkeit auffaßten, konnten die Frauensänger auch die Verehrung irdischer Frauenschönheit in ihr Gedankensystem einfügen."[2] True as this is, it does not follow that the poets as a matter of course retained the philosophical-theological insight to which Wechssler refers. We have seen, and shall see again, that beauty at times is clearly linked to the realm of earthly values and sharply contrasted with those of the religious sphere, and this contrast, too, stems from "die kirchlichen Gelehrten"—see, e.g., our discussion of "Si darf mich des zihen niet" (chapter VIII).

De Boor sees this lyric as an early one; he states: "Die Frau erscheint [dem Dichter] in ihrer seelisch und leiblich vollendeten Schönheit als die Krone von Gottes Schöpfungswunder." This comes in conjunction with the view regarding "das neue vertiefte Aufbrechen des Zwiespalts Welt-Gott, vertieft dadurch, daß ja nun auch die Welt in der hohen Minne einen transzendent erlebten und darum verpflichtenden Pol besitzt."[3] And, it is true, the lady's—for the moment perhaps "merely" physical —beauty is such as to cause the speaker sorrow. He welcomes it, however, as long as he can stay with her:

> 5 den kumber den ich des erlide,
> den wil ich gerne han,
> zediu daz ich mit ir belibe
> und al min wille süle ergan.[4]

> the sorrow which I suffer from that
> I shall gladly bear
> provided I can stay with her
> and all my will shall be satisfied.

Becker finds that this " 'kumber' nicht als ein Widerspruch erscheint, sondern als etwas Natürliches."[5] We agree on the basis of the axiom that love, anywhere and at any time, comes with sorrow,[6] but then read on: "Hier findet also die direkte Gegensatz zwischen altheimischer Auffassung vom Minnedienst statt." But "kumber," it would seem, is here a matter of physical yearning as much as of anything else, if not more so, and results from the lady's (still only) physical beauty.[7] This, to be sure, is something "Natürliches," but why it should be seen as a contrast "zur altheimischen Auffassung vom Minnedienst" remains obscure, for it is natural anywhere. In fact, the question arises what there is in the form of *Minnedienst* in this strophe. The speaker in the following lines is simply saying with an ironic twist that he will gladly suffer as long as he gets what he wants. The suffering thus undertaken cannot possibly be equated with suffering of the mind:

> 9 min frowe sehe waz si des tuo:[8]
> da stat dehein scheiden zuo.

> let my lady see what she (can) do about it;
> it allows no separation.

These lines have evoked some comments. Müllenhoff translates the last one as: "ein Abkommen ist hier nicht möglich."[9] Kraus finds this "doppelsinnig. Der Dichter hat gewiß nur an die Trennung des Verhältnisses gedacht. Also: 'Meine Herrin mag sehen, was sie dabei zu tun hat, eine Trennung ist unter diesen Umständen nicht möglich.' "[10] Schönbach renders it, "da gibt's weiter nichts zu deuten," and he continues, "Der Dichter mißt diesem Satz solches Gewicht bei, daß er ihn in den Refrain nimmt, und betont in der zweiten Strophe alle Umstände, die nunmehr Klarheit erwarten lassen."[11] Schönbach, although usually an intelligent and sensitive reader, forces these lines to conform to a preconceived view regarding their meaning, away from the obvious and toward something which simply is not there.

Instead of the above we would suggest that the refrain—or rather, what turns out to be the refrain[12]—reflects the mood created; it is playful and unproblematic; it does not press for a solution, but leaves the stanzas open-ended. Brinkmann sees this differently also; placing it as number I in the Hausen corpus—"Schmerz und Treue, erste Variation"—he states: "Es beginnt mit einem Bewundern des Erstaunens über die Schönheit der Frau, die Gott schuf. Ein Ergriffener redet, der den ehrfürchtigen Aufblick kennt. Er sieht die Strahlen, die vom Überirdischen ins Irdische fallen und alles Menschliche verklären. Was den Dichter bewegt, kommt von oben."[13] Lofty though this is, it exerts an unwarranted influence on the mood of this lyric, and in effect mutilates it. There is, in fact, nothing of "seelische Belastung" here.[14] We could even say that despite the frequent use of the first person singular—there are fourteen instances of it—the speaker is not very much involved, and certainly not in the way Brinkmann and other critics suggest. Nor, for that matter, is the lady, even though the speaker wants her to solve his "problem": "min frowe sehe waz si des tuo." It is clear that the closing lines restate in a negative way what "al min wille süle ergan" states positively. There is support for this view: de Boor finds in this strophe "das erotische Ziel des Werbens unverhüllt ausgesprochen."[15]

Isbǎşescu detects in the opening lines of the second strophe "den eigentlichen Begriff der hohen Minne, die einseitig ist und ohne Erfüllung bleibt":[16]

11 Si gedenke niht deich si der man
der si ze kurzen wilen minne.

She must not think that I am the man
who loves her for a short time (only);

But it is difficult to see what difference there exists between *hohe Minne* thus conceived and love unrequited. Schmid speaks of "totale Minne" and "negative Minne," and finds that "Mehrdeutigkeit zur vollständigen Entartung des Begriffs [der Minne] führen kann, wie etwa in MF 50,10, wo der Dichter 'ze kurzen wilen' minnt, das heißt, hier sich auf irgendwelcher Weise mit Damen unterhält."[17] Schmid, to be sure, may have misread the line by overlooking the negative in the eleventh. Mowatt makes this point: "The contrast here may be merely between a short and a long attachment, in which case the phrase would mean: 'for a short time only.' But another contrast could also be operative, namely 'seriously'/'lightheartedly,' in which case the familiar association of 'kurzewile'—leisure pastime—would be opposed to the lifelong dedication expressed in 'von kinde' line 13."[18] With Mowatt's suggestion taken into account, the lady is confronted with another problem: if, thus understood and intended, the speaker's statement is assumed ever to come to her ears, she must decide whether or not to believe the speaker.

The following lines have also received attention:

> 13 ich han von kinde an si verlan
> daz herze min und al die sinne.
>
> from childhood on I have surrendered to her
> my heart and all my senses.

Becker finds that the first of these constitutes "eine gewisse licentia poetica."[19] Kolb says in a statement into which he incorporates also a consideration of "Ich sihe wol daz got wunder kan": "Mit Sicherheit dürfen wir ein Glimmern der Fernliebe und der Sehnsucht . . . überall da annehmen, wo [die Dichter] in ihren Liedern [so etwas] sagen."[20] Baumgarten takes these lines to provide biographical information: "Wenn auch das Liebesverhältnis erst mit MF 48,23 begann, so war die Geliebte doch dem Dichter schon von Kind auf bekannt."[21] The credibility—or lack of it—of these statements needs no scrutiny. Wechssler advocates this: "wir brauchen das nicht immer wörtlich zu nehmen. . . . Doch eine so exakte Behauptung muß nicht in jedem Fall bloße Phrase gewesen sein. Im Gegenteil: der Sänger konnte sie vor einem Publikum, das ihn kannte, nur dann wagen, wenn sie in etwas die Wahrheit traf."[22] This half-hearted link between poetry and some kind of reality may contradict the view of "die Liebe . . . als poetische Fiktion,"[23] though a twist in the argument, consistently applied throughout his studies, enables Wechssler to harmonize these two views. Elsewhere he says: "nicht der buchstäbliche, sondern der allegorische Sinn. . . . sicherte den wunschbaren Erfolg. Den . . . Minnesängern wurden die feudalrechtigen Vorstellungen bald zu bloßen Stilmitteln."[24]

The fact is that "ich han von kinde an si verlan" is followed by a line with which it cannot possibly be taken to function in any other but a metaphorical sense: "das herze min und al die sinne" has an *adult* value. It enhances the emphatic statement that the speaker does not love "ze kurzen wilen," no matter whether the latter phrase refers to the past or the future (see Mowatt as cited above).

The second strophe tells us also that the lady's effect on the speaker is due not only to her outward beauty (which so far has been the driving force behind his statements), but also by her inward light:

> 15 ich wart an ir nie valsches inne,
> sit ich si so liep gewan.
>
> I never noticed anything false in her
> since I began to love her.

In connection with our ponderings elsewhere (see chapter II, p. 23) about the significance of public opinion regarding one's honor, loveworthiness, etc., Brinkmann makes an interesting comment about these lines: "In ritterlicher Sprache ist weniger wichtig, was ein Mensch ist, als die Wahrnehmung seines Wesens durch andere."[25] This could leave open the question whether the speaker evaluates the lady correctly, or whether he is so blinded by her outward appearance that his judgement is impaired. After all, he has long since surrendered "al die sinne" to the lady. But Brinkmann is sensitive to the ring of sincere simplicity that comes to him from these lines, and we may surmise that the speaker's feeling amounts to something like Schmid's "totale Minne" which is motivated not only by the lady's physical charms, but also by those that (to the speaker) gleam from within. In this way, we are allowed to think that "al min wille süle ergan" alludes to more than the short-lived satisfaction of the moment. Because of this would-be abiding quality in his feelings, the speaker can say:

> 17 min herze ist ir ingesinde,
> und wil ouch staete an ir bestan.
>
> my heart is her servant
> and will steadfastly remain true to her.

We make the same claim for "min herze ist ir ingesinde" as Brinkmann makes for "sit ich si so liep gewan": the metaphorical simple value of the line rings true and is immediately convincing. Less clear is the suggestion that the line is indicative of *hohe Minne*.[26]

The *staete* (18), then, occurs in an environment where love holds sway. It is ready to give and to serve and to receive, brooks no encumbrance in its way toward fulfillment. That is the reason why the refrain has an urgent quality despite its comfortable lilt:

> 19 min frowe sehe waz si des tuo:
> da stat dehein scheiden zuo.

As with a man's deep attachment to a woman anywhere and any time, it asks for a return on her part, and we may conclude that "Ich sihe wol daz got wunder kan" is a love poem, nothing more and nothing less.

Says Isbăşescu in a generalizing statement about Hausen's poetry: "Alles, was mit Wünschen niedriger Art in Berührung kommen konnte, wird sorgfältig vermieden."[27] "Wünschen niedriger Art" is opaque since we do not know what is meant with this phrase. Hence it is puzzling not only with respect to Hausen's poetry in general but also with regard to this particular lyric specifically. Indeed, we may put it more strongly and say that if this view touched upon the truth there would be something very wrong with this poem. As it is, its balance is there for all to enjoy.

XV. ICH LOBE GOT DER SINER GÜETE

50, 19 I 1 Ich lobe got der siner güete 37 B, 39 C
20   daz er mir ie verlech die sinne
    daz ich si nam in min gemüete:
    wan si ist wol wert daz man si minne.
    5 noch bezzer ist daz man ir hüete
    dan iegelicher sinen willen
25   spraeche, daz si gerne horte
    und mir die fröide gar zerstorte.

  II Noch bezzer ist daz ich si mide 38 B, 40 C
   10 dan si ane huote waere
    und ir deheiner mir ze nide
30   spraeche des ich gerne enbaere.
    ich hans erkorn uz allen wiben:
    laze ich iht durch die merkaere,
   15 frömed ich si mit den ougen,
    si minnet doch min herze tougen.

35 III Min lip was ie unbetwungen 39 B, 41 C
    und ungemuot von allen wiben:
    alrerste han ich rehte befunden
   20 waz man nach liebem wibe lide.
51, 1   daz ich muoz ze mangen stunden
    der besten frowen eine miden,
    des ist min herze dicke swaere,
    als ez mit fröide gerne waere.

5 IV 25 Swie dicke so ich lobe die huote, 40 B, 42 C
    deswar ez wart doch nie min wille
    daz ich in iemer in dem muote
    wurde holt, die dar die sinne
    gewendet hant daz si der guoten
10   30 entpfrömden wellent staete minne.
    deswar, tuon ich in niht mere,
    doch friesche ich gerne al ir unere.

  Opinions about this poem vary considerably. One of the commentators has this to say: "Das hervorragendste Beispiel [für Hausens Gewandtheit, mit entgegengesetzten Gedanken gleichsam zu spielen] ist das Lied 50,19: Jubel und Klage über die Liebe, Lob und Verwünschung über die huote sind durch die vier Strophen kunstvoll so verteilt, daß die erste und dritte, die zweite und vierte näher zusammen gehören."[1] On a different plane, the first strophe is closely linked to the fourth by means of echoing rhymes: over against "güete," "sinne," "gemüete," "minne," "hüete," "willen," "horte," and "zerstorte," of the first, we have "huote," "wille," "muote," "sinne," "guoten," "minne," "mere," and "unere" of the fourth.[2] The preponderance of feminine rhymes causes Becker to speak of "die Unvollkommenheit dieses Gedichts."[3] Neunteufel sees things Lehfeld's way: "Hier zeigt sich in dem feinen Spiel der Gedanken und der scharfsinnigen Dialektik die ganze Weise des Dichters."[4] Brinkmann finds that *Minne* "als geistige Liebe, Gedenken, Caritas zu verstehen [ist]."[5] Kraus disagrees: "Der Grundgedanke soll nur das Maß der Eifersucht [des Dichters] und seines Wunsches vor ihr in makelloser Treue darzustehen, zum Ausdruck bringen."[6] Seibold states: "Huote war [dem Dichter] eine menschliche Maßnahme, die zu Recht bestand bei der Unfähigkeit der Frauen staete minne von unstaeter zu unterscheiden."[7] Isbăşescu sees matters from a less earthly level: "Die Minne wird geläutert, von allem Erdhaft-sinnlichen entkleidet."[8] The reader is left with the impression that what with Seibold is a dearth of deference with regard to the stability of the weaker sex has turned into superabundance of it with Isbăşescu.

The opening statement lauds the deity for having granted the speaker the senses to take "her," the lady, into his "gemüete," that realm situated somewhere near the heart and the mind. For Brinkmann it represents "die Sphäre des Verlangens," but he does not say what that "Verlangen" amounts to.[9] Perhaps he gives a hint as to what he has in mind when he contrasts "gemüete" with "herze"; the latter he sees as "den bleibenden, ruhenden Innenraum." However, a phrase like MF 42,29—"min herze muos ir kluse sin" (chapter I)—is but one of several suggesting that to Hausen's speakers the difference between "gemüete" and "herz," if it exists at all, is negligibly small.

1 Ich lobe got der siner güete
daz er mir ie verlech die sinne
daz ich si nam in min gemüete:

I praise God for his goodness
that he granted me the senses
to take her into my mind.

Aarburg finds that "die Minne ausdrücklich als ein Vorgang im Inneren, als ein geistiges Geschehen gekennzeichnet wird."[10] She is correct of course, though it should be added that this is the only possible thing that *can* happen in an environment where the speaker can only report on his inner experience, there being nothing on the "outside" to report. Kolb goes further than Aarburg:

Die Sinne sind nach diesen Worten eine Fähigkeit, von Gott verliehen durch seine große Güte und auf das Hohe und Wertvolle gerichtet, die den Minnenden in den Stand setzt, die geliebte Frau in sein Innerstes hereinzunehmen und sein Herz zu erfüllen mit dem besten Teil ihrer selbst. Mit diesen drei Aufschlüßen über die Sinne—unmittelbare Herkunft von Gott als ein Geschenk seiner Gnade; Gerichtetsein auf das Wert-Habende und Wert-Machende; Hereinnehmen der Geliebte in das eigne Innere und damit Einswerden mit ihr in einem seelischen

Vollzug, der einer verweltlichten unio mystica gleichkommt—werden wir . . . in direkter Berührung an die christliche Seelenlehre augustinischen Gepräges herangeführt.[11]

Kolb leaves room for the view that the poem does not *have* to be read as imbued with mysticism, since he speaks of matters being secularized. And indeed, the senses do not even come close to acquiring mystical qualities. Their more natural (and hence preferable?) characteristics are laid bare in the fourth line which says that the lady's attributes are such as to make her worth loving:

> 4 wan si ist wol wert daz man si minne.
>
> for she is indeed worthy of being loved.

This line, we gather, declares that all right-thinking men must love the lady, cannot help loving her, and owe it to their God-given senses to love her. For this reason it is "good" that she be loved. Then comes the *anti*-mystical secularization *if* we read the first four lines in a mystically tinted vein: It is still better that she be guarded:

> 5 noch bezzer ist daz man ir hüete
> dan iegelicher sinen willen
> spraeche, daz si gerne horte[12]
> und mir die fröide gar zerstorte.
>
> it is still better that she be guarded
> than that anyone would speak his will
> which she would like to hear
> and would destroy my joy entirely.

These lines seem to say that many men would court the lady if the guardians were not there. And again, *if* things were mystical, why should the speaker's joy be destroyed if other men spoke to the lady? No matter what they said, they could not possibly do harm to his then impeccable relationship—or rather, perhaps, would-be relationship—with the lady, no matter whether wished by the speaker alone, or by the lady as well. The conclusion seems clear: there is no piety of any kind to be found in the stanza.

This statement may harbor truth: "Wenn der Dichter die huote rechtfertigt, die seine Frau vor Zudränglichen schützt, rechtfertigt er in ihr die Gesellschaft selbst."[13] Aarburg moves in Brinkmann's sphere; says the latter: "Wenn die Frau keine schützende Mauer umgibt, die sie für jeden unbefugten und zudringlichen Blick unerreichbar macht, wird ihre Reinheit entweiht."[14] This statement on the one hand comes close to supporting Becker's contention that the (young and unmarried) lady of the *Minnesang* needs close watching for reasons dealing with morality,[15] while on the other hand the statement implies something that from a different angle is also implied in the notion regarding love before first sight (see, e.g., chapter IV, p. 35): just as favorable public opinion can make a woman lovable, so, too, a lady's purity can be marred merely by the appreciative eye of a man gazing on her. Given Brinkmann's view, the honor and purity of the lady of the *Minnesang* is extremely delicate, so delicate as to render her stirringly vulnerable. This in turn suggests (again) the make-up of a society in which it is public opinion alone, even if represented only by an admiring glance coming a lady's way, that decides that she is "such and such." Society can bestow loveworthiness and other goods simply by saying that she has them. Conversely, it can take them away simply by saying they are not there. With society's opinion being what it is, untrustworthy because changeable as the wind, it is small wonder that ladies keep aloof, that they continue forever to doubt the proclaimed *staete* of their suitors, all because they must protect themselves from being marred. And it is small wonder that otherwise sturdy men turn inward to reflect rather than act when love is at stake,[16] even though love is the foremost and obvious way by which a person might seek to establish a trustworthy line of communication with another member of society. And so, if the individual is to keep himself intact, he must stand alone if—such is the paradox—he wishes to remain a member of this corporate body called society.

With this line of reasoning, the lines 7 f.—"daz si gerne horte/ und mir die fröide gar zerstorte"—acquire an edge. Instead of simply seeming illogical for a lover with lofty intentions, they now may also suggest that the speaker has indeed good reason to dread the lady's listening to the talk of other men. They might speak "[im] ze nide" (10; see below) and thereby harm him in the eyes of the lady who, such is the power of pronouncements made about someone's worthiness, could not help but be affected by such slander.

We must also take cognizance of Mowatt's view. Whereas Kraus emends the manuscripts' "ungerne" of MF 50,26 into "gerne" in order to convey the speaker's mistrust of the lady's constancy, Mowatt disagrees with this emendation:

The antithesis is good as it stands, "das si ungerne horte" and "des ich vil gerne enbere" . . . being variant formulations of the same reaction, from contrasting points of view. . . . The uniqueness of "ungerne" merely adds a formal significance to its obvious meaning. On one level, we have the conventional assumption that other people's attention must be "unwelcome." On another level, the form leads us to expect the word "welcome" at this point. The oft-repeated convention becomes in this case an exception to the rule. . . . It could be argued that Husen has managed to express what Jellinek and Kraus want him to, and has done it without the help of their emendation.[17]

Hausen, I think, deserves more credit than even Mowatt is ready to grant him: by accepting the latter's argument as well as the implications of Brinkmann's last cited passage, we are confronted with a startling *double entendre*. On the one hand it takes the lady off the pedestal, and on the other hand lays bare the innermost crack in the edifice of medieval society. Irony thus exercised readily becomes bitter.

Though Mowatt has a host of commentators on his side when he argues in favor of retaining the manuscripts' "ungerne" (Brinkmann,[18] Paul,[19] Schönbach,[20] Müllenhoff,[21] are but some of them), none applies his kind of reasoning according to which the speaker is in doubt about the lady's willingness to listen to other men. Whereas with Mowatt's reading we gain also by being sensitive to the speaker's irony, with Brinkmann and others the reason for retaining "ungerne" is motivated by the view that it reflects favorably on the lady (in a particular frame of reference). But it would seem that this notion traps them in a contradiction, for why from their point of view should the speaker's "fröide" be destroyed if the lady truly did not like to hear what others would have to say to her?[22] He would have nothing to be afraid of, and it would be much more sensible for him to wish the guardians away from the outset since, with the lady's being unwilling to listen to the talk of (all) other men, the speaker himself would then have the opportunity to speak his own "willen" (6) to her—unless, of course, the lady would not be interested in listening to any men, including the speaker.

The following statement:

> 9 Noch bezzer ist daz ich si mide
> dan si ane huote waere
> und ir deheiner mir ze nide
> spraeche des ich gerne enbaere.
>
> It is still better that I avoid her
> than that she were without guardians
> and anyone would speak ill of me to her
> which I would gladly do without.

is simple enough, though we may not feel too confident about its implications. Milnes sees this passage as an example of how "Schmach auf das Aufrechthalten der Ehre im sexuellen Sinne [deutet],"[23] but it is not clear whether he means this from the speaker's point of view or from that of the lady. However that may be, the question arises whether in view of the ambiguous reading obtained from the first strophe, we must understand from this passage also that a pronounced opinion makes someone what that opinion states him to be, even if it is patently and purposefully false.

The second part of this strophe states:

> 13 ich hans erkorn uz allen wiben:[24]
> laze ich iht durch die merkaere,[25]
> frömed ich si mit den ougen,
> si minnet doch min herze tougen.
>
> I have chosen her from all women:
> if I refrain from anything because of the guardians,
> if I avoid her with my eyes,
> my heart nevertheless loves her secretly.

Schönbach interprets the fourteenth line as "ein Zeichen der Vertraulichkeit";[26] he must be of the view that the lady knows of and reciprocates the speaker's feelings. Isbăşescu agrees and speaks about "heimliche gegenseitige Herzensneigung."[27] Many commentators agree with this, though it does not seem to make much sense to think that the sixteenth line means "she nevertheless loves my heart secretly." Brinkmann sees this more clearly; taking "herze" as the subject, he can appreciate the antithesis developed with respect to the fifteenth line: If I avoid her with my eyes, my heart nevertheless loves her secretly.[28] Indeed, the question is now warranted whether the lady must be assumed to know anything at all; that "tougen" may well have the value of "unknown to *anyone*," including the lady.

The third strophe's opening statement can hardly be said to contain an ambiguity if we adhere to the lines as transmitted by the manuscripts:

> Min lip was ie unbetwungen/ungebunden
> und doch gemuot von allen wiben
>
> I was always unconquered
> though desired by all women.

We cite Mowatt:

As far as "doch gemuot" BC is concerned, the implied opposition between this phrase and "unbetwungen"/"ungebunden" (free but worried) has been unacceptable to all editors. They prefer to locate the opposition elsewhere in the stanza, and write "hochgemuot" or "ungemuot" so as to produce a contrast between past insouciance (lines 1-2) and present involvement (lines 3-8).[29]

But why should "unbetwungen" or "ungebunden" not mean "unconquered," "not subdued?" And what is wrong with reading "gemuot" as "troubled" in the sense of "bothered" because desired? After all, though Becker,[30] Schönbach,[31] Arnold,[32] Jellinek,[33] Kraus,[34] and others advocate the emendation of "doch gemuot" into "hoch gemuot" or "ungemuot," which they then clarify this way or that, Brinkmann sees fit to prefer the manuscripts' reading, which he translates as "Ich selber war frei, aber von Frauen begehrt,"[35] thus suggesting the notion of the ladies' man that we have encountered before (see chapter I, p. 7).

> 19 alrerste han ich rehte befunden
> waz man nach liebem wibe lide,
>
> only now have I truly experienced
> what one suffers for a beloved woman.

Korn says this: "Der Dichter bekennt erst jetzt zur Klarheit über den seelischen Schmerz gelangt zu sein. 'Die Fröide' wird jetzt ein Betrachtungsgegenstand neben andern, die Funktion des Freudebegehrens wird dem Herzen zugewiesen."[36] But again we have reason to ask: what, in view of the possible values of "unbetwungen"/ "ungebunden" and "doch gemuot" (see above), prevents "lide" from simply conveying the distress of a man whose desires remain unfulfilled?

> 21 des muos ich ze mangen stunden[37]
> der besten frowen eine miden,
> des ist min herze dicke swaere,
> als ez mit fröiden gerne waere.
>
> for a long time therefore I must
> avoid one of the best of all women;
> because of that my heart is often heavy,
> whereas it would like to be joyful.

This passage is obscure insofar as it does not indicate whether "des" (21) refers to 19 f., whether avoiding the lady stems from the speaker's determination to act the wiser part (see 9 f.), or whether it results from the activity of the guardians who (would) prevent any attempt to see the lady.

The closing strophe is a *tour de force* and highlights the speaker's basic interest:

> 25 Swie dicke so ich lobe die huote,
> deswar ez wart doch nie min wille
> daz ich in iemer in dem muote
> wurde holt, die dar die sinne
> gewendet hant daz si der guoten
> entpfrömden wellent staete minne.
> deswar, tuon ich in niht mere,
> doch friesche ich gerne al ir unere.[38]

> However much I laud the guardians,
> nevertheless it was never my will
> that I would ever become sympathetic
> in my mind toward them who have turned
> their minds to tempting steadfast love
> away from the good one.
> in truth, though I do not do more harm to them,
> I would like to hear of their dishonor.

In these lines the speaker takes back whatever positive attributes he may seem to have granted the guardians, and he ends with a wish which according to Schönbach hopes for their "Eheschande."[39] The terms used seem vague enough to accomodate "unere" as something less clearly defined, and its exact value is perhaps of little consequence. After all, such dishonor would give the speaker a certain satisfaction, to be sure, but it would be purely intellectual, and quite impractical in the sense that it would not enable him to approach the lady *if* he heard of the guardians' dishonor. Though in this manner there would be no particular benefit coming his way, the speaker's wish is nevertheless a dire one in view of the suggestions made elsewhere, to the effect that "unere," no matter how it comes about, makes medieval man an outcast and constitutes his social shame. Seen in this light, the speaker's closing statement, in which he barely stops short of taking away the guardians' honor simply by actually saying that they do not possess it, stands in uneasy tension to Mowatt's dictum: "Husen never attacks the institution of 'huote.' "[40] And "doch friesche ich gerne al ir unere" gives the lie also to the suggestion, advanced by many critics in one way or other, that the speaker affirms and welcomes the guardians' watchful activity. The final statement by far outweighs all the statements preceding.[41]

It should be pointed out that in the state of affairs as developed in the fourth stanza "staete minne" becomes an obscure entity.[42] The guardians are said to have turned their "sinne"[43] on wishing to keep "staete minne" away from the lady. From the guardians' point of view, "staete minne"—or rather, perhaps, what the speaker *calls* "staete minne"—does not need to be anything more than a liaison of a duration long enough to warrant the use of the adjective "staete." If in addition to this we wonder once again whether the lady must be assumed to know of the speaker's condition, it becomes evident that there is a tight rationale at work in this lyric; it severely limits the speaker's ability to look at matters from various sides and objectively, even though it *seems* to take account of every possible aspect; a term like "compulsively single-minded logic" comes to mind.

In connection with the function of the guardians another matter calls for attention: several Hausen lyrics depict love for a lady as reprehensible insofar as the speakers commit themselves to it "ane sinne" (see, for example, chapter VI, p. 50). With this in mind, we must ask whether perhaps there is additional irony embedded in "Ich lobe got der siner güete": the guardians rather than the speaker may see matters as they *ought* to be seen. They may represent the realities of life by seeking to protect a lady from what the speaker calls "staete minne." For these realities may demand that love be confined to the bounds of publicly sanctioned arrangements. Society has an all-important stake in orderly arrangement; such orderliness is barely lower on the scale of values than society's commitment to the principle of "fröide" as discussed above (see, for instance chapter II, p. 23).

It stands to reason that with the above suggestions the lyric's opening line—"ich lobe got der siner güete"—need not be evaluated as bringing testimony to a deep faith. In fact, God's role in this lyric is as problematic as it is in "Sich möhte wiser man verwüeten."

XVI. SICH MÖHTE WISER MAN VERWÜETEN

51, 13	I 1	Sich möhte wiser man verwüeten	41 B, 43 C
		von sorgen der ich mange han.	
15		swie ich mich noch da vor behüete,	
		so hat got wol ze mir getan,	
	5	sit er mich niht wolte erlan,	
		ich naeme si in min gemüete.	
		jo engilte ich alze sere ir güete	
20		und ouch der schoene die si hat.	
		lit ich durch got daz si begat	
	10	an mir, der sele wurde rat.	
	II	Mich kunde niemen des erwenden,	42 B, 44 C
		in welle ir wesen undertan.	
25		den willen bringe ich an min ende,	

>   swie si habe ze mir getan.
> 15 sit ich des boten niht enhan,
>   so wil ich ir diu lieder senden.
>   vert der lip in enelende,
> 30 min herze belibet doch alda.
>   daz suoche nieman anderswa:
> 20 ez kunde ir niemer komen ze na.

The first line of the B manuscript—"Mich möhte wiser man verwüeten"—has a transitive verb; this is an exception to the rule that "verwüeten" is either intransitive or reflexive.[1] Since, in addition, the line makes little sense when read in conjunction with those that follow, the C version seems to be more trustworthy. To be sure, there is a problem with C; it implies a boast and as such seems objectionable, particularly since Neumann's article on *hohe Minne*.[2] As it is, however, the lack of modesty in C fits in with the tenor of some of the following lines as evaluated below.

> 1 Lichte ein unwiser man verwüete
>   von sorgen der ich mange han.
>
>   An unwise man could easily become deranged
>   by worries of which I have many.

Except for Schönbach (see below), the critics have interpreted "sorgen" as resulting from the speaker's relationship—or rather, lack of it—with a lady; God is seen as having in his goodness allowed him to remain sane:

> 3 swie ich mich noch da vor behüete,
>   so hat got wol ze mir getan,
>
>   as much as I (manage to) protect myself against that,
>   God has done well to me.

So, for instance, Lehfeld: "Man könnte vor Liebe rasend werden . . . aber ich danke Gott für diese Liebe."[3] Brinkmann takes this view on the basis of "Sich möhte *unwiser* man verwüeten" (italics added): "Hier setzt [der Dichter] sich von denen ab, die sich nicht zu beherrschen wissen (er nennt sie 'unwise')."[4] There is a contradiction in these lines between God's goodness and the speaker's claim that he can handle his affairs by himself—though he admits it is not easy. Either he is correct in saying that he manages to safeguard himself against becoming mad, or it is God who protected him against that fate. Siekhaus smooths matters out by translating the third line as "sowie ich mich auch immer noch so sehr . . . ," and states:

Es bedarf an dieser Stelle des Liedes eines deutlichen positiven Gegengewichts. Deshalb steht das bedeutsame Wort *got*. Aber noch etwas anderes fällt im Zusammenhang mit diesem Wort auf: Das *ich* ist Subjekt zu dem Wort *behüeten*, es taucht dann in Zeile 51,16 als Objekt einer höheren Gewalt—*got*—auf und kann erst nach einer komplizierten grammatikalischen Überleitung in Zeile 51,17 auch Subjekt zu dem inhaltlich dem *behüeten* entegegengesetzten *naeme* (ins gemüete) werden. Das heißt: zwischen den beiden gegensätzlichen Haltungen des Sprechers steht eine höhere Fügung, die es ihm unmöglich macht, die innere Spannung von sich aus aufzuheben.[5]

Schönbach's elucidation also obscures the contradiction somewhat, but in a different way: he identifies "sorgen" as those "der Welt, des Amtes—auf der Heerfahrt."[6] In Schönbach's view, then, "sorgen" are the worries of a man driven to distraction because he is too busy.

All commentators link the fourth line to the following one with a comma, and thus read:

> 4 so hat got wol ze mir getan,
> sit er mich niht wolte erlan,
> ich naeme si in min gemüete.

> God has done me well
> since he did not spare me from
> taking her into my mind.

Brinkmann makes a distinction between the poet's obligation to God and his obligation to the world—as indicated by his duty to *Minne*—and citing 3–6 he states: "Die sprachliche Fassung ist so gewählt, daß sie wie ein Zitat aus Nr. 3 wirkt. Wir sollen deutlich an dies Lied erinnert werden."[7] Reading in like manner, de Boor has this suggestion: "So zu Gott in Bezug gesetzt und in göttliche Ordnung eingebettet, ist der Wert der Minne unangreifbar."[8] This is Fischer: "Nur weil der Schöpfer die Minne wollte, kann sie vor Gott bestehen."[9]

It may be well, for the sake of contrast with our own evaluation, to cite Brinkmann at some length:

Der Dichter begreift sein Leiden als Folge des inneren Wertes und der äußeren Schönheit der Frau.... Gott, den er in Nr. 1 als Schöpfer der Frauenschönheit und in Nr. 3 als Veranlasser der Minne berief[10] bleibt gegenwärtig (zugleich als letztes Ziel menschlichen Lebens bewußt). Zu ihm setzt er sein Leben in Beziehung; wenn er die Schmerzen, die er um der Frau willen leidet, für Gott ertrüge, so würden sie seiner Seele zur Erlösung verhelfen.[11]

Isbăşescu finds that "des Dichters entsagende, sehnsüchtige Verehrung der Frau... ihren Grund nicht in seinem freien Willen zu haben [scheint],"[12] and Korn is of the opinion that "der Dichter sich damit zu trösten [sucht], daß das Herz nicht zum Verzicht auf die Liebe gezwungen werden könnte.... Gott wird als Zuflucht vor den Liebessorgen angerufen."[13] Schönbach, on the other hand, detects an undertone critical of God, and he proposes emending thus: "sone hat got mir niht wol getan," or "so hat mir got gewalt getan."[14] Even Brinkmann sees fit to speak of "das seelische Leiden, das sich zur Auflehnung zu steigern droht."[15]

There are certain difficulties with these evaluations. If love of a lady is seen as a God-imposed task, the following lines are so abrupt as to make little sense:

> 7 jo engilte ich alze sere ir güete
> und ouch der schoene die si hat.

> I suffer for her goodness all too much
> and also for her beauty.

It is true that the tension between "engilte" and "ir güete" results from an intrinsically ironic antithesis in any environment, but the evaluations cited above leave us totally unprepared for the sudden shift in emphasis. It places the speaker in a position which is not unlike Job's: God allows love to test him—to the greater glory of God? When the strophe's closing lines tell us:

> 9 lit ich durch got daz si begat
> an mir, der sele wurde rat.
>
> if I suffered for God what she inflicts
> upon me, my soul would be aided.

it is clear that this particular Job does *not* suffer for God's sake, but for love's, even though, according to the critics cited, this love must be seen as a God-imposed duty. In this manner, the strophe makes for difficult and in part illogical reading.

In contrast to the above remarks, it seems perfectly possible to call the strophe ironic; such irony fits in neatly with the second strophe as evaluated below. In addition, there is another possibility, though it depends on a slight emendation and therefore skirts our reluctance to "improve" the manuscripts. However questionable its merit, it nevertheless is fascinating to see how a small change fits in with the mood and tone that can readily be seen as imbuing the entire lyric. By placing a period after the fourth line, so that now each pair of lines in the strophe forms a sentence, and by recasting the sixth line, we may read:

> 3 swie ich mich noch da vor behüete,
> so hat got wol ze mir getan.
> sit er mich niht wolte erlan,
> so nim ich si in min gemüete.
>
> as much as I (manage to) protect myself against that,
> God has done me a good turn.
> since he did not want to set me free,
> I take her into my mind.

Admittedly, the dictionaries tell us that "erlan" should take a genitive or a subordinate clause. If that was a rule in Hausen's day, we could conform with it by suggesting that a genitive is understood. Something similar happens in MF 45,26 f.—"das si dem ungelonet lat/ der si vor al der werlte hat" (chapter V)—where, since "lonen" takes the dative, we have to imagine some impersonal object for "lat."[16]

If the emendation suggested for the sixth line seems far-fetched, we may wish to recall that reading the opening line as a boast now turns out to be fully justified, as does Schönbach's opinion that the speaker seems to be critical of God. Moreover, Brinkmann's rendering of "gemüete" as "Sphäre des Verlangens" is now allowed to retain its full force. Besides, by bringing the punctuation into line with that of the second strophe—as found in *Des Minnesangs Frühling*—we have a reading that should satisfy everyone, including the critics who advocate the view that there is a deeply religious faith at work in Hausen's confrontation of *Frauendienst* and *Gottesdienst*, though in a different way from the one they envisage (see below).[17] For the moment we can at least say that the passage leaves God without the blemish which offends Schönbach (see above), and it seems to speak of love of a kind that accords even with Neumann's view.[18]

It is worth pointing out emphatically that in the present reading God's remaining unblemished refers only to the view that he did *not* compel the speaker to love. This does not rule out the possibility of irony in the fourth line. Indeed, nothing prevents us from reading it thus: I do it but I am perfectly willing to give God the credit for maintaining my sanity. In view of the tenor of the second strophe, such irony may be mingled with a touch of bitterness, the bitterness of despair. In this manner, the material reads smoothly:

In so far as I (manage to) safeguard myself against going mad because I have so much to do, God has been good to me. Since he did not want to set me free [from the crusade duty], I take her into my mind.

It hardly needs pointing out that in this reading the speaker has committed himself to the crusade but has not yet departed; "so nim ich si in min gemüete" indicates that his resolve stretches into the future. Indeed, he would now prefer not to go.[19]

It is true that the following lines still amount to a surprising twist of thought:

> 7 jo engilte ich alze sere ir güete
> und ouch der schoene die si hat.
>
> I suffer for her goodness all too much
> and also for her beauty.

"In min gemüete nemen" contrasts with the verb in "ir güete engelten." Yet it is at least a twist within the realm of love; a direct connection is no longer possible between these lines and that in which God is thought, by the critics in general, to exert his merciful goodness by not setting the speaker free unless he takes the lady into his mind. Instead we now have a situation suggesting that the speaker's decision is an act of his own will[20] rather than a God-given duty. Furthermore, whereas with the views cited there is a contradiction between the strophe's closing lines and the task imposed by God of loving the lady, the strophe now presents a clear development, and we are ready to say that the last sentence indicates the basic theme treated in this lyric:

> 9 lit ich durch got daz si begat
> an mir, der sele wurde rat.
>
> if I suffered for God what she inflicts
> on me, my soul would be aided.

Since love is now not a God-given duty but is entered into by the speaker's own volition and, for all we know, *against* God's will, the soul will *not* benefit. The strophe's essential feature is therefore not that God mercifully compels the speaker to love, but that his readily available mercy goes unheeded.[21] For in the present framework God's unwillingness to set the speaker free (5) is an act of mercy since it means to safeguard the speaker by separating him from the lady.[22] Hence the closing lines show the speaker's self-indictment, and the following strophe shows the result of his stubborn will: a blind pursuit of love and a deaf ear to God's offer of mercy. This is not surprising when we remember that in "Wafena, wie hat mich minne gelazen" (chapter VI), too, "Minne nicht mehr von Gott kommt."[23]

The speaker thus plays the role which in "Min herze und min lip diu wellent scheiden" (chapter IX) is "acted out" by the heart. This is but another way of saying that the speaker is on the wrong path, that from God's point of view his decision to take the lady into his mind is reprehensible, that it endangers the soul. It is therefore inevitable that "sorgen" of a different kind than those of the second line will beset the speaker. Meanwhile, the second half of the first strophe has already indicated what happens to a man who surrenders to love. The "güete" of the seventh line may be "positive," but it has a negative effect: the speaker suffers it "al ze sere." There is therefore no equation of any kind possible between this "güete" and the goodness of God which is implied in the fourth line, as well as in the fifth,[24] whether ironically or not. Indeed, the lady's "güete" may harbor a demonic quality. This is not to say that she herself is indictable. After all, she is little more than a catalyst, "neutral" as such. What emerges, however, is that love as depicted here is reprehensible, is a force of darkness as contrasted to the forces of light that find their embodiment in God. *If*, then, the lyric is an endeavor to reconcile *Frauendienst* and *Gottesdienst*—thus the view of the critics—we must immediately add that the attempt is doomed since these two services in this particular case cannot possibly be reconciled. In the following strophe, the speaker goes the road he has indicated in "so nim ich si in min gemücte," and as long as he continues to follow it, he will have to face the consequences.

An attempt could be made to argue that the strophe just now investigated constitutes an independent unit and yields equally as much "value" as when it is read in conjunction with MF 51,23. No matter which way we read the latter, it brings little new in terms of "plot" development, except that it brings home the speaker's firm determination to love. If read independently, it would therefore amount to a little monument to his devotion. As it is, Brinkmann detects a break between the two strophes from *his* vantage point: "Als Liebender und von Gott Bestimmter fühlte sich der Dichter in der ersten Strophe gebunden. Aber er ist den Menschen und dem Leben gegenüber frei. Die zweite Strophe steht ganz im Zeichen seiner Freiheit."[25]

In conjunction with our reading of the first strophe, the opening of the second:

> 11 Min kunde niemen des erwenden,
> in welle ir wesen undertan.
>
> Nobody could prevent me
> from being subservient to her.

evokes the picture, not of laudible *staete*,[26] but of the speaker's determination (against his own better judgment?) to adhere to love. In this reading, "undertan" is equivalent to "being in bonds of love," and it has been suggested in previous discussions that such bondage may in the medieval outlook be tantamount to violating the concept that man is created in the image of God, since the passion coming with such servitude is the result of one's reason being suspended.[27] The speaker's determination must therefore lead to damnation, no matter what the outcome of his pursuit, whether he be successful in attaining the intended goal, or not. This stubborn determination is emphatically brought out throughout the strophe; it is not only against God's will, but also against all odds:

> 13 den willen bringe ich an min ende,
> swie si habe ze mir getan.

> I shall adhere to my will until my dying day,
> however she has treated me.

Come what may, the speaker says, I am bound to remain subservient to her. The C manuscript brings out this stubbornness more clearly still: "und wil min leben also verenden" ("and I want to end my life this way"), and may therefore be preferable to the B text for the very same reason that Mowatt advances for rejecting it: "B seems preferable on most counts. For the version in C to fit in, 'also' would have to be read as 'in this state of mind'; and even if we could justify reading it this way, we would still have to find a function for the heavy emphasis on the act of dying instead of on constancy."[28]

Brinkmann understands from the last lines cited that "über den Schmerz der Seele sich die Freiheit des Geistes [erhebt]."[29] By way of contrast, in the reading presented here the forms "welle" and "willen" do not harmonize but contrast with God's will, and consequently Brinkmann's following statement acquires a coloring not intended by Brinkmann himself: "Wie die eigne Lage aussieht, das wird abhängen von dem Standort, von dem aus [der Dichter] sie betrachtet."

Becker finds that the lady is "feindlich" to the speaker; he reads this from "swie si habe ze mir getan."[30] But this suggestion depends on another one, that she knows of the speaker's yearning. The strophe says nothing about such knowledge, however; *if* she knew, the speaker would have no reason to send her "diu lieder" (16). And "swie si habe ze mir getan" is little more than a restatement of 7 f.: "jo engilte ich alze sere ir güete/ und ouch der schoene die si hat." That "schoene," at any rate, affects the speaker without the lady's doing anything "active" beyond just being there for him to behold her beauty. The sorrow resulting from this beauty and the lady's "güete" thus suggest the pangs of love unanswered. On a different plane, of course, it may also be the sorrow of someone who has chosen the road leading to hell, and knows he has chosen it. Sorrow thus seen derives from one's self-alienation from God and his will.

The following lines imply bitter irony:

> 15 sit ich des boten niht enhan,
> so wil ich ir diu lieder senden.[31]

> since I have no messenger,
> I shall send her the song.

Is there nobody from amongst the speaker's friends available to help him because they all see what is happening to this victim of love and therefore refuse to help him meet his doom?[32] Becker surmises from these lines that "die Muse also ein Mittel der Mitteilung [ist],"[33] and Schönbach deduces from them that the lady lives in Hausen's vicinity.[34] From the present point of view the irony results from the fact that if this plan is carried out, the lady will come to see in writing what happens to a man so devoted to her as to endanger his soul. In this reading, the following two lines:

> 17 vert der lip in enelende,
> min herze belibet doch alda.
>
> if my body travels to alien lands,
> my heart nevertheless stays there;

also become ambiguous. While indicating the heart's devotion and *staete* on one plane, on a different one we become aware of the dreadful threat of a possible calamity: the heart, the seat of love, but also the organ symbolizing man's capability for spiritual devotion, may (in the future) have to go "in enelende" if it continues its alienation from, and recalcitrance against, God's will.

Kuhn's view is totally different, although it is readily acceptable to the reading advocated in these pages: "In the conventional agreement of the members of the *Minnesang* profession, and in the public mind as well, the earthly love of a lady did not mean simply the experience of love but included, as its living base, a moral claim upon the total personality, which must 'sich ellenden,' lose itself in order to gain itself."[35] Elsewhere he speaks of the act of distant love on the part of the singer as *hohe Minne*.[36]

Brinkmann states matters as he sees them this way; we could readily adopt his view also, and even incorporate it into our present argument: "Der Geist und die Innenwelt sind nicht an die Schwere und Enge des Raumes gefesselt. Der Körper aber kann sich ihr nicht entziehen."[37] To this we need only add that "der Geist an die Frau gefesselt ist, an sie gefesselt sein *will*, und der Körper auch." From this follows the restated decision to serve the lady until the end, come what may. For, as the closing lines state regarding the speaker's heart:

> 19 daz suoche nieman anderswa:
> ez kunde ir niemer komen za na.
>
> let nobody seek it elsewhere;
> it never could come too close to her.

This "anderswa" excludes every other place—"die Heimat seines Herzens ist bei der Frau"[38]—therefore also the place where God dwells. It is a last defiant (and desperate?) note constituting a self-indictment, particularly if read in conjunction with "niemer." That "niemer" harbors the possible implication that the speaker, despite the high price he is willing to pay for his love, down to the point where he may be thought of as letting his soul go "in enelende,"[39] will never be satisfied, that there will be no end to his yearning, and therefore no end to his "sorgen." "Sorgen" of such a kind may easily result in despair, and despair, we remember, is in many a medieval drama the one sin of the fallen angel; it cannot be forgiven since it is a sin against the Holy Ghost.[40]

Siekhaus understands the closing lines very differently:[41] "Der Sprachvorgang bricht abrupt ab, der Zuhörer wird gleichsam mit der aufgebauten Kontrast alleingelassen, er ist aufgerufen, diesen Kontrast von sich aus aufzulösen. Diese Auflösung geschieht in dem Augenblick, in dem er sich des nur Artifiziellen dieser Problematik lächelnd bewußt wird."[42]

Many readers will be of the opinion that this discussion goes so much against the grain of established criticism of *Minnesang* in general and of Hausen's poetry in particular as to be totally unacceptable. It is not the purpose of these pages to stake out claims to the exclusion of any other. Instead our aim is to lay bare the ambiguity that pervades Hausen's poetry and thus to suggest that multiple readings and "meanings" and "values" are possible simultaneously.[43] Wechssler, after all, speaks of "die grundsätzliche Neigung des Mittelalters zu einem mehrfachen Sinn."[44] We therefore can readily accept a statement advanced by Langenbucher, though it seems superfluous to take his concept of *hohe Minne* as the only possible base: "Man muß von den Wandlungen des Inhalts der Minneidee aus lernen, den Zusammenhang neu zu sehen, auch auf Kosten alter, liebgewordener Vorstellungen."[45] Or, in Brinkmann's words: "Alles schon Untersuchte ist neu in Frage zu stellen."[46]

If in the particular case of "Lichte ein unwiser man verwüete" the suggested ambiguity leads to variant modes of reading that seem too drastically opposed to each other,[47] we can benefit from remembering that in "Min herze und min lip diu wellent scheiden" we have no choice but to agree that Hausen is a master not only in the way in which the speaker that he projects into the poem expresses his thoughts in antithetical statements, but also in the way he deals with sharply differentiated opposites when envisioning the heart's fate. In like manner, "Lichte ein unwiser man verwüete" mirrors the same preoccupation as "Min herze und min lip diu wellent scheiden," though from a different perspective.

In conclusion, it should be pointed out that with the reading here proposed Brinkmann's title for the poem—"Schmerz und Treue, zweite Fassung"—far from depicts the "message" of these two strophes. "Verfremdung" would be a more ambiguous and therefore more apt title: it would stand for (geographical as well as personal) distance from the lady, and also for alienation from God.

XVII. ICH DENKE UNDER WILEN

51, 33 I 1 Ich denke under wilen,   45 B, 47 C
           ob ich ir naher waere,
   35   waz ich ir wolte sagen.
           daz kürzet mir die milen,
52, 1   5 swenn ich ir mine swaere
           so mit gedanken klage.
           mich sehent mange tage
           die liute in der gebaere
    5   als ich niht sorgen habe,
        10 wan ichs also vertrage.

        II Het ich so hoher minne   46 B, 48 C
           nie mich underwunden,
           min möhte werden rat.
   10   ich tete ez ane sinne:
        15 des lide ich zallen stunden
           not diu nahe gat.
           min staete mir nu hat
           daz herze also gebunden,
   15   daz siz niht scheiden lat
        20 von ir als ez nu stat.

       III Ez ist ein grozez wunder: 47 B, 49 C
           diech aller serest minne,
           diu was mir ie geve.
   20   nu müeze solhen kumber
        25 niemer man bevinden,
           der also nahe ge.
           erkennen wande i'n e,
           nu kan i'n baz bevinden:
   25   mir was da heime we,
        30 und hie wol dristunt me.

        IV Swie kleine ez mich vervahe,   48 B, 50 C
           so vröuwe ich mich doch sere
           daz mir sin niemen kan
   30   erwern, ichn denke ir nahe
        35 swar ich landes kere.
           den trost sol si mir lan.
           wil siz für guot enpfan,
           daz fröut mich iemer mere,

52, 35   wan ich für alle man
               ir ie was undertan.

The critics have made sensitive statements about this poem. Langenbucher, for instance, speaks of "jene Haltung, die ein gezügeltes, meist leidenschaftsloses Sichversenken darstellt in Betrachtungen darüber, was die Minne dem Manne sein kann und darf, was sie ihm versagen muß und wird. Betrachtungen, die gedämpfte Stimmungen auslösen und ein Beharren in tagflüchtenden, dämmrigen Empfindungen; die nicht Gefühle auslösen, sondern zunächst nur Gedanken, denen er sich hingibt."[1] The descriptive quality of "tagflüchtende, dämmrige Empfindungen" allows the realistic notion that the speaker is plodding along on a heavy horse under a copper-colored, Italian sky. Wentzlaff-Eggebert says: "Raum und Welt, Abschied und Sehnsucht werden überwunden in der einen Gewißheit, daß die geistig-seelische Verbundenheit in Gedanken erhalten bleibt."[2] It remains to be seen, however, how much "Überwindung" there is in these stanzas, and "die geistig-seelische Verbundenheit" travels a one-way street, since the lady apparently knows nothing. Brinkmann finds "daß das Lied zur Waffe des Geistes gegen die Erschütterungen der Seele [wird],"[3] but our own reading leaves no room for such terms as "Erschütterungen" (see below); the very tone, mood and language of the poem work against Brinkmann's view.

   1 Ich denke under wilen,
       ob ich ir nahe waere,
       was ich ir wolte sagen.
       daz kürzet mir die milen,
       swenn ich ir mine swaere
       so mit gedanken klage.

      I think sometimes,
      if I were closer to her
      what I would say to her.
      that shortens the miles for me,
      whenever I lament to her about my
      troubles in my thoughts.

The auxiliary verb in the sixth line of the C manuscript is intriguing:

      swenne ich ir mine swere
      so mit gedanken mac klagen

It evokes the view that lamenting, as long as it is voiced without the benefit of an interlocution, is perfectly justified: it does not bother, annoy, or upset anyone, not even the speaker himself, who seemingly relishes the opportunity of cultivating thoughts of the kind he wishes to indulge in. The C wording thus fits neatly into the mood created.

   No matter which version we prefer, we may take it for granted that the miles to be covered are a nuisance.[4] The obvious thing to do therefore is to think of pleasant matters, not of depressing ones. Since it is explicitly stated that "klagen" shortens the trip, we must conclude that it cannot be taken seriously as "lamenting." Instead it reads as though it were a synonym to "composing," to "arranging my thoughts." "Klagen" at the same time reads as though it can be equated with "sagen" of the third line, except that it is one step further removed from whatever quasi-reality we may think is prevailing. Hence a rough equation becomes possible between "sagen," "klagen" and "arranging," and "Sublimierung" suggests itself as a title equally as deft as Brinkmann's "Auf fernem Ritt."[5] Langenbucher, we surmise, is correct when he speaks of "genießerisch auskosten."[6] This leaves open the question whether Hausen actually "sein Freud-Leidfühlen auf dem Hintergrund der sittlich verstandenen Minneidee problematisiert."[7] And it may be true from the speaker's point of view that much "unausgesprochenes zwischen den durch die Minne Verbundenen lebt in dem 'was ich ir wolte sagen,' "[8] but the lady is said to have always been antagonistic to the speaker—or so the latter thinks (23; see below). It *is* true "daß dichterisch gesehen[9] hier das gedankliche Innenerlebnis von der höfischen Konvention abrückt und sich echten Wirklichkeitsempfindungen nähert. Hier klingen Töne an, die über höfische Aussageweise hinausgehen. Modern und zeitlos zugleich wirkt dieses Gedicht."[10] We may ask, however, why we have encountered but little testimony of the courtly convention of which Wentzlaff-Eggebert speaks, unless, of course, he means by that a set of certain forms and motifs rather than what has been called *hohe Minne* and what he himself refers to when he suggests "daß es immer um die Erhebung des Herzens [ging]."[11]

The following opinion is similar to that of Wentzlaff-Eggebert: "Immer aussichtsloser wird [das Minnen], aussichtsloser darum, weil [der Dichter] eben aus reinmenschlichen Gründen Gedanken in das Minneverhältnis hineinträgt, die in seinem Bereich keinen Platz haben können, *wenn die Idee in ihrer Erhabenheit erhalten bleiben soll.* Es ist ein Klagen, das nicht aufhören darf, *wenn der Dichter der Idee treu bleiben will*" (italics added).[12]

As already stated, we encounter a development that remains strictly confined to the realm of "private" ponderings:

> 7 mich sehent mange tage
> diu liute in der gebaere
> als ich niht sorgen habe,
> wan ichs also vertrage.
>
> for many a day people
> see me
> as though I have no worries,
> for that is the way I bear it.

As Brinkmann puts it: "Es gilt . . . Haltung zu bewahren, gefaßt zu sein."[13] Indeed, once again we may be dealing with a phenomenon, unstressed because ingrained and a matter of course in the medieval mind, according to which sorrows are to be hidden because they do not contribute to the *fröide* which society *must* celebrate at all cost (cf. chapter II, pp. 23). The reading of the C manuscript seems to indicate this clearly and may by that taken be preferable to that of B:

> mich sehent ze mengen tagen
> diu liute in der gebere
> als ich niht sorgen müge tragen
> des muos ich verzagen

Hence joy becomes something totally other than "die gesellige Gemeinsamkeit."[14] By assuming a biographical connection between the stuff of poetry and the stuff of life, this statement places a different emphasis: "Zu *joi* und *freude* beizutragen das heißt, zur Erheiterung der Hofgesellschaft bei ihren Festen, das war . . . des Sängers Amt, dazu gab man ihm Kleider und Pelzwerk, Ross und Rüstung, Pfründe und Lehen, oder auch ließ man ihn darben."[15] It is awkward, however, to see this suggestion as applicable to the courtier-statesman-soldier-poet Friedrich von Hausen.

On a different plane, we are confronted once again with the paradox of sorrow put to the service of entertainment, and of the speaker's worries, to be kept private by his own account ("so *mit gedanken* klage"; italics added), being emphatically proclaimed in public. The paradox, to be sure, is similar to that confronting any lover at any time in the poetry of love.

The second strophe states:

> 11 Het ich so hoher minne
> nie mich underwunden,
> min möhte werden rat.
> ich tete ez ane sinne:
> des lide ich zallen stunden
> not diu nahe gat.

> Had I not subjected myself
> to such high love,
> there might be a way out for me;
> I did it senselessly;
> as a result I suffer woes
> that affect me keenly all the time.

According to Becker, 11 f. emphasizes the "Noth der hohen Minne."[16] Schmid speaks of "vornehme Resignation in der Minne."[17] Milnes, by way of contrast, cites several passages in which "rat werden" and "not" are thought to carry erotic overtones.[18] To accomodate his suggestion, the opening line of the strophe would have to stress the adjective: if only I had not subjected myself to the kind of love which makes it unlikely that I shall enjoy it in the way I like to.

With these divergent views taken into account, we receive no exact information from these lines about the circumstances in which love is envisaged or simply suffered. It may be meant as a contrast to something that at a later day was to be called "niedere Minne" and, in conjunction with "staete" (17; see below) is to be read as abiding love. Then again, it may be that love which dreams of engaging a lady of high social standing. At any rate, the second part of the strophe indicates that the speaker is not far from wishing that he had not done what he did. And the fact that this love is submitted to "ane sinne" (14) does not make it likely that we deal with an attempt "das ursprüngliche Individualerleben in ein hohes Minneverhältnis, das heißt, zu überpersönlicher, ideeller Wesenhaftigkeit aufzuhöhen."[19] Indeed, the speaker regrets whatever is "überpersönlich" in his relationship with the lady.[20] Nor does it make persuasive sense to say that in this strophe "höchste sittliche Eigenschaft der Wille zur Dauernden (staete) ist. . . . Der Dichter besitzt jenen Willen zur Dauer, ohne den kein Leben in Kultur bestehen kann. Die Minne aber wird so eine Schule des Willens zur Kultur."[21] There is, it would seem, nothing of "eine Aufgabe" in that direction.[22] Instead the speaker has thrown himself headlong into a situation of which the result, or rather, the lack of result, chagrins him. And he fails to live up to the standards that are presupposed by the principle of *hohe Minne*. Hence the speaker's suffering "not diu nahe gat" (16) may not stand for anything as abstract as some of the citations above suggest. We may equally well or perhaps even more plausibly argue that the speaker had become a slave of love. With reason suspended—"ich tete ez *ane sinne*" (14; italics added)—passion, understood in the medieval sense, held sway. The speaker is therefore not "das Opfer seiner eigenen Sittlichkeit,"[23] but the victim of his own senselessness; he himself seems to be aware of this for in the following lines he alludes to the possibility of turning away from the lady, if only he were able to do so:

> 17 min staete mir nu hat
> daz herze also gebunden,
> daz siz niht scheiden lat
> von ir als ez nu stat.
>
> my steadfastness now has
> bound my heart in such a way
> that it does not allow separation
> from her as things are now.

Here "staete" reads as though it is synonymous to "being hopelessly in love"; though spoken in a different environment from which to receive their exact value, these lines are a parallel to the refrain of "Ich sihe wol daz got wunder kan" (chapter XIV): "da stat dehein scheiden zuo."

The third stanza speaks of the lady's indifference:

> 21 Ez ist ein grozez wunder:[24]
> diech aller serest minne,
> diu was mir ie geve.
>
> It is very strange,
> she whom I love most of all
> has always been hostile to me.

There is no indication why the lady is "geve"; she may simply dislike the speaker and not have known anything about his feelings towards her; a sensitive lover feels slighted and experiences as enmity what actually is no more than benign indifference. (which led her to treat him the way she treats other men). The inward suffering portrayed in this lyric readily conforms to this view of the speaker as cultivating and nourishing his own pains ("genießerisch auskosten").

> 24 nu müeze solhen kumber
> niemer man bevinden,
> der also nahe ge.[25]
> erkennen wande i'n e,
> nu kan i'n baz bevinden:
> mir was da heime we,
> und hie wol dristunt me.
>
> no man should ever experience
> sorrow of this kind,
> which is so painful.
> I thought I knew it earlier,
> now I have experienced it better.
> back home I suffered,
> and here at least three times as much.

Brinkmann says of the opening lines: "Ganz in den Widersprüchen der eigenen Lage befangen, offenbart der Dichter noch die Kraft der Sympathie."[26] It seems equally possible, however, and perhaps more plausible, that the speaker simply laments that his experience is too much for any man, that he is made to suffer too much. Thus there may be moral indignation lurking beneath these words. That it remains anemic is due to the fact that in the state of affairs here depicted there is no room for any forward movement. A purposeful resolve, whatever its nature, would rupture this mood of refined masochism. That there is such wallowing in one's self-created misery is indicated by the tenor of the closing strophe:

> 31 Swie kleine ez mich vervahe,
> so vröuwe ich mich doch sere
> daz mir sin niemen kan
> erwern, ichn denke ir nahe
> swar ich landes kere.
> den trost sol si mir lan.
> wil siz für guot enpfan,
> daz fröut mich iemer mere,[27]
>
> However little it avails me,
> nevertheless I am happy that
> nobody can prevent me
> from thinking of her
> wherever I go.

> that solace she should allow me.
> if she is willing to consider it good,
> that makes me happier and happier.

The opening lines have led to the view that "[der Dichter] die innere Unabhängigkeit des Geistes endgültig gesichert [hat]."[28] By way of contrast, we read from them a reminder: the speaker comes as close here as he will ever get to saying "was [er] ir wolte sagen" (3). In this manner, the closing strophe leads back to the first with its "sagen" and "klagen"; and "nahe denken" (34) leads back to the same beginning of the circular arrangement—see "so mit *gedanken* klage" (6; italics added). The speaker thus can start all over again, and can continue shortening the miles by lamenting in another circular composition.

According to Mowatt, the notion of acceptable service in *Minnedienst* is alluded to in 37 f., and is said to constitute a pendant to 27 f. of "Min herze und min lip diu wellent scheiden"—"ich waere en gouch ob ich ir tumpheit hete/ für guot es engeschiht mir niemer mere" (chapter IX, p. 66)—"in which the poet is rejecting the lady because her contribution to the relationship is inadequate."[29] This is one of several occasions on which Mowatt shows himself to adhere to the view that the speakers in Hausen's lyrics are preoccupied with *Minnedienst* and concepts related to *hohe Minne*. The discussion presented in these pages must do without the enrichments that come with such a view.

The link between the above cited passage and the lyric's closing lines is a tenuous one:

> 39 wan ich für all man
> ir ie was undertan.
>
> for before all men
> I was always subservient to her.

On the one hand, they may intend to emphasize the validity of the poem's (circular) arrangement. On the other hand, in terms of logical development of thought, they read like a *non sequitur*. No matter how we rationalize the link, it remains difficult to acquiesce in this evaluation of the last line: "Schmerz liegt darin und Stolz und Freude."[30] Instead, we suggest, "undertan" reminds us that the speaker made himself subservient to the lady "ane sinne" (14).

Korn calls the closing strophe "ergreifend schlicht."[31] He is correct perhaps, but that does not mean that it is very clear. It is also true that "schon hier bei Hausen sich die scholastischem Denken urverwandte Art, Widersprüche zu lösen, [anbahnt],"[32] though with the lack of our knowledge of a specific sequential order in the Hausen poems it is not a matter of "schon" in the sense that we *know* this to be an early lyric. When Korn then continues: "Jedes Hausensche Minnelied wird fortan ein Streben nach der ideellen Wesenheit: Freude, die unabhängig von der Erlebnisrealität objektive Seinsqualität besitzt, sein; Leid wird auf dialektischem Wege in Freude übergeführt,"[33] then this is true because Hausen deals with the concept of love for the sake of (beautiful) poetry, and thus brings "fröide."

This lyric is an "as if" stance; anything can happen in this unreal world. The poem receives color from the very mood in which it is created; or rather, it receives color from the mood with which it is imbued. For instance, we tend to forget that the lady alluded to may never "es für guot enpfan" (37) simply because she is not informed. Consequently, as could be expected from an instance of pensive day-dreaming (deliberately evoked to shorten the miles), there is no forward movement here, no development, no activity other than that of the speaker's mind turning around the pondered problem—"genießerisch auskosten." The language itself, not only in the thoughts and term it employs, but also in its tone and timbre, is subdued. This subdued quality makes "Ich denke under wilen" a "thought" poem through and through, and it may also be the reason why some of the critics cited above allowed their sensitivity to turn into sentimentality. The "depth" of reading thus applied does not do to the poem the justice it deserves.

CONCLUSION

It is tempting to argue that little needs to be added because it is in the nature of the foregoing inquiries to allow the questions they raise to remain open-ended, and because the conclusions to be drawn are already inherent in the body of the work. It is obvious, for instance, that these chapters seek to thrust individualism upon each of the lyrics, and therefore upon Hausen himself, who has emerged as a multifaceted poet, capable of providing variety.

Because of the approach used in the preceding materials, one or two generalizing remarks can be made, however. These suggestions do not serve so much to impose unifying elements upon the lyrics as to reveal a type of consistency in Hausen's poetic procedure. In this connection it is interesting to note that all the lyrics share an antithetical quality. They reveal the poet's habit of employing a given motif and then illuminating it from various, often surprising, angles. Likely as not, to an argument worked out in one poem a counterbalance is provided in another, or one lyric continues a theme, with or without a twist in emphasis, dealt with elsewhere. Since the antithetical method is primarily a manner of delivering poetic statements, it does not indicate the *content* of such statements. We therefore are reminded of Schönbach, who has taught us again and again that many ecclesiastical tenets seem to be reflected in Hausen's lyrics. This ought to make us attentive, for scholastic philosophy and ecclesiastical tenets of the day are closely intertwined. Furthermore, it has been argued on several occasions that passion as defined and understood by medieval man is a sin because it unhinges the mind and thus violates the concept that man is created in the image of God. To be "ane sinne," to "fall" in love, to be love's "undertan" is therefore reprehensible. The concept of "dienen," too, easily acquires negative coloring. In short, all those terms we encounter that refer to love in whatever fashion, while generally seen as functioning in the *hohe Minne* system are valid also in a framework of reference that is antagonistic to that system. If we consider also that Andreas Capellanus was familiar with and elaborated on passion as sin, and that he and Hausen share other motifs as well (see chapter I, pp. 14), the conclusion must be drawn, even if only in the form of an open-ended question: Are not Hausen's poems held together and informed by scholastic principles and devices?

Hausen's possible awareness of the difference between contrition and attrition (see, for instance, chapter IX, pp. 71) is another matter that may qualify him as having received a scholastically colored training. With this, we might wish to wonder about the education Hausen enjoyed and about the kind of mentors he had. Beyond that, if we care to, we could even ask the unanswerable question whether the young Hausen was perhaps meant for a career in the church but for some reason veered into a different direction, perhaps because he was totally unsuited for such a calling, perhaps because the death of an elder brother made it mandatory that he remain "in the world."

To restate what has been suggested in several of the discussions: the concept of *Gottesdienst* does not testify to Hausen's devoutness. Rather, it seems, God here serves the (arbitrary) purpose of the moment. Even in the lyric that we saw as elaborating a theme more directly and closely concerned with religious tenets and values than any other of the poems—"Sich möhte wiser man verwüeten"—there is reason to wonder whether the poet evokes those values solely for the sake of entertainment (cf. chapter XVI, note 41). It thus becomes tempting to suggest that God is a "courtly" God, not unlike Gottfried's Christ who is as adaptable as a weather vane. For with Hausen, too, the idea of God seems to be malleable. It can accommodate poems like "Diu süezen wort hant mir getan" (chapter IV) or "Wafena, wie hat mich minne gelazen" (chapter VI) as well as "Si welnt dem tode entrunnen sin" (chapter VII).

There is also the problem of *Frauendienst*. The above inquiries suggest that the connotations accompanying this concept are so ambiguous in Hausen's poetry as to render them problematic. Indeed, these lyrics constitute an inhospitable environment for *Frauendienst* as defined in established criticism. Thus, since *Gottesdienst* and *Frauendienst* do not (yet) possess the brightness they acquire elsewhere—whether with other poets or in the minds of the critics—it seems unrewarding to think of Hausen's attempting to harmonize these two services. Rather, it would seem, these lyrics constitute a warning against such an attempt at harmonization.

On a different plane of evaluation, other results of the foregoing analyses could be mentioned, though they, too, are already inherent in the body of the work. The most important of these is that a number of manuscript readings do not seem to be in need of the emendations imposed upon them by various editors. As we have seen, the refusal to abide by all the alleged improvements propagated in the editions of *Des Minnesangs Frühling* has important results for the evaluations of these lyrics. "Min herze und min lip diu wellent scheiden" (chapter IX), for instance, which is generally regarded as Hausen's most important poem, acquires a meaning quite different from that found in established literary criticism. The same argument holds for a majority of the other lyrics. In this connection also, our discussions suggest again and again that irony is operating where it had not previously been assumed. No matter whether such irony is bitter or jocular, at the cost of the speaker or that of the lady, in each instance it colors the "message" which a given lyric brings. Furthermore, such a "message" is at times considerably affected by the essentially hypothetical nature of the relationships celebrated in these poems.

In conclusion, the above discussions imply that the concept of *hohe Minne* in Hausen's poetry is at best a problematic one. Despite the fact that Hausen is generally regarded as the first poet who is fully oriented towards *hohe Minne*, the disconcerting question must be raised whether the application of this concept to Hausen is productive at all (see also chapter XI, p. 82). Needless to say, should *hohe Minne* prove to be an unrewarding and frustrating criterion in the poetry of other *Minnesinger* such as Albrecht von Johansdorf, some of the presuppositions cherished for so long by scholarship may have to be considerably revised.

NOTES

INTRODUCTION

1. See, eg.g, Anton E. Schönbach, *Beiträge zur Erklärung altdeutscher Dichtwerke*, I: *Die älteren Minnesänger*. Sitzungsberichte der kaiserlichen Akademie der Wissenschaften in Wien, philosophisch-historische Klasse, 141 (Wien, 1894), p. 41.
2. By way of example, see the discussion of the opening line of "Sich möhte wiser man verwüeten" (chapter XVI).
3. Hennig Brinkmann, *Friedrich von Hausen* (Bad Oeynhausen, 1948), passim, esp. pp. 22 ff.
4. This in contrast also to Karl Müllenhoff, "Zu Friedrich von Hausen," *ZfdA*, 14 (1869), who uses the BC order to arrange the lyrics into three *Liederbüchlein*.
5. Oskar Baumgarten, "Die Chronologie der Gedichte Friedrichs von Hausen," *ZfdA*, 26 (1882), 480–82.
6. Müllenhoff, "Zu Friedrich von Hausen."
7. Eduard Wechssler, *Das Kulturproblem des Minnesangs: Studien zur Vorgeschichte der Renaissance*, I: *Minnesang und Christentum* (Halle, 1909; repr. Osnabrück, 1966).
8. For a recent discussion of this question, see David G. Mowatt, *Friderich von Husen: Introduction, Text, Commentary and Glossary* (Cambridge, 1971), pp. 12 ff.
9. See, e.g., Mowatt, *Husen*, pp. 156 ff.
10. It is naturally of consequence whether such ambiguity is deliberate or whether it results from the distance in time between the poet and the modern reader. To be sure, the *additional* levels of meaning suggested again and again in the chapters ahead presuppose that multiple readings are intrinsic to these poems. The following discussions will also suggest, however, that there are instances in which ambiguity may stem from an incomplete grasp of the poetic and syntactical data on which Hausen drew.
11. Wilhelm Scherer, *Geschichte der deutschen Literatur* (Berlin, 1929), p. 154.
12. Mowatt, *Husen*, p. 100, speaks of the irony inherent in "allegorical self-analysis."
13. In addition, though Mowatt has made the manuscript readings more easily accessible, the majority of readers will find it easier to consult a Kraus edition.
14. Günther Jungbluth, "Neue Forschungen zur mittelhochdeutschen Lyrik," *Euphorion*, 51 (1957), 193.

I. ICH MUOZ VON SCHULDEN SIN UNFRO

1. The citations are from Carl von Kraus, *Des Minnesangs Frühling* (Leipzig, 1959). The numbers in the first column correspond to those found in the left column of the Kraus edition, the Roman numerals indicate which strophe of the lyric is cited, the numbers in the third column are my own, and the right margin shows in which order the strophes appear in the manuscripts.
2. As will become evident, the translations can be no more than approximations. This is particularly the case in those instances in which more than one reading can be obtained from the original.
3. Hausen being a cerebral and quasi-autobiographically oriented poet, it becomes inevitable that the use of the first person singular occurs often. There are seventeen such references in "Ich muoz von schulden sin unfro." Of course, all speakers in *Minnesang* are "self-centered"; the genre demands it. But this does not prevent us from scrutinizing this egocentricity in a given poem and from drawing from it whatever inferences are available.

4. Speaking from within the framework of *hohe Minne* philosophy, Hellmuth Langenbucher, "Idealismus and Realismus im deutschen Minnesang," *ZfdB*, 6 (1930), 444, would see the line from the perspective of "Trauer als Pflicht." Hennig Brinkmann, *Friedrich von Hausen* (Bad Oeynhausen, 1948), p. 115, speaks of "höfische Dämpfung."

5. Anton E. Schönbach, *Beiträge zur Erklärung altdeutscher Dichtwerke*, I: *Die älteren Minnesänger* (Wien, 1894), p. 41, has an eye for what we call epic elements situated behind the largely reflective façade of Hausen's poetry. He says of the second line: "[Der Dichter] setzt . . . voraus, daß [die Frau] Schulbildung genossen hat." Regarding the possible origin of the Aeneas-Dido reference, he refers to Ovid's *Heroids* of which the seventh "ein Brief von Dido an Eneas ist, der das Thema nach allen Richtungen hin ausschöpft."

6. For a résumé of the arguments pro and con that Hausen borrowed the Aeneas-Dido motif from Heinrich von Veldeke, see Werner Friedrich Braun, "Hausens MF 42,1–27 und Veldekes Eneit," *ZfdA*, 93 (1964), 209–14, who speaks in favor of the Veldeke influence on Hausen in this matter. See also Richard Lehfeld, "Über Friedrich von Hausen," *Beiträge*, 2 (1876), 345–405.

7. Many critics have dealt with the problem of the relationship between speaker and audience and the game-character in *Minnesang*; see, e.g., Hugo Kuhn, "Zur Deutung der künstlerischen Form des Mittelalters," *SG*, 2 (1949), 114–21; "Dichtungswissenschaft und Soziologie," *SG*, 3 (1950), 622–26; "Soziale Realität und dichterische Fiktion am Beispiel der höfischen Ritterdichtung Deutschlands," *Soziologie und Leben*, ed. Carl Brinkmann (Tübingen, 1952), pp. 195–219; Wolfgang Mohr, "Minnesang als Gesellschaftskunst," *DU*, 6 (1954), 83–107.

8. Brinkmann, *Hausen*, p. 110.

9. Brinkmann, *Hausen*, p. 55: "Die Auslegung des Minnesangs [fordert] eine besondere Tiefe."

10. Brinkmann, *Hausen*, p. 111: "Sehr sanft erwidert er der Äusserung der Frau: wie konnte sie nur so sprechen?"

11. Lehfeld, "Über Friedrich von Hausen," 397, points out that there are several other occasions where Hausen depicts a lady as doubting her suitor's *staete*. Hausen is of course not the only poet to do this; indeed, it becomes one of the patterns used throughout *Minnesang*. Even so, it is well to heed Lehfeld's reminder.

12. Perhaps we should state that all this is not to suggest that actual love is involved; it only functions in a *quasi*-real, and illusory, situation, in a game. Says Kuhn, "Soziale Realität," 203: ". . . ein Spiel also, das ist die Tatsächlichkeit." Within this game, the term "love" is meant to encompass whatever kind of love we may think of, including the nebulous concept of *Minne*. And again, nothing prevents the audience from entering into the spirit of the game and from going along with the speaker's "as if" stance. From within this would-be frame of reference the audience can scrutinize the various statements and arrive at tentative and multiple conclusions regarding the motivations behind the "plot" line.

13. Many commentators speak of love from afar as *hohe Minne*. But *hohe Minne* thus defined hinges on a second criterion, that there is no personal acquaintance between speaker and lady; it is love *before* first sight. According to this definition, *hohe Minne* is not applicable to the situation developed in the present lyric.

14. See in this connection Hugo Bekker, *The Nibelungenlied: A Literary Analysis* (Toronto, 1971), p. 63.

15. Compare this with MF 45,22—"daz si der zwivel dar uf dringet"—in "Ich sage ir nu vil lange zit" (chapter V). Schönbach, *Beiträge*, p. 41, thinks that "zwivel" should be read as "Mangel an Glauben."

16. Despite the danger of being thought redundant, we state that we, too, have entered the game; this allows us to make inquiries about the possible motivations *within* the realm of quasi-reality in which the speaker develops his theme. Of course, if the speaker may get the best of his listeners in this guessing game, it is also possible that he gets the best of *us*, that we discover belatedly that we have erred and therefore must retrace our steps to seek a clearer understanding.

17. Schönbach, *Beiträge*, p. 41.

18. Günther Jungbluth, "Neue Forschungen zur mittelhochdeutschen Lyrik," *Euphorion*, 51 (1957), 219.

19. Hausen uses "lip" nineteen times—MF 54, 1 is not included in this counting. Fully half of these references may be thought to call for "person" or "body"/"life" as a correct term to render its value; four

demand the use of a pronoun; the remaining five cases are ambiguous and can be rendered either way, that is, by means of a pronoun or of "person," "body" and/or "life."

20. Brinkmann, *Hausen*, pp. 111 f.
21. Braun, "Hausen 42,1-27 and Veldekes Eneit," 213.
22. Olive Sayce, *Poets of the Minnesang: Edited with Introduction, Notes and Glossary* (Oxford, 1967), p. 30.
23. Schönbach, *Beiträge*, p. 41.
24. This line provides Kraus with one of many occasions on which to smooth the meter of the manuscripts' texts by changing things about, or by adding dips and stresses. Some of these changes seem questionable, but insofar as they do not affect the approach used in the present evaluations they are left unchallenged. Besides, matters of this kind have been treated by David G. Mowatt, *Friderich von Husen: Introduction, Text, Commentary and Glossary* (Cambridge, 1971).
25. Schönbach, *Beiträge*, p. 41.
26. The question may turn out to be warranted: exactly how astounded is the speaker?
27. See in this connection Max Ittenbach, *Der frühe deutsche Minnesang: Strophenfügung und Dichtersprache*, DVjs Buchreihe, 24 (Halle, 1939), pp. 190 ff.
28. Brinkmann, *Hausen*, p. 111.
29. Arnold Becker, "Der mittelalterliche Minnedienst in Deutschland," *Festschrift der Oberrealschule Düren* (Leipzig, 1895; repr. Halle, 1897), 58.
30. Friedrich Neumann, "Hohe Minne," *ZfDk*, 39 (1925), 81-91.
31. Brinkmann, *Hausen*, p. 55.
32. Hennig Brinkmann, "Der deutsche Minnesang," *Der deutsche Minnesang: Aufsätze zu seiner Erforschung*, ed. Hans Fromm, Wege der Forschung, 15 (Darmstadt, 1966), pp. 157 f.
33. Braun, "Hausen MF 42,1-27 und Veldekes Eneit," 214.
34. Schönbach, *Beiträge*, p. 41.
35. Sayce, *Poets of the Minnesang*, p. 30.
36. Mowatt, *Husen*, pp. 145 ff. It may be, though, that he is merely cleaning out some underbrush in order to make room for his own planting (see below).
37. Hermann Paul, "Kritische Beiträge zu den Minnesingern," *Beiträge*, 2 (1876), 423.
38. Schönbach, *Beiträge*, p. 41.
39. Gustav Ehrismann, "Die älteren Minnesänger," *ZfdPh*, 33 (1901), 402.
40. Franz Neunteufel, "Zu Friedrichs von Hausen Metrik, Sprache und Stil," *Progr. Czernowitz* (1884), 41.
41. Friedrich Vogt, *Des Minnesangs Frühling* (Leipzig, 1920), p. 332.
42. Kraus, *Des Minnesangs Frühling: Untersuchungen*, p. 141.
43. Sayce, *Poets of the Minnesang*, p. 30.
44. Brinkmann, *Hausen*, p. 11.
45. Mowatt, *Husen*, p. 146.
46. Mowatt does not actually offer his own translations; the closest he comes to doing so is in these words: "There was always plenty of room for 'elliu wip' in my heart. She, however, now occupies it fully by herself" (p. 147).
47. Says Schönbach, *Beiträge*, p. 42, about "rehte staete": "vgl. Albertus Magnus, De paradiso animae, lib. 1 cap. 42: 'perseverantia vera est in bonis operibus frequens exercitatio, continuum studium, etc.' Bonitas 27 ist die Mutter aller Tugenden ... und besteht aus sechs Theilen, deren fünften 'perseverantia' bildet. Man sieht aus diesem Beispiel, das Schema der Minnepsychologie deckt sich im Wesentlichen mit dem der Kirchenlehre und ist wohl auch aus diesem entstanden."
48. Schönbach, *Beiträge*, p. 42.
49. Mowatt, *Husen*, p. 146.
50. Brinkmann, *Hausen*, p. 112, speaks of this *staete* as having "eine Zukunft ohne Ende."
51. Eduard Wechssler, *Das Kulturproblem des Minnesangs: Studien zur Vorgeschichte der Renaissance*. I: *Minnesang und Christentum* (Halle, 1909; repr. Osnabrück, 1966), p. 85.
52. As already indicated as a possibility in note 16 above, the speaker did have the best of us.
53. This reading prompts a period after the seventh line.

54. Helmut de Boor, *Geschichte der deutschen Literatur von den Anfängen bis zur Gegenwart*, II (München, 1964), pp. 11 f.
55. *Untersuchungen*, p. 139.
56. As advocated by Mowatt; see above.
57. Andreas Capellanus, *The Art of Courtly Love*, ed. F. W. Locke (New York, 1969), p. 14. Compare Walther von der Vogelweide:

42,5   Diu mir enfremdet alliu wip
         wan daz ichs dur si eren muoz.

In a generalizing statement, Wechssler, *Kulturproblem*, p. 175, puts it as follows: "Der Lobdichter der Frauen widmete seine Huldigungen nicht einer einzigen Geliebten, die ihn jedes andere Weib hätte vergessen machen, sondern dem weiblichen Geschlecht überhaupt." He spoils it all by continuing and thus undoing the irony that Hausen's lack of explication creates, thus destroying the notion of the "game" character as we have conceived of it in the present argument: ". . . das heißt, den vornehmen Damen, die allein der Aufmerksamkeit würdig waren. Weder die Dichter noch ihr Publikum dachten an eine Untreue des Sängers, wenn dieser erklärte, um der Herrin willen alle andere Frauen ehren zu wollen: denn sie allein schon erhöhte ihr ganzes Geschlecht."

58. This suggests commas: "ich muoz, von schulden, sin unfro."
59. From this point of view it could be argued also that the speaker "inadvertantly" shows himself to be at fault because he was not persuasive enough and failed to convince the lady of his devotion. Because of his way with language, this alleged lack of persuasiveness would be irony at his own cost.
60. Lehfeld, "Über Friedrich von Hausen," 401.
61. Kraus, *Untersuchungen*, pp. 139 ff.
62. Karl Korn, *Studien über "Freude und Truren" bei mittelhochdeutschen Dichtern: Beiträge zu einer Problemgeschichte*, Von deutscher Poeterey, 12 (Leipzig, 1932), p. 43.
63. Presumably, the speaker's view would be that the lady's outlook is narrowly private. This, in turn, entails the conclusion that she has a "practical" mind when it comes to dealing with love and its problems.
64. See Andreas Capellanus as cited above.
65. Did he beg for it "do [er] bi ir was"?
66. Hans Spanke, "Romanische und mittellateinische Formen in der Metrik von *Minnesangs Frühling*," *ZfdPh*, 49 (1929), 289.
67. Gustav Ehrismann, "Die Grundlagen des ritterlichen Tugendsystems," *ZfdA*, 56 (1919), 137–216.
68. Ernst Robert Curtius, *Europäische Literatur und lateinisches Mittelalter* (Bern, 1954), pp. 508–25. Against Curtius, see Eduard Naumann, "Der Streit um 'das ritterliche Tugendsystem,'" *Festgabe Helm: Erbe der Vergangenheit* (Tübingen, 1951), pp. 137–53.

II. MICH MÜET DEICH VON DER LIEBEN QUAM

1. Franz Rolf Schröder, "Zu Friedrich von Hausen, 42,1," *GRM*, 42 (1961), 330 f.
2. Friedrich Maurer, "Zu den Liedern Friedrichs von Hausen," *NM*, 53 (1952), 149–70. Also in F.M., *Dichtung und Sprache des Mittelalters: Gesammelte Aufsätze*, Bibliotheca Germanica, 10 (Bern/München, 1963), pp. 80–94.
3. Ingeborg Ipsen, "Strophe und Lied im frühen Minnesang," *Beiträge*, 57 (1933), 381, speaks of "die kunstvolle, geschlossene Aufbau" of "Ich muoz von schulden sin unfro."
4. Anton E. Schönbach, *Beiträge zur Erklärung altdeutscher Dichtwerke*, I: *Die älteren Minnesänger* (Wien, 1894), p. 42.
5. Hennig Brinkmann, *Friedrich von Hausen* (Bad Oeynhausen, 1948), p. 12.
6. As we shall see, there are several other Hausen lyrics with this kind of time change between the first and second parts.

7. Humphrey M. Milnes, "Über die erotische Sprache in der mittelhochdeutschen höfischen Dichtung" (Diss. Ohio State University, 1949), p. 140.

8. Brinkmann, *Hausen*, pp. 114 ff.

9. Peter Schmid, "Die Entwicklung der Begriffe 'minne' und 'liebe' im deutschen Minnesang bis Walther," *ZfdPh*, 66 (1941), 141.

10. Hellmuth Langenbucher, "Idealismus und Realismus im deutschen Minnesang," *ZfdB*, 6 (1930), 444.

11. David G. Mowatt, *Friderich von Husen: Introduction, Text, Commentary and Glossary* (Cambridge, 1971), p. 164, does not accept the need for inserted punctuation after the fifth line; he reads the sixth line as "ever since I was engaged in this," and allows it to refer back, or forward, or both.

12. Brinkmann, *Hausen*, p. 115. It would not be fair to Brinkmann's intent to ask what that "Bereitschaft" amounts to: "Bereitschaft" to what?

13. This leaves open the question as to the exact meaning of the strophe's closing line (see below).

14. Carl von Kraus, *Des Minnesangs Frühling: Untersuchungen* (Leipzig, 1939), p. 141, follows a suggestion made by Schönbach: "v. 7 mag sich auf 42,24 ff. beziehen."

15. Helmut de Boor, *Geschichte der deutschen Literatur von den Anfängen bis zur Gegenwart*, II (München, 1964), 256.

16. Richard Lehfeld, "Über Friedrich von Hausen," *Beiträge*, 2 (1876), 358.

17. Brinkmann, *Hausen*, p. 116. See also Kraus, *Untersuchungen*, p. 142.

18. Mowatt, *Husen*, p. 194, gives as alternate "imagine mistakenly," but this value imputed to the verb does not seem desirable in this particular instance.

19. See chapter I, p. 13, where it is argued that "für" also means "for," "as a representative of."

20. The manuscripts are cited as they are given by Mowatt, *Husen*, pp. 106 ff. The spelling, but not the punctuation has been somewhat normalized.

21. Mowatt, *Husen*, p. 147.

22. Milnes, "Erotische Sprache," p. 117.

23. It is good to remember that "love" used throughout these discussions is meant to be an all-encompassing term, including *Minne*.

24. E.g., Brinkmann, *Hausen*, p. 80.

25. Is there a link here to the medieval concept of being "ellende"? See in this connection the discussion of "Sich möhte wiser man verwüeten" (chapter XVI).

26. Brinkmann, *Hausen*, p. 13. This is not to say that "das heitere Miteinander eines geselligen Kreises" is a null and void notion. On the contrary, it is highly important insofar as it suggests that medieval man, with the persona of the present lyric as his representative, is "korporativ," has no choice but to be corporate in his needs since as an individual he is not (yet) able to stand alone and must hence receive his worth from his environment rather than from within.

27. See chapter I, p. 12.

28. See Hugo Bekker, *The Nibelungenlied: A Literary Analysis* (Toronto, 1971), pp. 15 and 57. Admittedly, the suggestions advanced here must remain tentative until their implications have been more fully scrutinized than the present investigation warrants.

29. Eduard Wechssler, *Das Kulturproblem des Minnesangs: Studien zur Vorgeschichte der Renaissance*. I: *Minnesang und Christentum* (Halle, 1909; repr. Osnabrück, 1966), p. 31.

30. Brinkmann, *Hausen*, p. 18.

31. Brinkmann, *Hausen*, p. 17.

32. Brinkmann, *Hausen*, p. 17.

33. Wechssler, *Kulturproblem*, p. 35.

34. Compare Wechssler, *Kulturproblem*, p. 35, when he says that the Church was ahead of the courtly life and society in that the former recognized "den tiefen Ernst des Lebens." "Die cortezia hatte darin ihre Schwäche, daß sie die höchsten Dinge und Fragen wie ein anmutiges und unterhaltendes Spiel behandelte." From the present perspective it becomes possible to say that courtly society of Hausen's day used such play as the perhaps most effective way of dealing with "den tiefen Ernst des Lebens." This would be the case in part because, as Wechssler sees it, this society had lost its faith, but *knew* that life nevertheless had its ultimate questions; perhaps we could say that those questions became all the more pressing because the age had lost

faith and had to find the answers all over again now that traditional canons and tenets had lost value. In this sense, indeed, the courtly period is the form of early Renaissance it has been said to be.

35. Brinkmann, *Hausen*, p. 16.
36. See Bekker, *Nibelungenlied*, pp. 15 f.
37. Wechssler, *Kulturproblem*, p. v.
38. Wechssler, *Kulturproblem*, p. 85.
39. C manuscript: "wer si mir us der masse niht" ("if she did not mean so extravagantly much to me"). Schönbach, *Beiträge*, p. 43, sees "in der maze" as "ganz wenig."
40. Kraus, *Untersuchungen*, p. 142: "v. 21 f. enthält wohl . . . einen Bezug auf Strophe III des vorhergehenden Liedes, wo der Dichter sagte: 'Swie lihte si sich troeste min.' "
41. Milnes, "Erotische Sprache," pp. 112 f. suggests that "troesten" or "getroesten" often "eine bestimmte aber immerhin verhüllende Bedeutung haben." See also Paul Schulz, "Die erotischen Motive in der deutschen Dichtungen des 12. und 13. Jahrhunderts" (Diss. Greifswald, 1907), p. 78.
42. Is this possibility enhanced by the fact that 23 has "vergezzen," which would be merely redundantly similar to "sich getroesten" if the latter meant "to forget"? Incidentally, there is of course still the possibility that the matter pondered by the speaker is only in his mind and that the lady alluded to may have to be imagined as not even knowing of his feelings.
43. Oskar Baumgarten, "Die Chronologie der Gedichte Friedrichs von Hausen," *ZfdA*, 26 (1882), 126.
44. Baumgarten, "Chronologie," 126. He can say "diesmal" since he sees the Hausen poems as interrelated.

III. AN DER GENADE AL MIN FRÖIDE STAT

1. Eduard Wechssler, *Das Kulturproblem des Minnesangs: Studien zur Vorgeschichte der Renaissance*. I: *Minnesang und Christentum* (Halle, 1909; repr. Osnabrück, 1966), p. 396.
2. Hennig Brinkmann, *Friedrich von Hausen* (Bad Oeynhausen, 1948), p. 55.
3. Brinkmann, *Hausen*, p. 54.
4. Maurice Colleville, *Les chansons allemandes de croisade en moyen haut-allemand* (Paris, 1936), pp. 26 f.
5. Richard Lehfeld, "Über Friedrich von Hausen," *Beiträge*, 2 (1876), 385, states: "Die Redensart, die in der Fassung 'diu was im sam der lip' wohl zuerst in der Kaiserchronik erscheint, ist wohl zurückzuführen auf die Bibel, Gen. I, 2, 24." Here, too, however, the line of communication is down between the erstwhile alleged source and the actual value of the phrase as used here.
6. Of the meanings which David G. Mowatt, *Friderich von Husen: Introduction, Text, Commentary and Glossary* (Cambridge, 1971), p. 176, suggests for "kip" — "quarrel," "argument," "uncooperativeness" — the latter is least far removed from the attributes usually lent to the lady of *Minnesang*. Besides, this term allows an open question to remain open: whether she is informed about the speaker's state. If she is not, her uncooperativeness exists only in his mind.
7. This happens rather regularly with Hausen's speakers, and this occurrence casts an interesting light on the adjective when Wechssler, *Kulturproblem*, p. 133, speaks of Hausen as engaging the style "der inneren Welt." The delineation of this "inner" man is not complete, and the question arises whether he is aware of this lack of full clarity.
8. Lilli Seibold, *Studien über die Huote*, Germanische Studien, 123 (Berlin, 1932), p. 52.
9. Seibold, *Studien über die Huote*, p. 53.
10. Brinkmann, *Hausen*, p. 56.
11. Brinkmann has little choice but to delve as deeply as he can: "Hausens Schaffen muß ganz begriffen sein bevor ein wirklicher Einblick in die Geschichte des Minnesangs gelingen kann" (p. 20).
12. From Brinkmann's point of view it is a change since he places "An der genade al min fröide stat" as the second poem in a series in which each component deals with the poet's experiences with one woman.

13. Brinkmann, *Hausen*, p. 56.
14. Karl Korn, *Studien über "Freude und Truren" bei mittelhochdeutschen Dichtern: Beiträge zu einer Problemgeschichte*, Von deutscher Poeterey, 12 (Leipzig, 1932), p. 45.
15. Mowatt, *Husen*, p. 148.
16. Mowatt, *Husen*, p. 76, indicates his stand in the matter when he speaks of the traditional role played by the *ich* in *Minnesang* "which is that of a man who courts a lady with song."
17. Brinkmann, *Hausen*, p. 54.
18. Willy Sanders, *Glück: Zur Herkunft und Bedeutungsentwicklung eines mittelalterlichen Schichsalsbegriffs*, Niederdeutsche Studien, 13 (Köln/Graz, 1965), p. 103.
19. Anton E. Schönbach, *Beiträge zur Erklärung altdeutscher Dichtwerke*, I: *Die älteren Minnesänger* (Wien, 1894), p. 44, has a different reading; he too, however, finds that "[C] den Sinn des Satzes mit dem reinen Reim 'tumber' getroffen [hat]."
20. Carl von Kraus, *Des Minnesangs Frühling: Untersuchungen* (Leipzig, 1939), p. 135.
21. Schönbach, *Beiträge*, p. 44, finds this line to incorporate "das Hauptthema der asketischen Literatur des Mittelalters."
22. This reading suggests that the concept of love being inevitably linked with sorrow, as we find it repeatedly stated throughout *Minnesang* and elsewhere, is not a matter of course to the speaker of this lyric. For him, it applies only to his particular case, and he rationalizes himself into this view. Indeed, he makes it sound as though the others, the lucky ones, are missing something desirable because they do not have this kind of experience. This forced line of reasoning contrasts markedly with what he himself would ultimately favor if he had things his way (see below).
23. Brinkmann, *Hausen*, pp. 56 f.
24. Brinkmann, *Hausen*, p. 54.
25. Brinkmann, *Hausen*, p. 56.
26. Brinkmann, *Hausen*, p. 56.
27. Peter Schmid, "Die Entwicklung der Begriffe 'minne' und 'liebe' im deutschen Minnesang bis Walther," *ZfdPh*, 66 (1941), 150.

IV. DIU SÜEZEN WORT HANT MIR GETAN

1. Hennig Brinkmann, *Friedrich von Hausen* (Bad Oeynhausen, 1948), p. 84.
2. See in this connection Hugo Bekker, *The Nibelungenlied: A Literary Analysis* (Toronto, 1971), p. 105. For contrast see Eduard Wechssler, *Das Kulturproblem des Minnesangs: Studien zur Vorgeschichte der Renaissance*, I: *Minnesang und Christentum* (Halle, 1909; repr. Osnabrück, 1966), p. 105.
3. It is true, however, that "gedenken" to medieval man seems to come inevitably with troubles—see "angest" (5) as discussed below. This does not give us license, of course, to think that medieval man finds the exercise of the brain painful.
4. Brinkmann, *Hausen*, p. 85.
5. Says David G. Mowatt, *Friderich von Husen: Introduction, Text, Commentary and Glossary* (Cambridge, 1971), p. 148: " 'Liebe' could be an adjective agreeing with 'enkeine' (hence: 'lieb gewinnen': 'I never loved anyone so much'); or it may be a noun with 'enkeine' as adjective: 'I never knew such love before.' "
6. Walter Fischer, *Liedsang aus deutscher Frühe: Mittelhochdeutsche Dichtung übertragen und herausgegeben* (Stuttgart, 1939), p. 37.
7. Istvàn Frank, *Trouvères et Minnesänger: Recueil de textes pour servir à l'étude des rapports entre la poésie lyrique romane et le Minnesang au XIIe siècle* (Saarbrücken, 1952), p. 22.
8. Humphrey M. Milnes, "Über die erotische Sprache in der mittelhochdeutschen höfischen Dichtung" (Diss. Ohio State University 1949), pp. 49 f. See also Paul Schulz, "Die erotischen Motive in der deutschen Dichtung des 12. und 13. Jahrhunderts" (Diss. Greifswald, 1906), p. 78.

9. Anton E. Schönbach, *Beiträge zur Erklärung altdeutscher Dichtwerke*, I: *Die älteren Minnesänger* (Wien, 1894), p. 44.
10. Cf., for instance, the value of "genade" as discussed in chapter III.
11. Kraus, *Untersuchungen*, p. 136.
12. Reference is made to "Min herze und min lip diu wellent scheiden" (chapter IX).
13. Kraus, *Untersuchungen*, p. 136.
14. Brinkmann, *Hausen*, p. 87.
15. Kraus, *Untersuchungen*, p. 136.
16. Karl Korn, *Studien über "Freude und Truren" bei mittelhochdeutschen Dichtern: Beiträge zu einer Problemgeschichte* (Leipzig, 1932), p. 30.
17. Mowatt, *Husen*, p. 148.
18. Brinkmann, *Hausen*, p. 19.
19. Kraus, *Untersuchungen*, p. 136, cites some of them.
20. Brinkmann, *Hausen*, p. 85, speaks of "Gott, der bei Hausen nie leerer Name, sondern immer lebendige Macht ist."
21. Wechssler, *Kulturproblem*, as cited above (chapter II, p. 24), has a different opinion.
22. I hope to deal with this matter on a later occasion.
23. See Bekker, *Nibelungenlied*, pp. 154 f.
24. Arnold Becker, "Zu Friedrich von Hausen," *Germania*, 28 (1883), 272.
25. So, for instance, Fischer, *Liedsang*, p. xix: "Hausen war es heiliger Ernst mit der hohen Minne als Erziehungsmacht im Leben wie im Dichten."

V. ICH SAGE IR NU VIL LANGE ZIT

1. Ingeborg Ipsen, "Strophe und Lied im frühen Minnesang," *Beiträge*, 57 (1933), 372.
2. Hennig Brinkmann, *Friedrich von Hausen* (Bad Oeynhausen, 1948), p. 10.
3. Friedrich Maurer, "Zu den Liedern Friedrichs von Hausen," *NM*, 53 (1952), 149-70.
4. Carl von Kraus, *Des Minnesangs Frühling: Untersuchungen* (Leipzig, 1939), pp. 136 f.
5. Brinkmann, *Hausen*, p. 96.
6. Brinkmann, *Hausen*, p. 96.
7. See chapter I, note 11.
8. With "Bearbeiter" Jungbluth does not intend us to think of Kraus, but of the scribe of the manuscript.
9. Günther Jungbluth, "Neue Forschungen zur mittelhochdeutschen Lyrik," *Euphorion*, 51 (1957), 197.
10. Jungbluth, "Neue Forschungen," 194, has a warning: "Man sollte sich nur keiner Täuschung darüber hingeben, daß die Forderung 'Zurück zur Überlieferung'—in voller Strenge—das Unverantwortliche, ja Unmögliche verlangt und daß selbst ihre eifrigsten Fürsprecher auf . . . Dispensationen nicht verziehen können."
11. Brinkmann, *Hausen*, p. 10.
12. Jungbluth, "Neue Forschungen," 198.
13. Brinkmann, *Hausen*, p. 96. The insights regarding the value of *zwivel* advanced by Helen Adolf, "Theological and Feudal Background of Wolfram's *zwivel*," *JEGP*, 49 (1950), 285-303, and Thomas Perry Thornton, "Love, Uncertainty and Despair: The Use of 'zwivel' by the Minnesänger," *JEGP*, 60 (1961), 213-27, do not seem applicable to the occurrence of the term in this Hausen poem.
14. In "Ich muoz von schulden sin unfro" these terms are not used, but from the speaker's point of view they could readily apply to the lady.
15. Jungbluth, "Neue Forschungen," 198.
16. We take "verstan" of the manuscript rather than Kraus' emended "verslan."

17. David G. Mowatt, *Friderich von Husen: Introduction, Text, Commentary and Glossary* (Cambridge, 1971), p. 148, gives this as a possible alternate reading: "Nobody should understand me to have said that she could not...."

18. Kraus, *Untersuchungen*, p. 138.

19. Brinkmann, *Hausen*, p. 97, gives "ouch" the value of "also" and comes to a different way of understanding the strophe and with that the entire lyric.

20. Either reading remains valid also if we assume that the lady knows nothing; in this case the speaker would be tilting, once again (see chapter III, p. 29), against windmills.

21. Peter Schmid, "Die Entwicklung der Begriffe 'minne' und 'liebe' im deutschen Minnesang bis Walther," *ZfdPh*, 66 (1941), 150.

22. Eduard Wechssler, *Das Kulturproblem des Minnesangs: Studien zur Vorgeschichte der Renaissance*, I: *Minnesang und Christentum* (Halle, 1909; repr. Osnabrück, 1966), p. 173. See also Friedrich-Wilhelm Wentzlaff-Eggebert, *Kreuzzugsdichtung des Mittelalters: Studie zu ihrer geschichtlichen und dichterischen Wirklichkeit* (Berlin, 1960), p. 185.

VI. WAFENA, WIE HAT MICH MINNE GELAZEN

1. Hennig Brinkmann, *Friedrich von Hausen* (Bad Oeynhausen, 1948), pp. 88 ff.
2. Samuel Singer, "Studien zu den Minnesängern," *Beiträge*, 44 (1920), 433.
3. Why does Kraus capitalize?
4. Oskar Baumgarten, "Die Chronologie der Gedichte Friedrichs von Hausen," *ZfdA*, 26 (1882), 122.
5. Arnold Becker, "Zu Friedrich von Hausen," *Germania*, 28 (1883), 281.
6. Carl von Kraus, *Des Minnesangs Frühling: Untersuchungen* (Leipzig, 1939), p. 124.
7. Anton E. Schönbach, *Beiträge zur Erklärung altdeutscher Dichtwerke*, I: *Die älteren Minnesänger* (Wien, 1894), p. 52.
8. Schönbach, *Beiträge*, p. 52.
9. See Heinrich Götz, *Leitwörter des Minnesangs*, Abhandlungen der sächsischen Akademie der Wissenschaften zu Leipzig, philosophisch-historische Klasse, 49, 1 (Berlin, 1957), pp. 145 f., for the various possible meanings of "wan."
10. Mihail Isbăşescu, *Minne und Liebe: Ein Beitrag zur Begriffsdeutung und Terminologie des Minnesangs*, Tübinger germanistische Arbeiten, 27 (Stuttgart, 1940), p. 19.
11. Says Brinkmann, *Hausen*, p. 91, of 5 f.: "Das ist ein Motiv der Leidenschaft, das Morungen später besonders pflegt." One could wonder, by the way, whether "güete" of the fourth line refers to the lady or to the abstract figure *Minne;* the answer is of some consequence, though love's "güete" can only become manifest through the "güete" of the lady.
12. Brinkmann, *Hausen*, p. 91.
13. Richard Lehfeld, "Über Friedrich von Hausen," *Beiträge*, 2 (1876), 355. See also Baumgarten, "Chronologie," 121.
14. Helmut de Boor, *Geschichte der deutschen Literatur von den Anfängen bis zur Gegenwart*, II (München, 1964), p. 257.
15. Hellmuth Langenbucher, "Idealismus und Realismus im deutschen Minnesang," *ZfdB*, 6 (1930), 443 f., too, has a different opinion when he places a dividing line between Hausen and the poets of older *Minnesang* who deal with "echte Liebe."
16. This is of course not to suggest that anything other than quasi-reality is delineated in this poem.
17. For reasons applied by Brinkmann, *Hausen*, p. 87, the strophes II and III are presented here in a reverse order from that found in *Des Minnesangs Frühling*. Due to this reversal, lines 8–14 become lines 15–21, lines 15–21 become lines 8–14.

18. See Hugo Bekker, *The Nibelungenlied: A Literary Analysis* (Toronto, 1971), p. 111, for the possible implications of love as passion, and of reason suspended.

19. Kraus, *Untersuchungen*, p. 123.

20. Peter Schmid, "Die Entwicklung der Begriffe 'minne' und 'liebe' im deutschen Minnesang bis Walther," *ZfdPh*, 66 (1941), 150.

21. Brinkmann, *Hausen*, p. 92.

22. Brinkmann, *Hausen*, p. 93: "Das ist mit einem Seitenblick auf Veldeke gesagt . . . eine scherzhafte Schlußpointe." Brinkmann sees this as the closing line of the poem; he regards MF 53,24 as a separate item, or at least as one written in a different mood, whether by Hausen or someone else.

23. Schönbach, *Beiträge*, p. 52.

24. Kraus, *Untersuchungen*, p. 123.

25. Lehfeld, "Über Friedrich von Hausen," 354.

26. Brinkmann, *Hausen*, p. 92.

27. Schönbach, *Beiträge*, p. 52.

28. This is based on the manuscript's "verkeren."

29. Is there irony in the imperative and emphatic "seht" with which the speaker implants his allegedly firm determination in the minds of his listeners?

30. Friedrich Vogt, *Des Minnesangs Frühling* (Leipzig, 1920), p. 330, introduced the term.

31. Kraus, *Untersuchungen*, pp. 123 f.

32. Friedrich Neumann, "Rezension zu Kraus, *Des Minnesangs Frühling: Untersuchungen*," *GGA*, 206 (1944), 26.

33. Günther Jungbluth, "Neue Forschungen zur mittelhochdeutschen Lyrik," *Euphorion*, 51 (1957), 196.

34. Whereas in many a Hausen poem the speaker seems forever to be teetering on the edge of sanity in his privately contrived "reality"—"ane sinne" and the like occur rather often—here he presents himself as losing his balance. Incidentally, we might gain from amplifying the definition of *revocatio* in Heinrich Siekhaus, "Revocatio: Studie zu einer Gestaltungsform des Minnesangs," *DVjs*, 39 (1971), 237–51, in such a way as to enable us to view the entire closing strophe of this lyric as an example of a special kind of *revocatio*. If we do, Siekhaus' statement on p. 241 of his study remains fully valid: "In der revocatio tritt nun der fiktionschaffende Dichter hinter dem fiktiven Vorgang hervor, zeigt sich als der, der diesen Vorgang lenkt. . . ."

VII. SI WELNT DEM TODE ENTRUNNEN SIN

1. David G. Mowatt, *Friderich von Husen: Introduction, Text, Commentary and Glossary* (Cambridge, 1971), p. 97.

2. For a recent study of the various attempts made to smooth matters that have been thought to be in need of smoothing, see Mowatt, *Husen*, pp. 36 ff. His argument leads to the suggestion that Kraus occasionally emends for the sake of clarifying what is not in need of clarification. It is not clear, for instance, what is gained by inserting "got" into the sixth line.

3. Günther Jungbluth, "Neue Forschungen zur mittelhochdeutschen Lyrik," *Euphorion*, 51 (1957), 197.

4. Mowatt, *Husen*, p. 39.

5. As we shall see, this fear of eternal punishment may play a role also in "Si darf mich des zihen niet" (chapter VIII) and "Min herze und min lip diu wellent scheiden" (chapter IX).

6. MF 46,28 of "Si darf mich des zihen niet" (chapter VIII).

7. Anton E. Schönbach, *Beiträge zur Erklärung altdeutscher Dichtwerke*, I: *Die älteren Minnesänger* (Wien, 1894), passim.

8. Acts VII: 1 ff.

VIII. SI DARF MICH DES ZIHEN NIET

1. Carl von Kraus, *Des Minnesangs Frühling: Untersuchungen* (Leipzig, 1939), p. 143.
2. Hennig Brinkmann, *Friedrich von Hausen* (Bad Oeynhausen, 1948), pp. 6 f.
3. Hennig Brinkmann, *Entstehungsgeschichte des Minnesangs*, DVJs. Buchreihe, 8 (Halle, 1926), pp. 136 f.
4. Gustav Ehrismann, *Geschichte der deutschen Literatur bis zum Ausgang des Mittelalters*, 2: *Die mittelhochdeutsche Literatur* (München, 1935), p. 229.
5. Helmut de Boor, *Geschichte der deutschen Literatur von den Anfängen bis zur Gegenwart*, II (München, 1964), p. 258.
6. Günther Jungbluth, "'Min herze und min lip diu wellent scheiden': Zu Friedrich von Hausen 47,9." *Euphorion*, 47 (1953), 258 f.
7. Eduard Wechssler, *Das Kulturproblem des Minnesangs: Studien zur Vorgeschichte der Renaissance*, I: *Minnesang und Christentum* (Halle, 1909; repr. Osnabrück, 1966), pp. 424 f.
8. Peter Schmid, "Die Entwicklung der Begriffe 'minne' und 'liebe' im deutschen Minnesang bis Walther," *ZfdPh*, 66 (1941), 150.
9. Olive Sayce, *Poets of the Minnesang: Edited with Introduction, Notes and Glossary* (Oxford, 1967), p. 142.
10. Kraus, *Untersuchungen*, p. 142.
11. The C manuscript, perhaps to make things rhyme, has "min herze hete si in pfliht."
12. All the same, it is remarkable how often this motif of the lady's *zwivel* seems to lie at the base of a given Hausen lyric. Though this is not the only one to mention it explicitly (it is also clearly indicated in "Ich sage ir nu vil lange zit"—chapter V), it is merely mentioned in order then to be "forgotten." See in this connection the possible motivation of the lady's bearing as alluded to in the last strophe of "Min herze und min lip diu wellent scheiden" (chapter IX). Whereas this motif of the lady's lack of belief places the speaker in isolation, elsewhere this isolation is brought about by his failure to inform the lady.
13. Anton E. Schönbach, *Beiträge zur Erklärung altdeutscher Dichtwerke*, I: *Die älteren Minnesänger* (Wien, 1894), p. 45.
14. Maurice Colleville, *Les chansons allemandes de croisade en moyen haut-allemand* (Paris, 1936), p. 28.
15. The lovers in Plautus' plays reveal similar symptoms.
16. Herbert Kolb, *Der Begriff der Minne und das Entstehen der höfischen Lyrik*, Hermaea, NS, 4 (Tübingen, 1958), p. 68.
17. Brinkmann, *Hausen*, p. 63: "So mächtig ist die Liebe geworden, daß sie [den Dichter] der Wirklichkeit enthebt."
18. Wechssler, *Kulturproblem*, p. 253.
19. Wechssler, *Kulturproblem*, p. 268.
20. Andreas Capellanus, *The Art of Courtly Love*, ed. F. W. Locke (New York, 1969), and Felix Schlösser, *Andreas Capellanus: Seine Minnelehre und das christliche Weltbild des 12. Jahrhunderts*, Abhandlungen zur Kunst-, Musik- und Literaturwissenschaft, 15 (Bonn, 1960), served as background materials.
21. Friedrich-Wilhelm Wentzlaff-Eggebert, *Kreuzzugsdichtung des Mittelalters: Studie zu ihrer geschichtlichen und dichterischen Wirklichkeit* (Berlin, 1960), p. 181.
22. Kolb, *Begriff der Minne*, p. 68.
23. Friedrich Vogt, *Des Minnesangs Frühling* (Leipzig, 1920), p. 333.
24. Brinkmann, *Hausen*, p. 74.
25. Brinkmann, *Hausen*, p. 72.
26. Brinkmann, *Entstehungsgeschichte*, p. 136.
27. Genesis III:12.
28. C: "gerungen alles umb ein wip/ ich hete ein leben das mir vil nahe gie."
29. C: "darumbe ich nit an got verzage."
30. Wechssler, *Kulturproblem*, p. 220, note.
31. David G. Mowatt, *Friderich von Husen: Introduction, Text, Commentary and Glossary* (Cambridge, 1971), p. 31.
32. Hennig Brinkmann, "Der deutsche Minnesang," *Der deutsche Minnesang: Aufsätze zu seiner*

Erforschung, ed. Hans Fromm (Darmstadt, 1966), p. 105: "'Liep' ist Inbegriff aller menschlichen Wünsche, verwirklicht, wo sich zwei Menschen glückhaft verbinden."

33. Schmid, "Entwicklung," 150.

34. See in this connection Karl Bartsch, "Nachahmung provenzalischer Poesie im Deutschen," *Germania*, 1 (1856), 481 f.

35. Is it possible to wonder in retrospect whether the opening statement of the second strophe tells us that in contrast to the heart the mind *is* ready to forego the struggle, thus hinting at the development that does not come fully into the open until "Min herze und min lip diu wellent scheiden" (chapter IX)?

36. Brinkmann, *Hausen*, p. 72.

37. Richard Lehfeld, "Über Friedrich von Hausen," *Beiträge*, 2 (1876), 399: "Die schon von H. v. Melk in 'Von des todes gehügede' ausgesprochene Auffassung 'von der frouwen sul wir nicht übel sagen' findet sich unter den Minnesingern zuerst bei Hausen."

38. Wechssler, *Kulturproblem*, p. 185.

39. Humphrey M. Milnes, "Über die erotische Sprache in der mittelhochdeutschen höfischen Dichtung" (Diss. Ohio State University, 1949), pp. 85 f. See also the value of the term as discussed above (chapter III, p. 27).

40. C: "und wil es iemer vor allen dingen klagen/ und im dar nach ein holdes herze tragen."

41. Schmid, "Entwicklung," 150.

42. The irony thus implied would be highlighted by the speaker's endeavor to convey the "seriousness" of his statement by becoming repetitive: cf. 33: "von der enspriche iht niht wan allez guot."

IX. MIN HERZE UND MIN LIP DIU WELLENT SCHEIDEN

1. Particularly the lengthy discussion of David G. Mowatt, *Friderich von Husen: Introduction, Text, Commentary and Glossary* (Cambridge, 1971), and his survey of the criticism dealing with this lyric seems to make such an attempt superfluous.

2. Helmut de Boor, "Zu Hausens Kreuzzugslied 47,9," *Beiträge*, 87 (Tübingen, 1965), 392, speaks of four characters: "Herz," "Leib," "Dichter," and "staetekeit."

3. Friedrich Panzer, *Das Nibelungenlied: Entstehung und Gestalt* (Stuttgart, 1955), p. 187. For the view regarding "Kampfwut" coming with the mind being unhinged, see Hugo Bekker, *The Nibelungenlied: A Literary Analysis* (Toronto, 1971), p. 33.

4. C: "ie doch dem herzen ein wip so nahen lit."

5. Carl von Kraus, *Des Minnesangs Frühling: Untersuchungen* (Leipzig, 1939), p. 155: "Warum 'volgent' hier juristisch als 'zustimmen,' 'übereinstimmen' zu fassen sei (Schönbach) ist nicht einzusehen: Hausen beklagt doch die räumliche Trennung der beiden." But clearly, there is no separation as yet!

6. Anton E. Schönbach, *Beiträge zur Erklärung altdeutscher Dichtwerke*, I: *Die älteren Minnesänger* (Wien, 1894), p. 46.

7. Consider this villanelle of 1576 by Regnart as published by Robert Heitner, *Deutsche dreistimmige Lieder nach Art der Neapolitanen*, Publikation älterer praktischer und theoretischer Musikwerke der Gesellschaft für Musikforschung, 5 (München, 1895):

> Lieb und vernunfft die hand bey mir ein streit,
> Lieb nach begier, mit sporrens streich mich reit,
> Vernunfft helt mich, im zaum zurucken weit,
>
> Gwalt thu ich mir zu dempfen liebes gwalt,
> Darzu vernunfft sich brauchet manigfalt,
> Doch hilffts nicht vil, der schad ist gar zu alt.

> Ich bsorg, ich werd solchs nit mehr treiben lang:
> Dann mir oft wird inn meinem sinn so bang,
> Als wann mir leg um halss des todes strang.
>
> Gott rüff ich an, dass er mir bey wöll stehn
> Und weisen mich, dieweil der weg sind zwen,
> Wohin ich soll nach seinem willen gehn.

8. Mowatt, *Husen*, p. 83.

9. As the following pages seek to make acceptable, there seems to be nothing wrong with the order in which the strophes occur in the C manuscript; we therefore follow it.

10. Karl Korn, *Studien über "Freude und Truren" bei mittelhochdeutschen Dichtern: Beiträge zu einer Problemgeschichte* (Leipzig, 1932), p. 12: " 'truren' heißt fast: seelisch tot sein, weshalb das Wort vielfach zur Bezeichnung der seelischen Erschütterung angesichts des Todes dient."

11. Mowatt, *Husen*, p. 85.

12. In addition to all this, Mowatt's interpretation would have to confront the statement of 15 f., to the effect that the speaker only, not God, can put an end to the heart's problem by helping it to a successful conclusion of its courtship. See below.

13. Mowatt, *Husen*, p. 90.

14. Compare Mowatt, *Husen*, p. 85, when he says that this term "neither requires nor receives any particularized antecedent."

15. Richard Lehfeld, "Über Friedrich von Hausen," *Beiträge*, 2 (1876), 359, believes that the lyric was written far away from the lady. See also Kraus as cited above, note 5.

16. Mowatt, *Husen*, p. 119.

17. Otto Ludwig, "Zum Text von MF 45, 19 f.," *ZfdA*, 93 (1964), 65.

18. Kraus, *Untersuchungen*, p. 150.

19. Mowatt, *Husen*, pp. 81 f.

20. Mowatt, *Husen*, pp. 92 f.

21. See in this connection Vera Vollmer, "Die Begriffe der Triuwe und der Staete in der höfischen Minnedichtung" (Diss. Tübingen, 1949), pp. 76–94, where she gives examples of *staete* used in the latter part of the twelfth century in writings other than those incorporated into *Des Minnesangs Frühling*: several of these examples are cited from religious-ecclesiastical writings.

22. This distinction was formulated by the Council of Trent which stated that attrition, though less desirable than contrition, was sufficient unto salvation. The matter had been a topic of debate long before its official formulation (see below, note 24).

23. Mowatt, *Husen*, p. 93. As already stated, Mowatt's pun relates to his view that the heart was not in the decision since it was with the lady; in the present argument it is meant in the sense that the decision was perhaps only made in the fear of God.

24. The word—*attritio*—occurs first in a popular penitential, *Theologicae regulae*, written by Alan of Lille, whose life spans the last eight decades of the twelfth century. He uses the term in such a way as to indicate that it was already an accepted term in the language of the schoolmen. See in this connection Reinhold Seeberg, *Lehrbuch der Dogmengeschichte*, III: *Die Dogmengeschichte des Mittelalters* (Leipzig, 1930), pp. 532 ff.

25. See, e.g., Karl Müllenhoff, "Zu Friedrich von Hausen," *ZfdA*, 14 (1869), 137: "eine angehängte Strophe"; Mowatt, *Husen*, p. 94, says this: "The four stanzas may have been intended to be performed together, but attempts to interpret them all as one poem in the modern sense have not so far been justified by the results."

26. Peter Schmid, "Die Entwicklung der Begriffe 'minne' und 'liebe' im deutschen Minnesang bis Walther," *ZfdPh*, 66 (1941), 150, finds that this line is "ein schönes Beispiel für den Fall einer völlig verfließenden Bedeutung des Wortes 'Minne.' "

27. This rejects without further ado Kraus' emendation "vor ir oren" for "sumer von triere." For a recent and rather exhaustive résumé of the many efforts made to clarify this term see Mowatt, *Husen*, Introduction and pp. 49 ff. It seems useless to seek to add to the confusion. All we know for certain is that the phrase reflects negatively on the lady, as does the passage in which it occurs.

28. See the tense of "minnet" and the time element "e" in 26.

29. The device used is similar, then, to that encountered in "Si darf mich des zihen niet" (chapter VIII). As with the closing strophe in that poem, it is tempting to argue that the closing strophe in this lyric, too, constitutes in its entirety a kind of *revocatio*.

30. Günther Jungbluth, " 'Min herze und min lip diu wellent scheiden': Zu Friedrich von Hausen 47,9," *Euphorion*, 47 (1953), 241–59, has a much lengthier discussion of this lyric. The reader would gain from consulting it on a comparative basis with the present evaluation to arrive at his own conclusions.

31. It is tempting to wonder whether the mind, because of the quality of its decision to take the cross— "in gotes ere"—is to be seen as only at a half-way station during an arduous journey; this journey may lead from fear of God to love of God, from attrition to contrition. For this journey to reach its desirable and intended end, the mind must be cleansed and purified before it is fit to start on the next tract of the process. If this is a viable possibility, Hausen's poetry would partake of the meditative tradition.

X. MIN HERZE DEN GELOUBEN HAT

1. Richard Lehfeld, "Über Friedrich von Hausen," *Beiträge*, 2 (1876), 359.
2. Friedrich-Wilhelm Wentzlaff-Eggebert, *Kreuzzugsdichtung des Mittelalters: Studie zu ihrer geschichtlichen und dichterischen Wirklichkeit* (Berlin, 1960), p. 185.
3. Kraus capitalizes.
4. This line is a pendant to MF 48,34 in the C manuscript: "als mir diu minne widerriet."
5. Hennig Brinkmann, *Friedrich von Hausen* (Bad Oeynhausen, 1948), p. 128.
6. Brinkmann, *Hausen*, pp. 130 f.
7. We follow the B manuscript for reasons touched upon by David G. Mowatt, *Friderich von Hausen: Introduction, Text, Commentary and Glossary* (Cambridge, 1971), p. 150.
8. C: "das si den heten liep der von uns schiet." Apparently, this version suggests that some knights did not simply stay behind but abandoned the crusade at one of its (early?) stages.
9. C has "iet," B has "ir."
10. Is it tempting to wonder whether a lyric dealing with this development has been lost?
11. C: "und gruesse si als ich beste mac."
12. Wentzlaff-Eggebert, *Kreuzzugsdichtung*, p. 185.

XI. IN MINEM TROUME ICH SACH

1. Eduard Wechssler, *Das Kulturproblem des Minnesangs: Studien zur Vorgeschichte der Renaissance*, I: *Minnesang und Christentum* (Halle, 1909; repr. Osnabrück, 1966), pp. 229 ff.
2. Herbert Kolb, *Der Begriff der Minne und das Entstehen der höfischen Lyrik* (Tübingen, 1958), pp. 13 and 82 ff.
3. Max Ittenbach, *Der frühe deutsche Minnesang: Strophenfügung und Dichtersprache* (Halle, 1939), p. 190, finds that the language in this strophe is sign-like and mediary rather than immediate. If I understand him correctly, he means that the individual lines or passages say something more and other than what they seem to say.
4. Heinrich Siekhaus, "Revocatio: Studie zu einer Gestaltungsform des Minnesangs," *DVjs*, 39 (1971), 242: "Die Dame ist lediglich als Ziel [seiner Minne] gegenwärtig."

5. Hennig Brinkmann, *Friedrich von Hausen* (Bad Oeynhausen, 1948), p. 119, speaks of "die verhüllende Art des archaischen Stils."

6. Brinkmann, *Hausen*, p. 118.

7. Ittenbach, *Der frühe deutsche Minnesang*, p. 191.

8. Anton E. Schönbach, *Beiträge zur Erklärung altdeutscher Dichtwerkem* I: *Die älteren Minnesänger* (Wien, 1894), p. 49.

9. Carl von Kraus, *Des Minnesangs Frühling: Untersuchungen* (Leipzig, 1939), p. 116.

10. Does the verb "si" indicate the speaker's introvertedly reliving the dream event and his consequent lapse into the present tense? Kraus, *Untersuchungen*, p. 393, translates: "so daß ich nicht weiß wohin sie entschwunden ist."

11. Suspense of disbelief is of course an integral and important part of acquiescent reading.

12. Kolb, *Begriff der Minne*, p. 13.

13. Siekhaus, "Revocatio," 244, speaks of "diese in einer komischen Verzweiflung des Sprechers zu seiner eigenen Situation gekennzeichnete Haltung."

14. Kraus, *Untersuchungen*, p. 115.

15. The equation again between the poet as *Dichter* and the poet as *persona*.

16. Brinkmann, *Hausen*, p. 119. He refers to MF 45,19 ("Ich sage ir nu vil lange zit"—chapter V) and MF 47,9 ("Min herze und min lip diu wellent scheiden"—chapter IX).

17. Oskar Baumgarten, "Die Chronologie der Gedichte Friedrichs von Hausen," *ZfdA*, 26 (1882), 111.

18. Baumgarten, "Chronologie," 110.

19. Brinkmann, *Hausen*, p. 118.

20. See chapter I, note 20.

21. The prevailing opinion that Hausen engages but little in metaphorical language is only partly acceptable. In many instances we encounter statements in which we are hardly aware of the metaphorical values because they have been overexposed and become sunken images. In Hausen's own day, however, such statements may have been vibrant with poetic value. In the opening line of "In minem troume ich sach," for instance, the very verb has a metaphorical value, it being the mind's eye that is said to do the seeing.

22. Karl Korn, *Studien über "Freude und Truren" bei mittelhochdeutschen Dichtern: Beiträge zu einer Problemgeschichte* (Leipzig, 1932), 44, sees "fröide" as "völlig vag und vom Ich des Dichters ungeschieden als Ziel des liebenden Werbens bezeichnet." Ittenbach, *Der frühe deutsche Minnesang*, p. 192, says of the seventh line: "Diese Zeile ist aus der übrigen Dichtung Hausens als Gebärde der Sehnsucht zu verstehen und hat auch hier keinen anderen Sinn."

23. Brinkmann, *Hausen*, p. 119.

24. Günther Jungbluth, "Neue Forschungen zur mittelhochdeutschen Lyrik," *Euphorion*, 51 (1957), 200.

25. In this framework, Helmut de Boor, *Geschichte der deutschen Literatur von den Anfängen bis zur Gegenwart*, II (München, 1964), p. 257, states: "All dieses ist weder nur angelernt, *noch spielerisch verwendet;* dahinter steht das Erlebnis der Minne als eines *echten Problems*, mit dem *eine echte Auseinandersetzung* folgt" (italics added). None of the italicized items seems to be relevant with respect to "In minem troume ich sach" as read in these pages.

26. Baumgarten, "Chronologie," 109; Wechssler, *Kulturproblem*, p. 85, speaks of "poetische Fiktion."

27. Wechssler, *Kulturproblem*, pp. 85 ff.

XII. DEICH VON DER GUOTEN SCHIET

1. Max Ittenbach, *Der frühe deutsche Minnesang: Strophenfügung und Dichtersprache* (Halle, 1939), p. 191.
2. Helmut de Boor, *Geschichte der deutschen Literatur von den Anfängen bis zur Gegenwart*, II (München, 1964), p. 256.
3. Hennig Brinkmann, *Friedrich von Hausen* (Bad Oeynhausen, 1948), p. 49.
4. Hennig Brinkmann, "Der deutsche Minnesang," *Der deutsche Minnesang: Aufsätze zu seiner Erforschung*, ed. Hans Fromm (Darmstadt, 1966), p. 104.
5. Richard Lehfeld, "Über Friedrich von Hausen," *Beiträge*, 2 (1876), 397.
6. For a discussion of the function of the "hüeter," see Lilli Seibold, *Studien über die Huote* (Berlin, 1932). Brinkmann, *Hausen*, p. 124, sees "hüete" as "die hochmittelalterliche Situation der Menschen in der ritterlichen Gesellschaft," and he gives this definition a metaphorical value which comes to stand for the "human condition" then prevailing—for polite men.
7. For discussions of the *Wechsel*, see Theodor Frings, "Frauenstrophe und Frauenlied in der frühen deutschen Lyrik," *Festschrift Korff* (Leipzig, 1957), pp. 13–28, and the literature there mentioned.
8. The version in C:

> Do ich von der guoten schiet
> und ich zir niht ensprach
> als mir diu minne widerriet
> des lide ich ungemach

is more explicit than that of B, and its speaker is motivated by his love for the lady; this in possible contrast to what exactly motivates the speaker in B (see below).

9. Karl Korn, *Studien über "Freude und Truren" bei mittelhochdeutschen Dichtern: Beiträge zu einer Problemgeschichte* (Leipzig, 1932), p. 44. David G. Mowatt, *Friderich von Husen: Introduction, Text, Commentary and Glossary* (Cambridge, 1871), does not agree.
10. Hausen refers to honor only four times throughout his lyrics, and in each instance he does so in a negative way, or he refers to "ere" with respect to God. This does not mean that Hausen is but little concerned with the concept of honor. More likely, it is of consequence to him as a matter of course, so as to make it unnecessary for him to draw explicit attention to it.
11. See, however, above, note 8. Eduard Wechssler, *Das Kulturproblem des Minnesangs: Studien zur Vorgeschichte der Renaissance*, I: *Minnesang und Christentum* (Halle, 1909; repr. Osnabrück, 1966), p. 170, states: "Zwischen den Wünschen des dienenden Frauensängers und der eigentlichen Bestimmung seines Liedes klafft ein Widerspruch. Aber wenige, meist nur Dichter der Spätzeit, haben ihn klar gesehen und ohne Zögern die allein mögliche Konsequenz gezogen: ihre Persönlichkeit der Herrin zu öpfern und statt ihrer eigenen *onor* allein die der Herrin zu fördern."
12. Brinkmann, "Der deutsche Minnesang," p. 158.
13. Anton E. Schönbach, *Beiträge zur Erklärung altdeutscher Dichtwerke*, I: *Die älteren Minnesänger* (Wien, 1894), p. 49: " 'Qui confregit claustra (portas) inferni' ist ein ungemein häufiger Ausdruck, dem Nicodemusevangelium, bezw. Descensus entnommen."
14. Ittenbach, *Der frühe deutsche Minnesang*, p. 194. We could argue instead that with the lady's words being more strident than those of the man, we have indication that this is an early lyric; such strength of language on her part is in line with the "old" habit of having the woman make the more explicit statement about love.
15. Brinkmann, "Der deutsche Minnesang," p. 156. It could be suggested also that instead of the speaker's courtly waiting for the lady to acknowledge the relationship, he is merely displaying some of the egocentricity we have encountered elsewhere, together with the posture of the daunted lover.
16. Brinkmann, *Hausen*, p. 124: "Die Gewißheit, die [dem Dichter] verwehrt bleibt, wird dem Hörer zuteil."
17. Mowatt, *Husen*, p. 150 f.
18. Brinkmann, *Hausen*, p. 127.
19. Schönbach, *Beiträge*, p. 49.

20. See in this connection Arnold Becker, "Zu Friedrich von Hausen," *Germania*, 28 (1883), 272–96.
21. Schönbach, *Beiträge*, p. 43: "Die Sache ist unsterblich, nur das Wort dafür wechselt."
22. Schönbach, *Beiträge*, p. 49.
23. Karl Müllenhoff, "Zu Friedrich von Hausen," *ZfdA*, 14 (1869), 133–43.
24. Becker, "Zu Friedrich von Hausen."
25. Oskar Baumgarten, "Die Chronologie der Gedichte Friedrichs von Hausen," *ZfdA*, 26 (1882), 105–45.
26. Becker, "Zu Friedrich von Hausen," 281.
27. Baumgarten, "Die Chronologie," 111 f.
28. Mowatt, *Husen*, pp. 7 ff., presents an up to date history of this approach and the accompanying *Liederbüchleintheorie*.

XIII. MIR IST DAZ HERZE WUNT

1. Hennig Brinkmann, "Der deutsche Minnesang," *Der deutsche Minnesang: Aufsätze zu seiner Erforschung*, ed. Hans Fromm (Darmstadt, 1966), p. 127.
2. Brinkmann, "Der deutsche Minnesang," pp. 127 f.
3. This inference can be avoided only if we read the lyric Ittenbach's way, to the effect that each statement says something other than what it is saying on the obvious plane. In this case, at any rate, Ittenbach's approach seems to lose something.
4. Hennig Brinkmann, *Friedrich von Hausen* (Bad Oeynhausen, 1948), p. 66.
5. Brinkmann, *Hausen*, p. 72.
6. Brinkmann, *Hausen*, pp. 67 f.
7. Anton E. Schönbach, *Beiträge zur Erklärung altdeutscher Dichtwerke*, I: *Die älteren Minnesänger* (Wien, 1894), p. 49.
8. Oskar Baumgarten, "Die Chronologie der Lieder Friedrichs von Hausen," *ZfdA*, 26 (1882), 105–45.
9. Arnold Becker, "Zu Friedrich von Hausen," *Germania*, 28 (1883), 272–96.
10. David G. Mowatt, *Friderich von Husen: Introduction, Text, Commentary and Glossary* (Cambridge, 1971), pp. 7 ff.
11. See Becker, "Zu Friedrich von Hausen," 283, as well as those who think of multiple love affairs being celebrated in the Hausen poems.
12. Richard Lehfeld, "Über Friedrich von Hausen," *Beiträge*, 2 (1876), 345–405, gives more than forty examples showing that "dem Dienste Lon geziemt." Of these, Heinrich Götz, *Leitwörter des Minnesangs* I (Berlin, 1957), p. 128, sees a considerable number as referring to love's pains being alleviated.
13. See about such "gan" Ernst Lesser, "Das Verhältnis der Frauenmonologe in den lyrischen und epischen Dichtungen des 12. und ausgehenden 13. Jahrhunderts," *Beiträge*, 24 (1899), 365.
14. Baumgarten, "Chronologie," 143.
15. A. H. Touber, *Rhetorik und Form im deutschen Minnesang* (Groningen, 1964), p. 20.
16. Brinkmann, *Hausen*, p. 67.
17. Schönbach, *Beiträge*, p. 49.
18. Carl von Kraus, *Des Minnesangs Frühling: Untersuchungen* (Leipzig, 1939), p. 119.
19. The capitalization in *Des Minnesangs Frühling* seems once again unwarranted.
20. Becker, "Zu Friedrich von Hausen," 281.
21. August Arnold, *Studien über den Hohen Mut*, Von deutscher Poeterey, 9 (Leipzig, 1930), p. 14.
22. Götz, *Leitwörter*, p. 115.
23. Brinkmann, *Hausen*, p. 67.
24. Franz Neunteufel, "Zu Friedrichs von Hausen Metrik, Sprache und Stil," *Progr. Czernowitz* (1884), 34.

25. Mowatt, *Husen*, p. 151.
26. Hennig Brinkmann, *Entstehungsgeschichte des Minnesangs*, DVjs. Buchreihe, 8 (Halle, 1926), p. 138.
27. This is the case according to Schönbach, *Beiträge*, p. 50.
28. Brinkmann, *Hausen*, p. 68.
29. Brinkmann, *Hausen*, p. 66.
30. Mihail Isbăşescu: *Minne und Liebe: Ein Beitrag zur Begriffsdeutung und Terminologie des Minnesangs* (Stuttgart, 1940), p. 17.
31. Mowatt, *Husen*, p. 151.
32. Brinkmann, *Hausen*, p. 67.
33. Götz, *Leitwörter*, p. 174.
34. Schönbach, *Beiträge*, p. 49.

XIV. ICH SIHE WOL DAZ GOT WUNDER KAN

1. Anton E. Schönbach, *Beiträge zur Erklärung altdeutscher Dichtwerke*, I: *Die älteren Minnesänger* (Wien, 1894), p. 50.
2. Eduard Wechssler, *Das Kulturproblem des Minnesangs: Studien zu der Vorgeschichte der Renaissance*, I: *Minnesang und Christentum* (Halle, 1909, repr. Osnabrück, 1966), p. 279.
3. Helmut de Boor, *Geschichte der deutschen Literatur von den Anfängen bis zur Gegenwart*, II (München, 1964), p. 257.
4. C: "und an ir min wille müesse ergan."
5. Arnold Becker, "Zu Friedrich von Hausen," *Germania*, 28 (1883), 294.
6. This may be true no matter whether we think of "niedere," "echte," "hohe," or any other form of "Minne."
7. Compare Humphrey M. Milnes, "Über die erotische Sprache in der mittelhochdeutschen höfischen Dichtung" (Diss. Ohio State University, 1949), pp. 117 f.
8. C puts it more directly: "min frowe sehe was si *mir* tuo" (italics added).
9. Karl Müllenhoff, "Zu Friedrich von Hausen," *ZfdA*, 14 (1869), 139.
10. Carl von Kraus, *Des Minnesangs Frühling: Untersuchungen* (Leipzig, 1939), p. 394.
11. Schönbach, *Beiträge*, p. 50.
12. Olive Sayce, *Poets of the Minnesang: Edited with Introduction, Notes and Glossary* (Oxford, 1967), p. 219, reminds us that this is the first lyric attested with a refrain.
13. Hennig Brinkmann, *Friedrich von Hausen* (Bad Oeynhausen, 1948), p. 51. By one criterion Brinkmann may have been correct when he placed this lyric as the first in the Hausen sequence, though he himself does not make use of it, but arranges the lyrics to accomodate what he sees as the interrelated "plot" development between them. According to this criterion Hausen deals with love pure and simple in this poem, but in later lyrics becomes more involved in his verbal arrangements. There is, in other words, no possibility of ambiguous reading in this lyric.
14. Brinkmann, *Hausen*, p. 52.
15. De Boor, *Geschichte*, p. 258.
16. Mihail Isbăşescu, *Minne und Liebe: Ein Beitrag zur Begriffsdeutung und Terminologie des Minnesangs* (Stuttgart, 1940), p. 19.
17. Peter Schmid, "Die Entwicklung der Begriffe 'minne' und 'liebe' im deutschen Minnesang bis Walther," *ZfdPh*, 66 (1941), 150.
18. David G. Mowatt, *Friderich von Husen: Introduction, Text, Commentary and Glossary* (Cambridge, 1971), p. 152.
19. Becker, "Zu Friedrich von Hausen," 283.
20. Herbert Kolb, *Der Begriff der Minne und das Entstehen der höfischen Lyrik* (Tübingen, 1958), p. 76.

21. Oskar Baumgarten, "Die Chronologie der Gedichte Friedrichs von Hausen," *ZfdA*, 26 (1882), 111.
22. Wechssler, *Kulturproblem*, pp. 144 f.
23. Wechssler, *Kulturproblem*, p. 85.
24. Wechssler, *Kulturproblem*, p. 177.
25. Brinkmann, *Hausen*, p. 52.
26. Kraus, *Untersuchungen*, p. 119.
27. Isbăşescu, *Minne und Liebe*, p. 17.

XV. ICH LOBE GOT DER SINER GÜETE

1. Richard Lehfeld, "Über Friedrich von Hausen," *Beiträge*, 2 (1876), 401.
2. See Olive Sayce, *Poets of the Minnesang: Edited with Introduction, Notes and Glossary* (Oxford, 1967), p. 219, for further remarks on echoing rhymes in this lyric.
3. Arnold Becker, "Zu Friedrich von Hausen," *Germania*, 28 (1883), 295.
4. Franz Neunteufel, "Zu Friedrichs von Hausen Metrik, Sprache und Stil," *Progr. Czernowitz* (1884), p. 31.
5. Hennig Brinkmann, *Friedrich von Hausen* (Bad Oeynhausen, 1948), pp. 137 f.
6. Carl von Kraus, *Des Minnesangs Frühling: Untersuchungen* (Leipzig, 1939), p. 121.
7. Lilli Seibold, *Studien über die Huote*, Germanische Studien, 123 (Berlin, 1932), p. 52.
8. Mihail Isbăşescu, *Minne und Liebe: Ein Beitrag zur Begriffsdeutung und Terminologie des Minnesangs* (Stuttgart, 1940), p. 17.
9. Brinkmann, *Hausen*, p. 90.
10. Ursula Aarburg and Hennig Brinkmann, "Sinn und Klang in Hausens Lied 'Ich lobe got der siner güete,'" *WW*, 9 (1959), 141.
11. Herbert Kolb, *Der Begriff der Minne und das Entstehen der höfischen Lyrik* (Tübingen, 1958), pp. 65 f.
12. B: "noch besser ist das man ir hüete/ danne iegelich sinen willen spreche/ das si ungerne horte"; C: "noch besser ist das man ir hüete/ danne ieglicher si brehte inne/ des das si ungerne horte."
13. Aarburg and Brinkmann, "Sinn und Klang," 142.
14. Brinkmann, *Hausen*, pp. 59 f.
15. Arnold Becker, "Der mittelalterliche Minnedienst in Deutschland," *Festschrift der Oberrealschule Düren* (Leipzig, 1895; repr., Halle, 1897).
16. Compare Siegfried's bearing in the *Nibelungenlied* prior to his marriage to Kriemhild.
17. David G. Mowatt, *Friderich von Husen: Introduction, Text, Commentary and Glossary* (Cambridge, 1971), pp. 27 f.
18. Brinkmann, *Hausen*, p. 5.
19. Hermann Paul, "Kritische Beiträge zu den Minnesingern," *Beiträge*, 2 (1876), 424.
20. Anton E. Schönbach, *Beiträge zur Erklärung altdeutscher Dichtwerke*, I: *Die älteren Minnesänger* (Wein, 1894), p. 50.
21. Karl Müllenhoff, "Zu Friedrich von Hausen," *ZfdA*, 14 (1869), 139.
22. Let it be noted that according to Mowatt the use of "ungerne" is a matter of tongue-in-cheek, whereas with the other commentators who wish to retain "ungerne" it is taken seriously.
23. Humphrey M. Milnes, "Über die erotische Sprache in der mittelhochdeutschen höfischen Dichtung" (Diss. Ohio State University, 1949), p. 127.
24. C: "Ich han si erkorn swas ich lide."
25. Brinkmann emends C this way: "*Si* lasse ich niht durch die merkaere" (italics added).
26. Schönbach, *Beiträge*, p. 50.
27. Isbăşescu, *Minne und Liebe*, p. 19.
28. Brinkmann, *Hausen*, p. 60.

29. Mowatt, *Husen*, pp. 152 f.
30. Becker, "Zu Friedrich von Hausen," 278.
31. Schönbach, *Beiträge*, pp. 50 f.
32. August Arnold, *Studien über den Hohen Mut*, Von deutscher Poeterey, 9 (Leipzig, 1930), p. 12.
33. Max Hermann Jellinek, "Zu Minnesangs Frühling," *ZfdA*, 55 (1917), 372.
34. Kraus, *Untersuchungen*, p. 120.
35. Brinkmann, *Hausen*, p. 96.
36. Karl Korn, *Studien über "Freude und Truren" bei mittelhochdeutschen Dichtern: Beiträge zu einer Problemgeschichte* (Leipzig, 1932), p. 44.
37. This line is the manuscript reading; it seems more acceptable than Kraus' emendation.
38. The closing lines of C:

>gewendet haben das si diu guote
>enpfremde mir ir stete minne
>deswar tuon ich in niht mere
>ich gefreische doch gerne alle ir unere

39. Schönbach, *Beiträge*, p. 51.
40. Mowatt, *Husen*, p. 148.
41. The closing statement reads like a *revocatio* in Siekhaus' sense of the term; see Heinrich Siekhaus, "Revocatio: Studie zu einer Gestaltungsform des Minnesangs," *DVjs*, 39 (1971), 237-51.
42. Isbăşescu, *Minne und Liebe*, p. 19, speaks of "ethisch vollwertige hohe Minne."
43. The use of this term is interesting; it is a contrast rather than a parallel to the occurrence of "sinne" in the second line. In view of the dire consequences for the guardians if the speaker's wish regarding their "unere" were fulfilled, and of the fact that his "sinne" are God-hallowed, the "sinne" of the guardians are anything but hallowed (from the speaker's point of view). Indeed, is he hinting that the guardians' activity is of the devil? See in this connection the discussion of the closing lines of the first strophe of "Deich von der guoten schiet" (chapter XII, p. 85). See also, however, the closing paragraphs of the present discussion.

XVI. SICH MÖHTE WISER MAN VERWÜETEN

1. David G. Mowatt, *Friderich von Husen: Introduction, Text, Commentary and Glossary* (Cambridge, 1971), p. 153.
2. Friedrich Neumann, "Hohe Minne," *ZfDk*, 39 (1925), 81-91.
3. Richard Lehfeld, "Über Friedrich von Hausen," *Beiträge*, 2 (1876), 401.
4. Hennig Brinkmann, *Friedrich von Hausen* (Bad Oeynhausen, 1948), p. 69.
5. Heinrich Siekhaus, "Revocatio: Studie zu einer Gestaltungsform des Minnesangs," *DVjs*, 39 (1971), 245.
6. Anton E. Schönbach, *Beiträge zur Erklärung altdeutscher Dichtwerke*, I:*Die älteren Minnesänger* (Wien, 1894), p. 51.
7. Brinkmann, *Hausen*, p. 70.
8. Helmut de Boor, *Geschichte der deutschen Literatur von den Anfängen bis zur Gegenwart*, II (München, 1964), p. 257.
9. Walter Fischer, *Liedsang aus deutscher Frühe: Mittelhochdeutsche Dichtung übertragen und herausgegeben* (Stuttgart, 1939), p. 3.
10. Brinkmann means "Ich sihe wol daz got wunder kan" (chapter XIV) and "Ich lobe got der siner güete" (chapter XV).
11. Brinkmann, *Hausen*, p. 70. This statement about "den inneren Wert" would nullify the notion, dealt with elsewhere, that medieval literature has little or no appreciation for such inner values in the face

of society's opposition. Then, too, the speaker does *not* relate his suffering to God, but to the lady, and that quite unmistakably and emphatically (see below).

12. Mihail Isbăşescu, *Minne und Liebe: Ein Beitrag zur Begriffsdeutung und Terminologie des Minnesangs* (Stuttgart, 1940), p. 18.

13. Karl Korn, *Studien über "Freude und Truren" bei mittelhochdeutschen Dichtern: Beiträge zu einer Problemgeschichte* (Leipzig, 1932), p. 43.

14. Schönbach, *Beiträge*, p. 51.

15. Brinkmann, *Hausen*, p. 70.

16. Cf. Mowatt, *Husen*, p. 148.

17. Of course, the view here expounded necessitates a strict separation which the critics have disregarded consistently, as many citations show, that of the poet as *persona* from the poet as *Dichter*.

18. Friedrich Neumann, "Hohe Minne," *ZfDk*, 39 (1925), 81–91.

19. There is a link here with MF 48,3:

> Min herze den gelouben hat
> solt ich oder iemer man beliben sin
> durch liebe oder der minne rat
> so ware ich noch alumbe den Rin.

For that matter, it would be very easy to place a direct connection between the present lyric and, say, "Min herze und min lip diu wellent scheiden" (as evaluated in chapter IX).

20. Mowatt, *Husen*, p. 154, speaks of the speaker's will as pervading, and hence presumably determining the mood of, the second strophe. As the suggestions below show, Mowatt's suggestion is applicable to the entire lyric.

21. This motif is treated from the opposite point of view in "Si darf mich des zihen niet" (chapter VIII), where the speaker comes to the conclusion that he will hence serve "dem der lonen kan."

22. Thus seen, God's role is similar to that of the mind-speaker in "Min herze und min lip diu wellent scheiden" (chapter IX).

23. Brinkmann, *Hausen*, p. 88.

24. Brinkmann, *Hausen*, p. 88, and others critics with him, sees the lady's goodness as a reflection of God's.

25. Brinkmann, *Hausen*, p. 70.

26. It does evoke the concept of *staete*, of course, but this is not necessarily to be interpreted as a praiseworthy feature in the present reading, since this *staete* violates values of a different magnitude, those dealing with matters of the soul's welfare.

27. Andreas Capellanus, *The Art of Courtly Love*, ed. F. W. Locke (New York, 1969), and Felix Schlösser, *Andreas Capellanus: Seine Minnelehre und das christliche Weltbild des 12. Jahrhunderts* (Bonn, 1960), served as background material.

28. Mowatt, *Husen*, p. 154.

29. Brinkmann, *Hausen*, p. 69.

30. Arnold Becker, "Zu Friedrich von Hausen," *Germania*, 28 (1883), 279.

31. Mowatt, *Husen*, p. 9: "The medieval poets do not even appear to have separate words for 'stanza' and 'poem.'"

32. Compare this with "friunde rat" (3) in "An der genade al min fröide stat" (chapter III). In either case, of course, such help, or lack of it, is part of purely poetic fiction.

33. Becker, "Zu Friedrich von Hausen," 279.

34. Schönbach, *Beiträge*, p. 51.

35. Hugo Kuhn, "Minnesang and the Form of Performance," *Formal Aspects of Medieval German Poetry: A Symposium*, ed. Stanley N. Werbow (Austin, Texas, 1969), p. 39. Obviously the reverse may occur also; Kuhn's explication goes the mystical way, whereas we argue, on quite different grounds, in terms of reason being suspended. Kuhn's is the more generally accepted approach. Witness, for example, Wechssler, *Kulturproblem*, p. 268, who, to be sure, starts with a little concession: "Nur wenige Motive sind an sich spezifisch mystisch. Bestimmt kann man das nur von den Vorstellungen des Entrücktsein und der Verzückung behaupten.... In der Verbindung mit den echt mystischen Motiven wurden auch die andern

ins Mystische transponiert." All the critics seem to share Wechssler's view that mystical influences affect the portrayal of love in *Minnesang*. It seems mandatory to argue that the transposition in this particular lyric (as well as in some of those discussed in the previous chapters) goes into the opposite direction, as suggested above.

36. Kuhn, "Minnesang and the Form of Performance," pp. 26 ff.
37. Brinkmann, *Hausen*, p. 71.
38. Brinkmann, *Hausen*, p. 71.
39. It would be somewhat disconcerting at this moment to remember an opinion pronounced by Wechssler, *Kulturproblem*, p. 54, to the effect that "keine Furcht vor Tod und Teufel, kein Bangen vor jüngstem Gericht und Höllenstrafen, kein memento mori" could subdue the *joie de vivre* of the *Minnesänger*. See, however, note 41 below.
40. We cite Barbara Könneker, *Wesen und Wandlung der Narrenidee im Zeitalter des Humanismus* (Wiesbaden, 1966), p. 18, though at first glance the title of her book seems hardly germane to the discussion at hand: "Ein *tumber*... so hieß... ein Mensch, der aus Unkenntnis oder bösem Willen gegen die Regeln der Gesellschaft verstieß, wie einer, der den Geboten Gottes zuwiderhandelte...."
41. This is not to say that the two views are incompatible. Such compatibility opens the door to yet another level of reading, that of humorous treatment. This, in turn, raises questions regarding Hausen's stand in religious matters now that he sees fit to depict the soul's possible damnation for the sake of entertainment by means of poetry.
42. Siekhaus, "Revocatio," passim.
43. Cf. Mowatt, *Husen*, p. 47: "In practice, an interpretation can have validity on two levels.... Progress towards greater completeness can only come if partial views are allowed to co-exist, of course on the understanding that they are internally consistent."
44. Wechssler, *Kulturproblem*, p. 156.
45. Hellmuth Langenbucher, "Idealismus und Realismus im deutschen Minnesang," *ZfdB*, 6 (1930), 442.
46. Brinkmann, *Hausen*, p. 1.
47. For instance, praise of God as well as (barely covered) criticism of God as found in "so hat got wol ze mir getan" (see above).

XVII. ICH DENKE UNDER WILEN

1. Hellmuth Langenbucher, *Das Gesicht des deutschen Minnesangs und seine Wandlungen* (Heidelberg, 1930), p. 28.
2. Friedrich-Wilhelm Wentzlaff-Eggebert, *Kreuzzugsdichtung des Mittelalters: Studie zu ihrer geschichtlichen und dichterischen Wirklichkeit* (Berlin, 1960), p. 180.
3. Hennig Brinkmann, *Friedrich von Hausen* (Bad Oeynhausen, 1948), p. 42.
4. Anton E. Schönbach, *Beiträge zur Erklärung altdeutscher Dichtwerke*, I: *Die älteren Minnesänger* (Wien, 1894), p. 51, without embroidering on the matter, has an eye for a little realistic detail in this ephemeral environment: "Der Dichter wird die Meilenzahl der Tagereisen gekannt haben."
5. Brinkmann, *Hausen*, pp. 7 f.
6. Langenbucher, *Gesicht*, p. 28.
7. Karl Korn, *Studien über "Freude und Truren" bei mittelhochdeutschen Dichtern: Beiträge zu einer Problemgeschichte* (Leipzig, 1932), p. 43.
8. Wentzlaff-Eggebert, *Kreuzzugsdichtung*, p. 180.
9. How else can we see it but "dichterisch"?
10. Wentzlaff-Eggebert, *Kreuzzugsdichtung*, p. 180. He seems to be saying that "Ich denke under wilen" is simply a love poem.

11. Wentzlaff-Eggebert, *Kreuzzugsdichtung*, p. 180.
12. Langenbucher, *Gesicht*, p. 27.
13. Brinkmann, *Hausen*, p. 36.
14. Brinkmann, *Hausen*, p. 80.
15. Eduard Wechssler, *Das Kulturproblem des Minnesangs: Studien zur Vorgeschichte der Renaissance*, I: *Minnesang und Christentum* (Halle, 1909; repr. Osnabrück, 1966), p. 215.
16. Arnold Becker, "Zu Friedrich von Hausen," *Germania*, 28 (1883), 281.
17. Peter Schmid, "Die Entwicklung der Begriffe 'minne' und 'liebe' im deutschen Minnesang bis Walther," *ZfdPh*, 66 (1941), 150.
18. Humphrey M. Milnes, "Über die erotische Sprache in der mittelhochdeutschen höfischen Dichtung" (Diss. Ohio State University, 1949), pp. 116 ff.
19. Korn, *Studien*, p. 43.
20. It is of course no more than a would-be relationship.
21. Hennig Brinkmann, "Dietmar von Eist und Friedrich von Hausen: Minnelieder," in *Gedicht und Gedanke: Auslegungen deutscher Gedichte*, ed. Heinz Otto Burger (Halle, 1942), p. 37.
22. This is not to prevent the view of medieval society as exercising "den Willen zur Freude"—see Brinkmann, "Dietmar von Eist und Friedrich von Hausen," 37.
23. Brinkmann, "Dietmar von Eist und Friedrich von Hausen," p. 37.
24. C: "es sint grossiu wunder."
25. C: "ich wünsche in kurzen stunden/ das niemer man gewinne/ kumber der also nahe ge."
26. Brinkmann, "Dietmar von Eist und Friedrich von Hausen," p. 37.
27. This line is missing in B.
28. Brinkmann, "Dietmar von Eist und Friedrich von Hausen," p. 37.
29. Mowatt, *Husen*, p. 156.
30. Brinkmann, "Dietmar von Eist und Friedrich von Hausen," p. 38.
31. Korn, *Studien*, p. 44.
32. Korn, *Studien*, p. 44.
33. Korn, *Studien*, p. 45.

BIBLIOGRAPHY

A. Materials Cited

Aarburg, Ursula and Brinkmann, Hennig. "Sinn und Klang in Hausens Lied 'Ich lobe got der siner güete.'" *WW*, 9 (1959), 139–47.

Adolf, Helen. "Theological and Feudal Background of Wolfram's *zwivel.*" *JEGP*, 49 (1950), 285–303.

Arnold, August. *Studien über den Hohen Mut*. Von deutscher Poeterey, 9. Leipzig, 1930.

Bartsch, Karl. "Nachahmung provenzalischer Poesie im Deutschen." *Germania*, 1 (1856), 480–82.

Baumgarten, Oskar. "Die Chronologie der Gedichte Friedrichs von Hausen." *ZfdA*, 26 (1882), 105–45.

Becker, Arnold. "Zu Friedrich von Hausen." *Germania*, 28 (1883), 272–96.

———. "Der mittelalterliche Minnedienst in Deutschland." In *Festschrift der Oberrealschule Düren*. Leipzig, 1895; rpt. Halle, 1897, 31–70.

Bekker, Hugo. *The Nibelungenlied: A Literary Analysis*. Toronto, 1971.

Boor, Helmut de, and Newald, Richard. *Geschichte der deutschen Literatur von den Anfängen bis zur Gegenwart*, II. München, 1964.

Boor, Helmut de. "Zu Hausens Kreuzzugslied 47,9." *Beiträge*, 87, (Tübingen, 1965), 390–93.

Brachmann, Friedrich. "Zu den Minnesängern." *Germania*, 31 (1886), 443–86.

Braun, Werner Friedrich. "Hausens MF 42,1–27 und Veldekes *Eneit*." *ZfdA*, 93 (1964), 209–14.

Brinkmann, Hennig. *Entstehungsgeschichte des Minnesangs*. DVjs Buchreihe, 8. Halle, 1926.

———. "Dietmar von Eist und Friedrich von Hausen: Minnelieder." In *Gedicht und Gedanke: Auslegungen deutscher Gedichte*. Ed. Heinz Otto Burger. Halle, 1942, pp. 29–42. Also in H. B. *Studien zur Geschichte der deutschen Sprache und Literatur*, II, 151–62. Düsseldorf, 1966.

———. *Friedrich von Hausen*. Bad Oeynhausen, 1948.

———. "Der deutsche Minnesang." In *Der deutsche Minnesang: Aufsätze zu seiner Erforschung*. Ed. Hans Fromm. Wege der Forschung, 15. Darmstadt, 1966, pp. 85–166.

Capellanus, Andreas. *The Art of Courtly Love*. Ed. F. W. Locke. New York, 1969.

Colleville, Maurice. *Les chansons allemandes de croisade en moyen haut-allemand*. Paris, 1936.

Curtius, Ernst Robert. *Europäische Literatur und lateinisches Mittelalter*. Bern, 1954.

Ehrismann, Gustav. "Die älteren Minnesänger." *ZfdPh*, 33 (1901), 393–406.

———. *Geschichte der deutschen Literatur bis zum Ausgang des Mittelalters*. II: *Die mittelhochdeutsche Literatur*. Schlußband. München, 1935.

———. "Die Grundlagen des ritterlichen Tugendsystems." *ZfdA*, 56 (1919), 137–216.

Fischer, Heinz. "Die Frauenmonologe der deutschen höfischen Lyrik." Diss. Marburg, 1934.

Fischer, Walter. *Liedsang aus deutscher Frühe: Mittelhochdeutsche Dichtung übertragen und herausgegeben.* Stuttgart, 1939.

Frank, Istvàn. *Trouvères et Minnesänger: Recueil de textes pour servir à l'étude des rapports entre la poésie lyrique romane et le Minnesang au XIIe siècle.* Saarbrücken, 1952.

Frings, Theodor. "Erforschung des Minnesangs." *FuF*, 26 (1950), 9–16, 39–43. Exp. ed. in *Beiträge*, 87 (Halle, 1965), 1–39.

――――. "Frauenstrophe und Frauenlied in der frühen deutschen Lyrik." In *Festschrift Korff.* Leipzig, 1957, pp. 13–28.

Götz, Heinrich. *Leitwörter des Minnesangs.* Abhandlungen der sächsischen Akademie der Wissenschaften zu Leipzig, philosophisch-historische Klasse, vol. 49, 1. Berlin, 1957.

Heitner, Robert (ed.). *Deutsche dreistimmige Lieder nach Art der Neapolitanen.* Publikation älterer praktischer und theoretischer Musikwerke der Gesellschaft für Musikforschung, vol. 5. München, 1895.

Ipsen, Ingeborg. "Strophe und Lied im frühen Minnesang." *Beiträge*, 57 (1933), 301–413.

Isbǎşescu, Mihail. *Minne und Liebe: Ein Beitrag zur Begriffsdeutung und Terminologie des Minnesangs.* Tübinger germanistische Arbeiten, 27. Stuttgart, 1940.

Ittenbach, Max. *Der frühe deutsche Minnesang: Strophenfügung und Dichtersprache.* DVjs Buchreihe, 24. Halle, 1939.

Jellinek, Max Hermann. "Zu Minnesangs Frühling." *ZfdA*, 55 (1917), 372–77.

Jungbluth, Günther. "*Min herze und min lip diu wellent scheiden:* Zu Friedrich von Hausen, 47,9." *Euphorion*, 47 (1953), 241–59.

――――. "Neue Forschungen zur mittelhochdeutschen Lyrik." *Euphorion*, 51 (1957), 192–221.

Kienast, Richard. "Hausens *scheltliet* (MF 47,33) und der *sumer von triere.*" *Sitzungsberichte der deutschen Akademie der Wissenschaften zu Berlin; Klasse für Sprache, Literatur und Kunst.* Berlin, 1961.

Kolb, Herbert. *Der Begriff der Minne und das Entstehen der höfischen Lyrik.* Hermaea, NS, 4. Tübingen, 1958.

Könneker, Barbara. *Wesen und Wandlung der Narrenidee im Zeitalter des Humanismus.* Wiesbaden, 1966.

Korn, Karl. *Studien über "Freude und Truren" bei mittelhochdeutschen Dichtern: Beiträge zu einer Problemgeschichte.* Von deutscher Poeterey, 12. Leipzig, 1932.

Kraus, Carl von. *Des Minnesangs Frühling: Untersuchungen.* Leipzig, 1939.

――――. *Des Minnesangs Frühling.* Leipzig, 1959.

Kuhn, Hugo. "Zur Deutung der künstlerischen Form des Mittelalters." *SG*, 2 (1949), 114–21. Also in H. K. *Dichtung und Welt im Mittelalter.* Stuttgart 1959, pp. 1–14. As "Zur inneren Form des Minnesangs" in *Der deutsche Minnesang: Aufsätze zu seiner Erforschung.* Ed. Hans Fromm. Wege der Forschung, 15. Darmstadt, 1966, pp. 167–79.

———. "Dichtungswissenschaft und Soziologie." *SG*, 3 (1950), 622–26.

———. "Soziale Realität und dichterische Fiktion am Beispiel der höfischen Ritterdichtung Deutschlands." In *Soziologie und Leben*. Ed. Carl Brinkmann. Tübingen, 1952, pp. 195–219. Also in H. K. *Dichtung und Welt im Mittelalter*. Stuttgart, 1959, pp. 22–40.

———. "Minnesang and the Form of Performance." *Formal Aspects of Medieval German Poetry*. Ed. Stanley N. Werbow. Austin, Texas, 1969.

Langenbucher, Hellmuth. *Das Gesicht des deutschen Minnesangs und seine Wandlungen*. Heidelberg, 1930.

———. "Idealismus und Realismus im deutschen Minnesang." *ZfdB*, 6 (1930), 441–49.

Lehfeld, Richard. "Über Friedrich von Hausen." *Beiträge*, 2 (1876), 345–405.

Lesser, Ernst. "Das Verhältnis der Frauenmonologe in den lyrischen und epischen Dichtungen des 12. und ausgehenden 13. Jahrhunderts." *Beiträge*, 24 (1899), 361–83.

Ludwig, Otto. "Zum Text von MF 45,19 f." *ZfdA*, 93 (1964), 65 f.

Maurer, Friedrich. "Zu den Liedern Friedrichs von Hausen." *NM*, 53 (1952), 149–70. Also in F. M. *Dichtung und Sprache des Mittelalters: Gesammelte Aufsätze*. Bibliotheca Germanica, 10. Bern/München, 1963, pp. 80–94.

Milnes, Humphrey M. "Über die erotische Sprache in der mittelhochdeutschen höfischen Dichtung." Diss. Ohio State University, 1949.

Mohr, Wolfgang. "Minnesang als Gesellschaftskunst." *DU*, 6 (1954), 83–107. Also in *Der deutsche Minnesang: Aufsätze zu seiner Erforschung*. Ed. Hans Fromm. Wege zur Forschung, 15. Darmstadt, 1966, pp. 197–228.

Mowatt, David G. *Friderich von Husen: Introduction, Text, Commentary and Glossary*. Cambridge, 1971.

Müllenhoff, Karl. "Zu Friedrich von Hausen." *ZfdA*, 14 (1869), 133–43.

Naumann, Eduard. "Der Streit um 'das ritterliche Tugendsystem.' " In *Festgabe Helm: Erbe der Vergangenheit*. Tübingen, 1951, pp. 137–53.

Neumann, Friedrich. "Hohe Minne." *ZfDk*, 39 (1925), 81–91.

———. "Rezension zu Kraus, *Des Minnesangs Frühling: Untersuchungen*." *GGA*, 206 (1944), 12–45.

Neunteufel, Franz. "Zu Friedrichs von Hausen Metrik, Sprache und Stil." In *Progr. Czernowitz* (1884).

Panzer, Friedrich. *Das Nibelungenlied: Entstehung und Gestalt*. Stuttgart, 1955.

Paul, Hermann. "Kritische Beiträge zu den Minnesingern." *Beiträge*, 2 (1876), 406–560.

Sanders, Willy. *Glück: Zur Herkunft und Bedeutungsentwicklung eines mittelalterlichen Schicksalsbegriffs*. Niederdeutsche Studien, 13. Köln/Graz, 1965.

Sayce, Olive. *Poets of the Minnesang: Edited with Introduction, Notes and Glossary*. Oxford, 1967.

Scherer, Wilhelm. *Geschichte der deutschen Literatur*. Berlin, 1929.

Schlösser, Felix. *Andreas Capellanus: Seine Minnelehre und das christliche Weltbild des 12. Jahrhunderts*. Abhandlungen zur Kunst-, Musik- und Literaturwissenschaft, 15. Bonn, 1960.

Schmid, Peter. "Die Entwicklung der Begriffe 'minne' und 'liebe' im deutschen Minnesang bis Walther." *ZfdPh*, 66 (1941), 137–63.
Schönbach, Anton, E. *Beiträge zur Erklärung altdeutscher Dichtwerke, I: Die älteren Minnesänger.* Sitzungsberichte der kaiserlichen Akademie der Wissenschaften in Wien, philosophische-historische Klasse, 141. Wien, 1894.
Schröder, Franz Rolf. "Zu Friedrich von Hausen, 42,1." *GRM*, 42 (1961), 330 f.
Schulz, Paul. "Die erotischen Motive in der deutschen Dichtungen des 12. und 13. Jahrhunderts." Diss. Greifswald, 1907.
Seeberg, Reinhold. *Lehrbuch der Dogmengeschichte, III: Die Dogmengeschichte des Mittelalters.* Leipzig, 1930.
Seibold, Lilli. *Studien über die Huote.* Germanische Studien, 123. Berlin, 1932.
Siekhaus, Heinrich. "Revocatio: Studie zu einer Gestaltungsform des Minnesangs." *DVjs*, 39 (1971), 237–51.
Singer, Samuel. "Studien zu den Minnesängern." *Beiträge*, 44 (1920), 426–73.
Spanke, Hans. "Romanische und mittellateinische Formen in der Metrik von Minnesangs Frühling." *ZfdPh*, 49 (1929), 190–235. Also in *Der deutsche Minnesang: Aufsätze zu seiner Forschung.* Ed. Hans Fromm. Wege der Forschung, 15. Darmstadt, 1966, pp. 255–329.
Sperber, Hans. "Der 'Sumer von Triere' (MF 47,36)." *Monatshefte*, 45 (1953), 1–22.
Thornton, Thomas Perry. "Love, Uncertainty and Despair: The Use of 'zwivel' by the Minnesänger." *JEGP*, 60 (1961), 213–27.
Touber, A. H., *Rhetorik und Form im deutschen Minnesang.* Groningen, 1964.
Vogt, Friedrich. *Des Minnesangs Frühling.* Leipzig, 1920.
Vollmer, Vera. "Die Begriffe der Triuwe und der Staete in der höfischen Minnedichtung." Diss. Tübingen, 1914.
Wechssler, Eduard. *Das Kulturproblem des Minnesangs: Studien zur Vorgeschichte der Renaissance.* I: *Minnesang und Christentum.* Halle, 1909; repr. Osnabrück, 1966.
Wentzlaff-Eggebert, Friedrich-Wilhelm. *Kreuzzugsdichtung des Mittelalters: Studie zu ihrer geschichtlichen und dichterischen Wirklichkeit.* Berlin, 1960.
Werbow, Stanley N., ed. *Formal Aspects of Medieval German Poetry.* Austin, Texas, 1969.

B. Materials Consulted

Ackermann, Friedrich. "Zum Verhältnis von Wort und Weise im Minnesang." *WW*, 9 (1959), 300–11. Also in *WW*, Sammelband 4 (1962), 177–88.
Allen, Philip S. "The Origins of German Minnesang." *MP*, 3 (1905), 411–44.
Amoretti, Giovanni V. *Il Minnesang.* Milano, 1949.
Arens, Hans. *Frühe deutsche Lyrik: ausgewählt und erläutert; mit einer Einleitung von Arthur Hübner.* Berlin, 1935.
Armknecht, Werner. *Geschichte des Wortes "süß" I: Bis zum Ausgang des Mittelalters.* Germ. Studien, 171. Berlin, 1936.
Baecker, Linde. "Herze und Lip in Friedrich von Hausens Gedicht MF 47,9." *Festschrift Wagner.* Gießen, 1960, pp. 34–37.

Bartsch, Karl. "Der Strophenbau in der deutschen Lyrik." *Germania*. 2 (1857), 257–98.

———. *Deutsche Liederdichter des zwölften bis vierzehnten Jahrhunderts: Eine Auswahl.* Leipzig, 1893.

Becker, Reinhold. *Der altheimische Minnesang*. Halle, 1882.

Behagel, Otto. "Zur Technik der mittelhochdeutschen Dichtung." *Beiträge*, 30 (1905), 431–564.

Benezé, Emil. *Das Traummotiv in der mittelhochdeutschen Dichtung bis 1250 und in alten deutschen Volksliedern.* In *Sagen- und literarhistorische Untersuchungen*, I. Halle, 1897.

Betz, Werner. "Andreas Capellanus und der Minnesang." In *Festschrift Kunisch*. Berlin, 1961, pp. 16–19.

Boor, Helmut de, "Friedrich von Hausen: *Min herze und min lip*. . . ." In *Die deutsche Lyrik: Form und Geschichte; Interpretationen.* Ed. Benno von Wiese. Düsseldorf, 1946, pp. 35–42.

Brinkmann, Hennig. "Zur geistesgeschichtlichen Stellung des deutschen Minnesangs." *DVjs*, 3 (1925), 615–41.

———. *Geschichte der lateinischen Liebesdichtung im Mittelalter*. Halle, 1925.

———. "Erscheinung und Entfaltung des deutschen Minnesangs." *ZfDk*, 50 (1936), 503–19.

Brodführer, Richard. "Untersuchung über die Entwicklung des Begriffes "guote" in Verbindung mit Personenbezeichnungen im Minnesang." Diss. Leipzig/Halle, 1917.

Bumke, Joachim. *Studien zum Ritterbegriff im 12. und 13. Jahrhundert.* Supplements to *Euphorion*, 1. Heidelberg, 1964.

Burdach, Konrad. "Das volkstümliche deutsche Liebeslied." *ZfdA*, 27 (1883), 343–67. Also in K. B., *Reinmar der Alte und Walther von der Vogelweide*. Halle, 1928, pp. 243–62.

———. "Über den Ursprung des mittellateinischen Minnesangs, Liebesromans und Frauendienstes." *Sitzungsberichte der Berliner Akademie der Wissenschaften, philosophisch-historische Klasse.* Berlin, 1918, 994–1029, 1072–1098.

Closs, August. "Minnesang and its Spiritual Background." In A. C. *Medusa's Mirror: Studies in German Literature.* London, 1957, pp. 43–56.

Closs, Hannah M. N. "Courtly Love in Literature and Art: An Enquiry into its Deeper Significance and the Secret Heresy of the Middle Ages." *Symposium*, 1 (1946/47), 3, 5–19.

Denomy, Alexandre Joseph. *The Heresy of Courtly Love: Boston College Candlemas Lectures on Christian Literature.* New York, 1947. Also, translated in: *Der provenzalische Minnesang: Ein Querschnitt durch die neuere Forschungsdiskussion.* Ed. Rudolf Baehr. Wege der Forschung, 6. Darmstadt, 1967, pp. 362–84.

Eis, Gerhard. *Mittelhochdeutsche Lieder und Sprüche.* Germanistische Bücherei, 2. München, 1949.

Ertzdorff, Xenja von. "Das Ich in der höfischen Liebeslyrik des 12. Jahrhunderts." *Archiv*, 197 (1961), 1–13.

Falke, Jacob. *Die ritterliche Gesellschaft im Zeitalter des Frauenkultus*. Deutsche Nationalbibliothek, 2. Berlin, n. d.
Fourquet, Jean. "Thèses sur le Minnesang." *EG*, 9 (1954), 1–15.
Frings, Theodor. "Die Anfänge der europäischen Liebesdichtung im 11. und 12. Jahrhundert." *Sitzungsberichte der Bayerischen Akademie der Wissenschaften, philosophisch-historische Klasse*. München, 1960.
———. "Minnesänger und Troubadours." *Vorträge und Schriften der deutschen Akademie der Wissenschaften zu Berlin*, 35. Berlin, 1949. Also in *Der deutsche Minnesang: Aufsätze zu seiner Erforschung*. Ed. Hans Fromm. Wege der Forschung, 15. Darmstadt, 1966, pp. 1–37.
Gennrich, Friedrich. "Das Formproblem des Minnesangs: Ein Beitrag zur Erforschung des Strophenbaus der mittelalterlichen Lyrik." *DVjs*, 9 (1931), 285–349.
———. "Die musikalischen Formen des mittelalterlichen Liedes." *DU*, 11 (1959), 60–80.
Halbach, Kurt Herbert. *Walther von der Vogelweide und die Dichter von Minnesangs Frühling*. Tübinger germanistische Arbeiten, 3. Stuttgart, 1927.
———. "Geschichte der altdeutschen Literatur: Minnesang und klassische staufische Lyrik. Literaturbericht," *ZfdB*, 7 (1931), 534–40.
———. "Formbeobachtungen an staufischer Lyrik." *ZfdPh*, 60 (1935), 11–22.
Hatto, Arthur Thomas. "Gallantry in the Medieval German Lyric." *MLR*, 36 (1941), 480–87.
Heinisch, Klaus, J. "Antike Bildungselemente im frühen deutschen Minnesang." Diss. Bonn, 1934.
Kienast, Richard. "Die deutschsprachige Lyrik des Mittelalters." In *Deutsche Philologie im Aufriß*, II, 1–132. Ed. Wolfgang Stammler. Berlin, 1960.
Kluckhohn, Paul. "Der Minnesang als Standesdichtung." *Archiv für Kulturgeschichte*, 11 (1914), 389–410. Also in *Deutscher Minnesang: Aufsätze zu seiner Erforschung*. Ed. Hans Fromm. Wege der Forschung, 15. Darmstadt, 1966, pp. 58–84.
Koch, Hansjörg. "Zu den Minnesängern." *Beiträge*, 58 (1934), 241–56.
Köhler, Erika. *Liebeskrieg: Zur Bildersprache der höfischen Dichtung des Mittelalters*. Tübinger germanistische Arbeiten, 21. Stuttgart, 1935.
Kück, Eduard. "Der 'Sommer von Trier': Zu einer unerklärten Stelle Friedrichs von Hausen: MF 47,38." *AfdA*, 28 (1902), 294 f.
Kuhn, Hugo. "Die Klassik des Rittertums in der Stauferzeit." In *Annalen der deutschen Literatur*. Ed. Heinz Otto Burger. Stuttgart, 1952, pp. 89 ff.
Lucae, K. "Noch einmal MF 38,13 ff." *ZfdA*, 27 (1883), 88–90.
Ludwig, Erika. *Wip und frouwe: Geschichte der Worte und Begriffe in der Lyrik des 12. und 13. Jahrhunderts*. Tübinger germanistische Arbeiten, 24. Stuttgart/Berlin, 1937.
Ludwig, Otto. "Die Rolle des Sprechers in MF 47,9." *ZfdA*, 93 (1964), 65 f.
Maurer, Friedrich. "Neue Literatur zum Minnesang." *DU*, 5 (1953), 94–98; 6 (1954), 113 f.
——— "Der Topos von den Minnesklaven: Zur Geschichte einer thematischen Gemeinschaft zwischen bildender Kunst und Dichtung im Mittelalter." *DVjs*, 27 (1953), 182–206.

Mergell, Erika. "Die Frauenrede im deutschen Minnesang." Diss. Frankfurt, 1940.
Milnes, Humphrey M. "The Minnesinger and the Court." *GLL*, 21 (1968), 279–89.
Mohr, Wolfgang. "Vortragsform und Form als Symbol im mittelalterlichen Lied." In *Festschrift Pretzel*. Berlin, 1963, pp. 128–38.
Moret, André. "Le problème des origines du Minnesang." *EG*, 2 (1947), 22–41.
——— . *Anthologie du Minnesang: Textes avec introduction, notes et glossaire*. Paris, 1949.
——— . "Qu'est-ce que la Minne? Contribution à l'étude de la terminologie et de la mentalité courtoise." *EG*, 4 (1949), 1–12.
——— . *Les débuts du lyrisme en Allemagne des origines à 1350*. Lille, 1951.
Mowatt, David G. "A Critical Examination of the Various Methods of Interpreting Minnesang, with Special Reference to Friedrich von Hausen, together with a Complete Word Index of his Poems." Diss. King's College, London, 1962–63.
Müller, Günther. "Studien zum Formproblem des Minnesangs." *DVjs*, 1 (1923), 61–103.
——— . "Ergebnisse und Aufgaben der Minnesangforschung." *DVjs*, 5 (1927), 106–29.
Northcott, Kenneth J. " 'Tougen Minne' in the Genesis." *MLN*, 74 (1959), 151–53.
Patzig, H. "Zu Friedrich von Hausen." *ZfdA*, 65 (1928), 142–44.
Pfaff, Friedrich. *Der Minnesang des 12. bis 14. Jahrhunderts, Abt. I: Einleitung. Auswahl*. In *Deutsche National-Literatur* 8. Stuttgart, 1892.
Plenio, Kurt. "Bausteine zur altdeutschen Strophik." *Beiträge*, 42 (1916–17), 411–502; 43 (1917–18), 556–99.
Rieckenberg, Hans Jürgen. "Leben und Stand des Minnesängers Friedrich von Hausen." *Archiv für Kulturgeschichte*, 43 (1961), 163–76.
Roediger, Max. "MF 48,13 ff." *ZfdA*, 26 (1882), 293 f.
Rooth, Erik. "Zum Gebrauch vom mhd. *wenen*: Interpretationsversuch." In *Festschrift Wolff*. Neumünster, 1962, pp. 135–60.
Rougemont, Denis. *L'amour et l'occident*. Paris, 1946.
Scherer, Wilhelm. *Deutsche Studien, II: Die Anfänge des Minnesangs*. Sitzungsberichte der kaiserlichen Akademie der Wissenschaften in Wien, vol. 77. Wien, 1874.
Scheunemann, Ernst. *Texte zur Geschichte des deutschen Tageliedes*. Ed. Friedrich Ranke. Altdeutsche Übungstexte, 6. Bern, 1946.
Schirmer, Karl-Heinz. "Zum Aufbau des hochmittelalterlichen deutschen Strophenliedes." *DU*, 11 (1959), 35–59.
Schissel von Fleschenberg, Otmar. "Zur Stilkritik des deutschen Liebesliedes im Mittelalter." *Beiträge*, 26 (1910), 43–76.
Schlösser, Felix. "Die Minneauffassung des Andreas Capellanus und die zeitgenössische Ehelehre." *ZfdPh*, 79 (1960), 266–84.
Schneider, Hermann. "Eine mittelhochdeutsche Liedersammlung als Kunstwerk," *Beiträge*, 49 (1923), 225–60.
Schönbach, Anton, E. "Über den biographischen Gehalt des altdeutschen Minnesangs: Biographische Blätter." *Jahrbuch für lebensgeschichtliche Kunst und Forschung*, 1 (1895), 39–52.
——— . *Die Anfänge des deutschen Minnesangs: Eine Studie*. Graz, 1898.

Schröder, Edward. "Zu Minnesangs Frühling." *ZfdA*, 21 (1889), 98–107.
———. "Kleinigkeiten zu Friedrich von Hausen." *ZfdA*, 69 (1932), 301–2.
Schröder, Franz Rolf. "Der Minnesang, I: Die Forschung; Das Problem." *GRM*, 21 (1933), 161–87, 257–90.
Schwarz, Bertha. *Das Gottesbild in höfischer Dichtung.* Bonn, 1933.
Schwarz, Werner. "Notes on Formulaic Expressions in Middle High German Poetry." In *Festschrift Norman*. London, 1965, pp. 60–70.
Schwietering, Julius. "Singen und Sagen." Diss. Göttingen, 1908.
———. "Einwirkung der Antike auf die Entstehung des frühen deutschen Minnesangs." *ZfdA*, 51 (1924), 61–82.
Spirgatis, Max. *Die Lieder Friedrichs von Hausen.* Tübingen, 1876.
Strümpell, Regine. "Über Gebrauch und Bedeutung von saelde, saelic und Verwantem bei mittelhochdeutschen Dichtern." Diss. Leipzig, 1917.
Thomas, Helmuth. "Minnesang in neuer Gestalt." *WW*, 4 (1953–54), 164–77.
———. "Die jüngere deutsche Minnesangsforschung." *WW*, 7 (1956–57), 269–86.
Trost, Pavel. "Neue Forschungen zum Minnesang." *Philologica Pragensia*, 6 (1963), 298–300.
Tubach, Frederic C. "Zum Problem der inneren Struktur im Minnesang." *EG*, 28 (1963), 155–66.
Weinand, Heinz Gerd. *Thränen: Untersuchungen über das Weinen in der deutschen Sprache und Literatur des Mittelalters.* Abhandlungen zur Kunst-, Musik- und Literaturwissenschaft, 5. Bonn, 1958.
Wentzlaff-Eggebert, Friedrich-Wilhelm. "Geschichtliche und dichterische Wirklichkeit in der deutschen Kreuzzugslyrik." In *Festschrift Lortz*. Baden-Baden, 1958, II, 273–86.
———. "Kreuzzugsidee und mittelalterliches Weltbild." *DVjs*, 30 (1956), 71–88.
Wiercinski, Dorothea. *Minne: Herkunft und Anwendungsschichten eines Wortes.* Niederdeutsche Studien, 11. Köln/Graz, 1964.
Willson, H. Bernard. " 'Der sumer von triere' (Hausen, MF 47,38)." *MLR*, 51 (1956), 414–16.
Wilmanns, Wilhelm. *Untersuchungen zur mittelhochdeutschen Metrik.* Beiträge zur Geschichte der älteren deutschen Literatur, 4. Bonn, 1888.

www.ingramcontent.com/pod-product-compliance
Lightning Source LLC
Chambersburg PA
CBHW031314150426
43191CB00005B/233